Coming Full Circle

Honoring the Rhythms of Relationships

Nancy VanArsdall

Third Side Press

Chicago

Cover art copyright © 1995 by Sid Reger.
Cover and interior design and production by Midge Stocker.

Printed on recycled, acid-free paper in the United States of America.

Acknowledgments
We gratefully acknowledge the following for permission to quote passages, in
the chapters noted, from previously published work:
    Chapter 3: Poem from SACRED PATH CARDS by Jamie Sams. Copyright
© 1990 by Jamie Sams & Linda Childers. Reprinted by permission of
HarperCollins Publishers, Inc.
    Chapter 5: *The Prophet* by Kahlil Gibran. Copyright ©1923 by Kahlil
Gibran and renewed 1951 by Administrators C T A of Kahlil Gibran Estate
and Mary G. Gibran. Reprinted by permission of Alfred A. Knopf, Inc.
    Chapter 5: *All I Really Need To Know I Learned In Kindergarten* by
Robert L. Fulghum. Copyright © 1986, 1988 by Robert L. Fulghum.
Reprinted by permission of Villard Books, a division of Random House, Inc.
    Chapter 7: David Ignatow, "One Leaf" from *New & Collected Poems
1970-1985*, © 1986 by David Ignatow, Wesleyan University Press by
permission of University Press of New England.

Library of Congress Cataloging-in-Publication Data

VanArsdall, Nancy.
    Coming full circle: honoring the rhythms of relationships /
Nancy VanArsdall. — 1st ed.
        p. cm.
    Includeds bibliographical references and index.
    ISBN 1-879427-25-7 (alk. paper). — ISBN 1-879427-26-5 (alk.
paper)
        1. Intimacy (Psychology) 2. Interpersonal relations. 3. Women-
-Psychology. 4. Life cycle. Human.   I. Title.
    BF575.I5V37 1996
    158'.2—dc20   96-13845
        CIP

Third Side Press
2250 W. Farragut
Chicago, IL 60625-1802
312/271-3029

First edition, June 1996
10 9 8 7 6 5 4 3 2 1

Hail! Spirit of the East,
Powers of Air.
Through thoughts and ideas and possibilities
riding on soft summer breezes,
fluttering from feathered bird's wing
I invoke the power to speak the unspeakable
to know the unknowable.
By the air that is Her breath
be with me as I do Her work.
Blessed be!

Hail! Spirit of the South,
Powers of Fire.
Through energy and will and intuition
arising from glowing hearth fires,
sparking from blazing sun,
I invoke the power of courage to tend the heat of passion.
By the fire that is Her Spirit
be with me as I do Her work.
Blessed be!

Hail! Spirit of the West,
Powers of Water.
Through feeling and calm and daring
flowing in river and sea,
riding with anemone and dolphin,
I invoke the power to dive into the depths of emotion.
By the waters of Her womb
be with me as I do Her work.
Blessed be!

Hail! Spirit of the North,
Powers of the Earth.
Through life within all creation:
the smallest of agates and the greatest of lions,
the delicate moss of green,
I invoke the power of endurance and grounding.
By the earth that is Her body
be with me as I do Her work.
Blessed be!

For MG
whose love, light and gentle wisdom
have nurtured this journey

In Memoriam
Jeanine C. Rae
Lucas

Contents

Acknowledgments

I have learned that the experience of writing is a solitary one indeed. Yet, without community to sustain, support, and replenish, *Coming Full Circle* would not have come to fruition. So it is with enormous gratitude that I acknowledge the community that has blessed me throughout the waxings and wanings of this endeavor.

Merlin Stone's insistence that the Goddess "wants you to write this book" has sustained me more than I can say. Truly, She has guided me on the path. I am grateful to Sid Reger for not only lovingly, wisely, and respectfully editing the many words but for really *knowing* the spirit of this book and translating that spirit into the form of art on the cover. To Nan Brooks: thank you for challenging me to write again.

Clearly, the Goddess knew the perfect editor/publisher for Her work: Midge Stocker has been a valuable collaborator in the final birthing of this book. Her vision, respect, and patience have been remarkable. Thank you for *getting it* and for taking the risk to walk the edge.

I am very appreciative of the many women and men who, through the years, have entrusted me with their stories and their cycles, who have helped me confirm the rhythms of our lives, and who have said, "Oh yes, that does make sense."

To the many courageous, strong, and feisty women in the women's spirituality movement, I thank you for showing the way, for helping us to *re/member*.

And to MG, my partner and dearest friend, I am grateful for the gifts of love and laughter and for choosing to join me in honoring the cycles of our life together and dancing the sacred rhythms.

Introduction

I begin this book with three basic assumptions: first, that women intuitively know about cycles; second, that it is primarily women who "do relationships"; and third, that relationships are cyclical. Further, it is my belief that for relationships to be healthy and life-giving, they must be nurtured with intentionality, a purposeful mindfulness. *

We women know about cycles, although we may not always honor them. We know that there are times when our lives flow smoothly and times when they do not. We know that at some times we are growing and learning and changing at a rapid pace and that at other times we feel dull and flat and stuck—as if nothing in our lives ever changes. We know that our moods change as our bodies move through our hormonal cycles. For all our knowing, the larger truths remain hidden. We tend to have little appreciation or tolerance for the waning phases of our cycles as we move through them; we judge them unproductive or even destructive. But we have a choice in this; we can remember that when the tide goes out, following the pull of the moon, new treasures are revealed in the tide pools. And when we honor the cyclical process, our relationships with ourselves and with one another can be filled with growth, vitality,

---

* Integrating rituals into relationships provides such nurturance, for rituals make intentional that which can otherwise easily become unconscious or habitual. Rituals traditionally make sacred that which is mundane, serving as a celebration and affirmation of the spiritual, and for that reason *Coming Full Circle* includes several ritual suggestions. (I use the term *spiritual* rather than *religious*, advisedly. For some people, adherence to organized religion is a spiritual experience, but my observation is that too often the two experiences are mutually exclusive.)

1

and respect. When we attend to our rhythms, we can know, even as we wane, that we will wax once more.

Inviting another to join us in creating a healthy, loving relationship is a complex and exciting venture. What is required is that we be mindful of not only ourselves and our own individual rhythms—a challenge in and of itself—but that we be aware of the rhythms of those who participate in our lives. Life becomes increasingly intricate when we join our rhythms with another's in relationship, for we must also be aware of the rhythm of the relationship we are creating. While our meeting symbolizes a magical synchronistic moment in time, as the relationship grows, we take notice—if we are willing—that all the cycles ebb and flow, wax and wane. While moving simultaneously, the cycles will not always flow in that magical synchronicity. Indeed, we may find ourselves growing at different speeds: the rhythms of the three entities—the two individuals and the relationship—may, in fact, vary significantly. We are challenged to attend to all the cycles.

Developmental psychologists tell us that women are predisposed toward attachment to and connectedness with others, while men tend to be more oriented toward individuation and separateness from others.[1] Because women seem more able to establish intimate relationships and, further, are more likely to define themselves in the context of those relationships,[2] we also tend, quite naturally, to devote energy to the "care and feeding" of relationships. Perceiving relationships as cyclical allows us the opportunity to become more at home with our own rhythms, defining ourselves more fully and creatively and more rhythmically within the context of our relationships. Heightened awareness of the cyclical nature of life allows for an increased intentionality in our relationships with others and with ourselves. Further, to ritualize these cycles and their passages integrates the awareness and intentionality into our lives.

Human relationships can be creative. Healthy relationships must be both creative and dynamic: everchanging, growing, ebbing and flowing, waxing and waning. Relationships often die from either "overworking" or from lack of purposefulness. Integrating an understanding of rhythmic cycles into our lives and our relationships can enhance the creativity of being in partnership with other people and with the universe.

Coming Full Circle begins by exploring the lunar phases as a metaphor for cycles in women's lives. It goes on to examine the cyclical qualities within ourselves as individuals, considering the developmental life cycle and how, in all phases of our lives, we are learning about relationships. The major focus of the book is the phases and life cycle of the intimate relationship. Throughout this discussion, we approach relationship cycles from a personal perspective, considering specific issues that emerge in each cycle.

- The New Moon Cycle involves trusting, learning, testing—birthing the relationship. This cycle is about the romance, excitement, and sometimes terror of being in a new relationship. This is a time of intensity.
- The Waxing Moon Cycle is about the business of establishing the foundation of the relationship. Here, differences between the two principals begin to be acknowledged; while no consensus may yet have been established about how to resolve these differences, the differences are being named. Issues around values (money, spirituality) and boundaries (space, communication) begin to emerge.
- In the Full Moon Cycle, those differences are affirmed. The issues are being dealt with. Enough trust has developed so that the issues can not only be explored but resolved as well. In this cycle, the relationship has reached enough maturity to sustain throughout the inevitable and many changes of midlife.
- Through the Waning Moon Cycle, there is enough safety and intimacy to welcome and celebrate, rather than merely resolve, those inevitable differences between partners. Here, the relationship becomes the arena in which we can deepen our individual experience of life. The relationship is not over; it is in its elderhood. In a healthy relationship, wisdom, comfort, and intimate companionship have been achieved. This is the time for celebration of the individual in the context of the relationship; further deepening of intimacy with the self as well as with the other is nurtured.

At the same time that we are experiencing the rhythm of the cycles of the relationship, we are experiencing our own individual cycles as well. Each of us waxes and wanes individually as the relationship proceeds through its cycles. We experience cycles within cycles within cycles; and, like a hologram, each of us is a microcosm of the whole. To maintain respect and integrity for ourselves, our relationships, and our universe, we must honor the flow of all the rhythms.

● ○ ●

I can't remember not knowing of cycles; I *can* remember judging and negating those knowings.

Like most women, infused with patriarchal values, I believed my cycles were further evidence of an innate weakness. To have *ups* and *downs* (a linear, patriarchal concept) was to be overreactive, too sensitive, too dramatic: too much.

Nearly 16 years ago, I began to explore the notion that cycles, not just ups and downs, influence women's lives. Mirrored in the cyclical experience of women are the seasonal rhythms of Mother Earth and those of the moon. Human relationships, I noticed, seem to have a rhythm, are cyclical, as well.

Through the ensuing years, I tested this concept, becoming mindful of my monthly, seasonal, even daily cycles. For example, between 4 and 5 p.m., my energy usually ebbed, yet I often awoke at 4 a.m. with an inexplicable surge of energy. I realized that through each autumn I seemed to "go crazy" with a restlessness of spirit—starting large projects, inevitably stirring up my marriage—demanding we *do something* about that relationship; then by Christmas, I'd settle down, returning to my "place" as good wife/mother.

Though I had never been plagued by serious premenstrual symptoms, I began to notice monthly changes in my body: increased wakefulness, muscle spasms, swollen (new moon) belly, surging energy the day before my period followed by depleting energy the day of my menses. (I am now convinced that modern-day PMS is simply our bodies' primitive need to go to the "menstrual hut!"*)

---

*   It is theorized that prior to the use of artificial light, all women
     menstruated at New Moon and ovulated at Full Moon. During the
     dark of the moon, women gathered together in menstrual huts, outside
     the village, resting, tending one another. Menstruating women,
     considered taboo in many tribes, were isolated during their menses.

Fifteen years ago, I left the city of my birth and relocated to a lovely and sacred wooded corner of the world where a stream happily accommodates the beaver and her dam, where possum shyly play in the woods, where raccoons arrogantly invite themselves to the herb garden, and where pileated woodpeckers lead a noisy parade of other birds to the feeders. Fifteen years ago, I became a country woman—and an ecofeminist.

As an ecofeminist, I joined the growing number of women who embrace a philosophy that integrates feminist and ecological and spiritual values. Ecofeminists share the conviction that a profound shift in perception and practices is essential to the survival of our planet, as well as to the healing of our dis/eased society. This paradigm shift must occur on a multitude of levels. The ecology movement cannot be separate from feminism, and neither can be sustained without a spiritual foundation. If equality for women is achieved while the planet continues catapulting toward destruction, what good is that equality? If the planet becomes pollution-free and safe from nuclear threat while women remain disenfranchised, then Earth remains unsafe for all its habitants.

Ecofeminism is a philosophy that confronts not only the domination of the earth by polluters but domination in all of its many and pervasive forms: whites over people of color, men over women, heterosexuals over lesbians and gays, adults over children, humans over animals and nature are but a few of the kinds of domination that must be challenged. Starhawk, writer and midwife to the women's spirituality movement, names this philosophy of domination *estrangement* because we see ourselves as separated from and as actors upon the world. We are strangers to nature, to our fellow human beings, even to parts of ourselves. We perceive the world to be made up of nonliving, disintegrated entities without inherent value. As a result, we've come to view all relationships as things to be manipulated and dominated.[3]

As a woman, my knowing of cycles has always and quite naturally been keen; as an ecofeminist, my sensitivity to the natural rhythms of life and the integration of all living things became enhanced as I began living in syncopation with the rhythm of the land. Indeed, I become aware of the new year waxing in March around the Spring

Equinox: to the accompaniment of a tree frog symphony by the creek, new life bursts forth. Soon, the finches, dressed in their summer finery, having gradually exchanged their winter browns for brilliant yellows, are celebrating with me the lushness of Summer Solstice in June as the earth ripens into fullness. By August, I notice a subtle sadness within myself as the buzzing cicadas remind me that summer is waning. The light changes; shadows deepen. Autumn Equinox, in its golden light, suggests an urgency of preparation, and I observe the squirrels frantically collecting walnuts, readying themselves for winter. I watch as the birch tree outside my window shamelessly drops all her amber leaves in a single morning. The year is waning. Suddenly, nature's bright canvas, brushed with raucously brilliant oil paints, becomes transformed into a quiet watercolor landscape awash in subtle hues of blacks, grays, and browns. Yet it is in the barrenness of winter that I more deeply appreciate the gentle contours of the land. I glimpse deer, previously hidden among the thick leaves of summer, ambling elegantly through the woods. I now can see all the way through the trees and watch as a coyote lopes across the meadow on the far side of the grove.

My relationship with the land changes as the seasons change: the energy of springtime lazily relaxes into the fullness of summer. In early fall, my energy heightens with an urgency matching that of the busy squirrels performing their autumnal foraging ritual. Inevitably, winter means retrieving an unfinished weaving project, journaling more regularly, slowing my pace, quieting into reflection. I find myself baking bread, savoring the blend of delicious fragrances emanating from the wood fire over which a hearty soup simmers and gurgles. I've become intrigued with the sounds of the seasons, as well: how the morning birds' songs differ from the evensongs. I tune in to the hum of the locusts as their buzz crescendos then diminishes to a drone. All around me life is in rhythm.

I begin to see more clearly how I've related with the moon, recognizing what phase she's in, feeling soothed by her presence. I thrill at the sight of the baby moon—the sliver of the waxing phase. I feel filled with passion in her fullness. Lucas, my dear black cat (a symbol of the new moon, I learn) and my familiar, becomes a significant teacher: he inevitably celebrates the night of the full moon by stubbornly refusing to come indoors at all.

I remember how increasingly intimate my relationship with the moon seemed as we anticipated the first landing of humans on her surface (only dimly acknowledging that with sadness and anger I felt excluded, along with all my sisters, by the famous "One small step for man, one giant leap for mankind"). I became fascinated with the movement of the moon as she glides across the sky; how in winter her brilliant glow awakens me in the pre-dawn hours shining into my west window. The moon and I began to seem even more intimate when I am at the beach, knowing that time at the ocean is an imperative for me: the ebb and flow of the tides, the power of the sea, is a source of both empowerment and healing.

As I began to notice, and then affirm, the cycles, the rhythms around me, becoming more aware of my relationship with the universe, I became increasingly curious about my relationships with Mother Earth and Grandmother Moon, with all there is. Are *all* my relationships cyclical? Does this concept apply simply to my intimate partner or does it apply also to my children? my parents? friends?

Through the years, my relationships with friends, my sister, my mother and father, my children have all seemed to ebb and flow, to wax and wane. Times of closeness and gentleness are often followed by conflict or distance that are in turn followed by a deepening intimacy. This rhythm is even more sharply defined in my more intimate relationship.

During what I now name *the waning times*, I even questioned my love for my life partner. Those times of introspection and separateness were fraught with feelings of fear and doubt, restlessness and loss. I often felt lost and abandoned, as though groping my way through darkened passages. Inevitably, the waning time is followed by a waxing time— when the relationship feels renewed and flows into greater depths. As I reflected on my own history, it began to make sense to me that the waning, however distressing, is as necessary a phase of the cycle as is the waxing, just as winter is as significant a season as is summer. What, I wondered, might it be like to experience these rhythms without fear or judgment?

Coming Full Circle is a woman's book, because it is my contention that women are more likely to *do* relationships. It is inclusive of men and relationships with men. I have, however, chosen to use, wherever possible, feminine pronouns. This convention is not intended to negate the masculine experience but to provide male and female readers alike with the opportunity to honor women's "ways of knowing." The perspective known as "womanspirit" is more subjective, emotional, relationship-centered.[4] Yet the patriarchal culture stubbornly continues to devalue that womanspirit, rejecting the very resource that may save us and our planet. Achieving and sustaining a life-giving, healing perspective becomes our greatest challenge. All of us—women and men alike—must commit ourselves to remembering and honoring the knowings of the ancient ones, of our foremothers, of those who honored the earth, who related intimately *with* the rhythms of the seasons, who participated *with* the cycles of all living things, when magic was afoot.

I confess to you, dear reader, that I do believe in magic. This book in many ways is an affirmation of that belief. My wish for you is that within yourself, within those relationships you hold dear, you will reclaim the magic, the mystery of life. As one of my favorite role-models, Trudy, the bag lady, suggests most articulately (via Lily Tomlin), "So maybe we should stop trying to figure out the *meaning* of life and sit back and enjoy the *mystery* of life."[5] There is something magical and mysterious about two people joining together in their loving and living. The possibilities are wondrously infinite when we unite with others to create relationships.

I invite you to surrender to the magic, to honor the rhythm, the cycles that surround you, for by honoring our own cycles, those of each other and of our planet, we may heal—ourselves and our Mother Earth.

Chapter 1

Moon as Metaphor

Each of us, woman and man alike, has, to a greater or lesser degree, a relationship with the moon. Who has not taken some moments to stand humbled in her shimmering glow, soothed in the cool presence of the full moon? Who has not felt reassured by her return when the tiny sliver at waxing moontime lightens the early nighttime sky? Who has not felt awed by the huge, amber fullness of the harvest moon as she rises over vast fields of corn? And who has not yearned for someone especially dear with whom to share the moon's promise of romance?

Symbols help make that which is implicit in our lives explicit; symbols aid in our making sense of our lives, giving order and meaning to the abstract and ambiguous. Symbols, then, give us a means by which we can connect with community, with nature, conjoined with the universe, with the Spirit. We connect with that which is greater than ourselves, giving meaning, affirming the awe, the wonder, the mystery, and the magic of being.

The moon is such a symbol. Throughout time, the moon has held deep and complex meaning for people. In ancient moon-centered cultures, the moon goddess was fully integrated into people's lives; the moon was a life-giving presence that determined the process for all growing things. People planted their crops, had their babies, organized their religions—lived their lives—by the light (and darkness) of the moon. The cycles of the moon determined the cycles of their lives.

The moon continues to enlighten us. If we're willing, through her phases we can be guided through our own phases. Magically, mysteriously, the moon appears, then disappears, pulling the tides—of the earth and the blood tides of woman—with her, as she waxes and wanes

9

through her cycles. We cycle inward into aloneness and introspection; then outward, accessible to others. "The moon is the Sun of Night, the eye of the Goddess that opens and shuts throughout the month."[1] The moon, she is wise—teaching us of the passage of time, of calendars, and moving us into deeply unconscious, psychic realms. If we are willing.

● ○ ●

Symbolizing fertility, the moon has held deep significance for women since the beginning of time. Woman was, for the ancient ones, the moon incarnate. The moon represented the very essence of womanhood: cyclical, changeable, soft, and whimsical.

Woman has been attuned, on both psychic and physical levels, to the cycles of the moon. In both a physical sense and a metaphorical one, woman and the moon are intricately and inextricably related. In fact, that which has, more than any other, symbolized woman most distinctively and uniquely is the moon. While the sun is representative of the masculine, the moon has, through the ages—continuing into contemporary times—symbolized the feminine aspect in each of us. In myth and poetry, first by influencing fertility, later as the Goddess Herself, the moon has been related to—in relationship with—woman.

The status of woman in any culture is often correlated with the status of the moon. Even the fates of woman and the moon are entwined. Attitudes and knowledge of woman and the feminine principle have paralleled attitudes and knowledge of the moon. As the moon was revered, so was woman; as the sun gods, representing the male principle and personified by the conquering patriarchy, prevailed, woman lost favor. In spite of the fact that many of us grew up being told of the "man in the moon" (another patriarchal theft!), the moon—she is female!

So the moon is a powerful female symbol, while the sun seems more to symbolize male. Of course, the constancy of the sun provides heat and light, while the moon is changeable—some say fickle. The sun—either present in the sky or not—shines during the day and disappears into the night, predictably appearing in the east once more at dawn. Not so the moon: she follows a different pattern as she rules the night. We may expect her to light the night skies, but she does so only through the full moon phase. At other times, she withdraws, leaving the night heavens in darkness. Nor is her rising predictable. Whimsically, she may not rise until dawn and she may set as the sun sets. She may even appear at midday—or not at all.[2]

Metaphors point to something that transcends ourselves. The moon serves as a metaphor for the rhythmic cycles of change and growth. Starhawk, in *The Spiral Dance*, her comprehensive "rebirthing of the ancient religion," helps us to re/member that the myths of the earth-centered religions used metaphors to define their obscured reality—to make sense of the movement of those celestial orbs, to explain birth and growth and death. Metaphors speak to us on many levels: we are touched both psychically and emotionally, both intellectually and intuitively. "If we describe the vagina as a flower, we feel differently about it than if we call it a 'piece of meat' or a 'genital orifice.' If we call the ocean 'Our Mother, the womb of life,' we may take more care not to pump Her full of poisons than if we see the ocean merely as a 'mass of H2O.'"[3]

To see more clearly the metaphorical significance of the moon and the integral part she plays in people's lives, we must re/member simpler times, when survival depended on being attuned with the cycles of the earth and of the moon. Ancient agricultural people commonly held the belief that there was a connection between the moon and woman. Woman's power to bear children, seen as a gift from the moon, seemed obvious, with her 28-day menstrual cycle mirroring the lunar cycle of 28-1/2 days. In many languages, the words for menstruation and moon are the same or similar: *mens* means moon. Menstruation is defined as "moon change."[4] Ancient peoples noted that animals mated seasonally and that crops grew seasonally, and their own lives depended on learning to abide by those cycles.

The cycles were both obvious *and* mysterious. It is no wonder, then, that the mystery of the moon was deified. Nearly every ancient culture has its moon goddess.

Honoring the spirit world was essential in early civilizations; attending to the cycles of the moon, the rhythms of the seasons, was imperative and was maintained by the priestesses of the Moon Goddesses. The survival of any community depended on the fertility of women and the fertility of the crops: fertility rites were integrated with the reverence of the moon. Conversely, to turn away from the goddesses meant certain death and destruction.

In these moon-centered cultures, the relationship between the unconscious (through visions) and conscious activities, between dreams and daily life, was a given. One's energy and vitality were assumed to be related to the extent to which one lived by the cyclical principles of fertility. Furthermore, because night is the special sphere of the moon, bringing sleep and, with it, dreams and visions, those were seen as messages and directives for the day's activities. Moon, then, was synonymous with guidance and creativity.[5]

The earliest object of spiritual worship was the Great Mother, who from the beginning was associated with the moon and was defined in terms of nurturing and the provision of food. Furthermore, archaeological finds reveal ancient artifacts substantiating the female as the primal power and center of what is sacred and necessary.[6] Ancient people saw the moon not only as a favorable influence, but as indispensable for growth—a fertilizing force. The moon caused seeds to germinate, plants to grow, women to bear young. In fact, most ancient people believed that only women could make things grow, because they alone were under the protection of the moon. Her ability to swell up, like the moon, and her monthly cycle, like the moon's, confirmed their belief in woman's at-oneness with the moon.

Woman's blood was seen as a source of life, symbolic of her connection with the life-giving, life-taking Moon Goddess. A symbol of fertility, her blood was held sacred. Menstrual blood was given to the fields for increased yield, making the land more fertile; it was even used as a lure to bring animals to hunters.

Fertility beyond a woman's childbearing years was also held sacred. The postmenopausal woman was said to withhold menses, thus turning her blood into power. The older woman, therefore, was revered and honored for her wisdom and power.[7] Attending to and honoring of the menstrual cycle in modern times is attending to the life cycle, the life force. It is symbolic of the reclaiming of womanpower.

Many of the myths of the earliest moon deities serve as powerful metaphors for women's contemporary experience. In *Ancient Mirrors of Womanhood*, a comprehensive work on goddesses and heroines, Merlin Stone artfully recounts stories of the many aspects of moon goddesses celebrated in ancient cultures. Our cycles are affirmed, our autonomy reclaimed; we celebrate ourselves as healers and weavers. We re/member to embrace ourselves as wisewomen.

Described as the first woman of the world, the Mayan goddess Ix Chel bestowed to Her people many gifts, not least of which was knowledge of healing and the easing of childbirth. By observing a spider spin her intricate web, Ix Chel was able to birth Her own daughter Ix Chebel Yax. The younger one later taught women the art of weaving and the art of dying cloth—red from rust, purple from pupura shell, and black from carbon. Ix Chel taught Her women, by Her own example, that they must be free to come and go, that even though they need to disappear from time to time, inevitably they will return. "Mother of all deities, it is She who causes the blood to gather so that it may flow with the passage of the month."[8]

The lessons we draw from the Mayan myth are rich and plentiful, for we re/member we are indeed the weavers, lending our many talents and skills, our colors of earth and blood, to the texture of the cloth of relationships. At the same time, we are confirmed in our need to "be free to come and go," to move inward and outward, to honor our cycles, to be respectful of our "moontimes." When we honor our autonomy, we disappear from time to time, yet, inevitably, we shall—like the moon—return.

Changing Woman teaches us of cycles, of birth and death, of waxing moon into waning, young to old, seed into fruit. Changing Woman, Estan Atlehi, creator of the Navajo people, is Mother of all the seasons; She is Mother Earth. It is She who teaches us "the flow of life, the restlessness of the sand as it flies with the wind, the wisdom of the ancient rocks that never leave their home, the pleasure of the tiny sapling that had risen through them." So it is into the House of Changing Woman that each young girl enters at menarche—her passage into womanhood.[9] It is Changing Woman's wisdom we must honor in our search for the wisdom of life. When we honor the ways of Changing Woman, when we sing Her sacred songs, we honor all of life, for She teaches us that to defy Her ways is to destroy all of life, "but those who understand the ways of Changing Woman, forever walk The Trail of Beauty."[10]

As the ancient stories unfold, surely we begin to reclaim the earthy wisdom and rhythm of those ancient times. The teachings of the goddesses have much to offer us, many gifts to bestow, as we journey on a path of re/membering the cycles.

Huitaca, the Colombian moon goddess, teases us to reclaim our outrageousness. Wild and wonderful, lusty and beautiful, Huitaca leads "us into merriment, encouraging us to drink the juices of intoxication, encouraging us to feel the wonder of the touch of our bodies against another."[11] We are in dire need of Huitaca's nudgings, for one of the most grave of our losses to the patriarchy has been our ability to freely celebrate our bodies. In Huitaca, we are gifted with a happy, laughing image—Mother of Joy, She was called—with whom we can dance and play and celebrate ourselves.

● ○ ●

The moon goddess in early Greek culture evolved into a deity of three forms, a trinity: Artemis, the waxing moon; Selene, full moon; and Hecate, goddess of the waning moon. The tri-form of the moon goddess was the Mother of us all, giver of all, taker of all. Representing the three phases of the moon—the waxing, full, and waning—the moon goddess is also the tri-form goddess of Maiden, Mother, and Crone.* Exploration of the moon goddess yields insights for us in contemporary life as we attempt to reclaim and strengthen the tri-form connections not only within ourselves but with one another and with our planet as well.

Known by the ancient Romans as Diana, Artemis is the virgin, the Maiden Moon Goddess, ruler on earth. She is the waxing, crescent moon, symbol of youth and newness. Having been a midwife to Her mother, She is the Goddess of childbirth. She is complex, having many identities, and like the variable and sometimes contradictory energies of the women She came to symbolize, She is seen as an "image of woman moving through life assuming different roles at different times: a compendium of feminine possibility."[12] Perhaps most beloved of the Greek goddesses, Artemis instinctively ruled reproduction, both sexuality and childbirth. She was the force of creation upon whom Greek mothers called for comfort in childbirth. Often portrayed as a light bearer, with moon and stars encircling her head, this Waxing Moon Goddess symbolized the beginning phase of the instinct to live and produce and reproduce constantly, to devour and to die, to begin again.

Artemis—strong and nurturing, fiercely protective and sexual, Goddess of the swelling moon—loved new life. She is an empowering way-

---

* We can see in this pre-patriarchal trinity the model for all subsequent trinities, including Christianity's "Father, Son, and Holy Spirit."

shower for us contemporary women as we struggle to balance our strength and our gentleness in our complex, multifaceted lives.

Selene, Goddess of the Full Moon, was one deity who, like the moon, changed appearance from light to dark. Often seen as a predecessor of the Virgin Mary, Selene, the Great Mother, was adult, sexual, powerful, and fertile. Ruling in heaven, Selene is pictured as a winged being, crowned with a crescent, driving the lunar chariot across the night sky. "When She was not visible, Selene was said to be in Asia Minor, visiting Her human lover, Endymion, for whom She had won the prize of eternal life and youth."[13] Invariably, Selene pulls the full moon steadily across the sky and then guides it downward into the seas once more. As the moon slips away, there are no celebrations as the nights grow black and mortals defend themselves against the ghosts and spirits of the underworld.[14] Certainly Selene, brightening the heavens, flooding the earth in light, offers us permission to be *fully* woman, to embrace our sexuality, our lusty earthiness, our creative fertility. Descending toward the darkness, she invites us into ourselves.

Ruler of that uncanny and mysterious underworld is Hecate. Goddess of the Waning Moon, Hecate is known as the Greek Goddess of witches,* of magic; She is the dark side of the moon, a mirror image of Artemis. "Holy Enchantress, Mother who brings birth and rebirth, forever renews the cycle of existence—as the frog brings forth the tadpole, as the tadpole turns to frog, so Hecate guides the transformations, giving power to the spoken word of sacred incantation."[15] The story of Hecate reveals Her accompanied by her baying hounds, roaming the earth on moonless nights, leading hoards of ghosts. Yet those who honored Her and observed Her rites were protected. The power of Her wrath swept over the earth as She unleashed storms and destruction. Until the new moon reappeared, however, Hecate shared Her secrets and "those who believed understood. They saw that form was not fixed, watched human become animal become tree become human. . . . Awesome were Her skills but always Hecate taught the same lesson: *Without death there is no life.*"[16]

---

* Z Budapest defines *witch* as "a woman or a man who considers the Earth a living, breathing, conscious being—part of the family of the vast universe—to be regarded and respected as God herself. To be a witch, you have to see yourself as part of God, who is present in, not separate from, us and all living beings" (*Holy Book of Women's Mysteries*, p. 57).

To the Greeks, the *power* of the moon was symbolized in Hecate, Goddess of the Waning Moon. Related to menopause, Hecate represents the old wise woman, the Crone, the final stage of woman's growth. As queen of death, Goddess of the underworld, She ruled the magical powers of regeneration and over the realm of the soul. "Rebirth is not understood as the return of the same but as metamorphosis, transformed consciousness. Death and new vision are closely intertwined."[17]

Hecate is the giver of dreams and omens, of intuition. She is the source of vision, of *lunacy*.* Through Hecate, we are transformed, and, perhaps most significantly in our youth-centric culture, as we age we can reclaim our crone-selves, as true wise women, honored for our skills, our life experience, our wisdom, and our intuition. It is Hecate who teaches us to honor the dark side, our own underworld, to walk with Her through the waning of our cycles.

The moon is a salient symbol for women. Further, it serves as a metaphor for both personal and relationship cycles. In pre-patriarchal times, there was no doubting the connection among the tides, the seasons, the lunar cycle, and woman's menstrual cycle; there was no denying the relationship between fertility and the moon. Inevitably, woman was the moon incarnate: women served as the moon goddess' priestesses and were ascribed additional powers as healers, herbalists, timekeepers. More than 5000 years ago, women, as oracles, prophets, and priests, ritualized the moon and her gifts through festivals and ceremonies, honoring fertility and the changing seasons. Rituals were vital for honoring what was a most precious commodity: the life force and all its aspects.

As we re/member the myths of the moon goddesses, we are reminded that to honor the cycles is to remember the necessity of balance, of

---

*   *Lunacy* is reclaimed here as "altered vision" rather than the patriarchal definition of "craziness."

renewal. We re/member that there is—must be—life with death, light with dark, rest with work, pleasure with hardship. Like the moon, all is cyclical: waxing into fullness, then waning into darkness, and waxing once more.

The moon shines only by reflecting the light of the sun. Viewed from the earth, it appears to change shape, going through phases. The changing cycles of the moon phases are caused by the changing of relative positions of the sun, moon, and earth. Each of the four phases lasts approximately seven days, with no definitive moment when one phase ends and the next begins. As with our own cycles, there are no sudden shifts; there is simply a flowing from one phase to another.

The moon rises about 51 minutes later from one day to the next because it is moving eastward, appearing at a slightly different point on the horizon each day during the month. When the moon is between the earth and the sun, it is not visible to us on earth; this is the dark side of the moon, the *new moon*. It rises and sets with the sun. Through the two weeks between the new and full phases, the moon passes through *waxing* crescent phase, reaching its first quarter phase, and then through *waxing gibbous* phase (more than a quarter and less than full).

When the earth is between the sun and moon, we see the *full moon* illuminated. When full, the moon rises when the sun sets and we are able to see it all night. From full moon to new, the phases wane in reverse order, illuminating the eastward edge while the western part is dark. It also starts rising later and later in the evening.[18]

Like the changing of the seasons, each phase of the moon brings its own opportunities for growth and change. Unlike societies where women's lives are focused on and dictated by the moon cycles, "civilized" women have psychically fallen under the rule of men and have lost touch with their own feminine instinct. Woman's nature is cyclic. To understand ourselves as women, it is necessary to seriously consider our moonlike character in order to gain insight into the law of change that governs us.

We have lost sight of the truth of wholeness the moon has to offer us, focusing instead on the sun's increasing and decreasing light affecting each day's length. In honoring moontime, and our own moontimes as well, we honor the length of each night, re/membering that both darkness and lightness belong to the moon and to ourselves. We must integrate and appreciate rather than debase and deny the cycles inherent in our very existence. We must attend to the tasks relevant to each phase of each cycle.

In general, the waxing phase is characterized by its activity, by nurturing the seeds of ideas into action. The full moon phase is a time of abundance—of manifesting those creative efforts. The waning phase is a time for withdrawing, moving within the self, honoring the dark side of ourselves. As we move toward the new moon, we pause to reflect in the darkness, to integrate what has occurred.

● ○ ●

Another lesson to be learned from our foremothers is the significance of supporting and nurturing our cyclic nature by integrating rituals into our daily lives. The thread that strengthens our relationships is a spiritual one, and we celebrate our connection with that which is greater than ourselves through ritual, through creating an alternative perception in order to maintain our integrity in what, for many, is an unnatural and inharmonious culture.

In rituals, we have opportunities to align our inner selves with the greater cycles of the earth, affirming an inner balance in rhythm with the changing seasons, celebrating the many life transitions as well as the moon phases. Ritual is about honoring outward, obvious changes, such as births and deaths, adolescence and aging, and about affirming the inner mythic flow within the depths of our souls.

Ritual helps us re/member our spiritual center—the core of our self-esteem. All transitions signify a movement through the cycles—the waxing, experienced as positive change; the waning, as movement toward the unfamiliar, a loss of what was. The purpose of creative ritual is to foster increased connection within ourselves, with one another, and with the universe—connection with the greater rhythms and energies that provide stability through the ever-changing cycles of our lives. Ritual is a way of affirming our connection with the rhythm and passages we all share.

Ritual gives us a context in which to "dive into the dark," discovering, perhaps, the magic. Like the moon cycle, the seasonal cycle is one of the most obvious ways in which we see and experience the process of birth, growth, death, and rebirth. Just as the ancient ones found guidance and nurturance through ritual, so may we affirm the magical cycles of life.

There are consequences to negating our cycles. We become psychologically and even physically ill when we fail to honor our internal rhythms. When we neglect the energy of the waxing phase, our sense of worth suffers; we negate the creative spirit that is life-giving and empowering. When we deny our need to move deeper into ourselves through the waning phase, we miss opportunities for affirming our autonomy, another source of self-esteem. Indeed, we suffer not only a psychological but a spiritual alienation almost certain to be manifested in some physical way.

To be healthy, self-empowered adults, capable of life-giving, loving, and respectful relationships, we must begin by honoring our own individual cycles. We must discover, or perhaps reclaim from our foremothers, the power that lies in all phases of our cycles. We cannot have life without death, day without night, light without dark, waxing without waning. We can take the opportunity of this moment to come to new awareness of the inevitability of our cycles and to let that awareness lead us out of fear of the waning and into understanding that all things come full circle in their time.

Chapter 2

Cycles of the Individual

The extent to which each of us experiences a sense of harmony and wholeness within ourselves determines how healthy, harmonious, and life-giving our relationships can be. Having an internal balance is critical to sustaining an external relationship. Any relationship between two people—whether between lovers, siblings, friends, or parent and child—can only be as healthy as the individuals in that relationship. Before exploring the cycles of relationships, we need to examine two kinds of personal cycles:

- Our internal cycles—daily, monthly, yearly. Attention to our individual cycles yields important information for each woman as she attempts to join another—who is also cyclical in nature—in partnership.
- Our developmental cycles—where we are on the wheel of personal development. As we become aware of where we are in our own individual developmental cycles, we begin to realize the places from which we draw strength and the aspects that threaten to debilitate us and thereby sabotage the very relationships we so desire.

Attending to our individual cycles, both internal and developmental, yields self-awareness from which we can make healthy and informed choices. This works on various levels. If we know about our internal cycle that we are typically more creative in the early morning hours, then we know the frustration of any attempts to initiate a new project in the late afternoon when our energy is at a low ebb. If we are aware that in an early developmental cycle of our lives we experienced a serious loss, then we are more likely to

21

understand why we feel intense fear when we are left alone. Exploration of those places in our lives that disturbed the natural progression of our development allows us to heal the wounds so that we may more fully engage in life-giving relationships—with ourselves and with others. Without that information available to us, we wander in a state of confusion, repeating unsatisfying patterns over and over and over.

In *Coming Full Circle*, the moon cycle is our guide as the metaphor for individual cycles, both internal and developmental. Through the waxing, we are ever moving into fullness and in the fullness, inevitably, we turn toward the waning and thence into the darkness—in an ever-changing spiral, light into dark into light, waxing, full, waning, new, waxing, full, and so on. Spirals are an ancient symbol of death and rebirth. There are many implications of the spiral, or cycle, including the shape of the DNA molecule that sets the pattern for an organism's growth to a spiral. It means that no form of energy can be exerted in only one direction; it will always peak, reaching a point of climax, and then turn. In the spiral, all activity is balanced by inactivity: excitement is followed by tranquillity, creativity by quiet. Contrary to patriarchal expectations, women are no more capable of living always in the passive any more than men can always be in the active mode; no one can be constantly in motion or constantly quiet or angry or happy or anything. In order to be whole, we must experience a balance of exertion and rest.[1]

Viewing life in the image of cycles and spirals dissolves dualities; opposites become complements. Restraint requires wildness; chaos, harmony. Diversity is the natural order of things. If both the waxing and waning are valued, then both poles of any polarity become valued and the cycle becomes the rhythm of the dance to which we, the dancer, the seeker are inevitably and quite naturally drawn.[2] The spiral/cycle is a universal symbol revealed to us in many forms—in galaxies, whirlpools, and moonshells. Just as the moon waxes and wanes, so do the tides, so does the energy of the economy, and so do our bodies. "As above, so below."[3]

Honoring the cycles in nature, in ourselves, and in others necessarily leads us to a place of honoring diversity—the differentnesses that, while potentially conflicting, are the foundation of creativity and growth, and a vital characteristic of any healthy relationship. When we extricate the idea of polarity from our culturally imposed images of male and female, we see that the male and female forces that represent differences are not really different; they are the same force flowing in opposite, albeit not opposed, directions. Neither is passive nor active, light nor dark: within each are all these aspects. As Starhawk describes it, "The Female is seen as the life-giving force, the power of manifestation, of energy flowing into the world to become form. The Male is seen as the death force, in a positive, not a negative sense: the force of limitation that is the necessary balance to unbridled creativity, the force of dissolution, of return to formlessness. Each principle contains the other: Life needs death, feeds on death; death sustains life, makes possible evolution and new creation. They are part of a cycle, each dependent on the other."[4]

Life is sustained by the cycling of forces, alternating, maintaining balance and flow. Starhawk's description continues, "Unchecked, the life force is cancer; unbridled, the death force is war and genocide."

Diversity is the stuff of which harmony is made: balance is maintained in the *both/and* of waxing and waning—not the patriarchal *either/or* perspective. The natural rhythm of the cyclic rhythm of birth, growth, death, decay, rebirth is seen in the changing seasons, in the life cycle of all living things, in the ecological balance of the natural world. Death is not an end but rather a necessary and inevitable stage in the cycle that evolves into rebirth. To be whole and complete is to be available to both aspects—creation and dissolution, growth and limitation, life and death, waxing and waning. The challenge is to honor all aspects in ourselves and in those with whom we relate—always drawing on the energy that leads us toward harmony. "All the tragedy in the world, in the individual and in the multitude, comes from lack of harmony. And the harmony is best given by producing harmony in one's own life."[5]

INTERNAL CYCLES

The lunar cycle serves as metaphor and model for the many cycles humans experience. In addition to the moon cycles, we experience, both personally and globally, seasonal and daily cycles; physical, emotional, and even spiritual cycles. When we attribute meaning to our life by attending to our cycles—whether those cycles are based on the calendar or on the body—we develop an intentional and inclusive attitude toward life, thus deepening our wisdom and understanding of ourselves, our universe, and our place in its context.

Time is one way we both measure and experience cycles. *Process time*, or subjective time, can be differentiated from *clock time*, or objective time. From a linear perspective, time is perceived as synonymous with the numbers on the clock: time is only that which the clock or calendar measures. From that view, being on time, being early or late, have real significance. From another perspective, time is perceived as a "process, a series of passages, or a series of interlocking cycles," to which the clock may or may not be relevant.[6] Process time eludes standardization and is normally an unconscious, organic experience. We just *feel* when it's time to eat, sleep, make love, write, walk, talk with a friend, visit Aunt Sadie, and so on, all based on our own individualized rhythms.

While both process time and clock time are valid, there are certainly circumstances where our own internal clock or process is what is most relevant—for instance, in childbearing and childrearing, and in relationships. The ability to move between the process time and clock time is vital, but we may experience great conflict in our attempts to balance both. Many of us struggle continually between honoring our own desire to participate in, yet not be slave to, the collective—the social groups to which we belong—while honoring our own individual needs and affirming our own identity. Each of us struggles between the need to be a part of a larger whole (community) and the deep sense that one (individual) is whole and self-contained. The struggle is further complicated in the context of an intimate relationship when we are trying to honor our own cycle while also being respectful of our partner's rhythms.

Many of us have times during the day when we feel more energetic, creative, than other times. Often, someone is heard to say, "I'm a real night person" (the owl) or, "I'm at my peak in the early morning" (the lark) Learning to appreciate the idiosyncrasies of our individual and unique time pattern is essential to our well-being.

Every bodily function has its own rhythmic cycle. Daily rhythms, known as *circadian rhythms*, those located within a 24-hour scale, include the waking and sleeping cycle, the rise and fall of body temperature (as much as 1.5 to 2 degrees, reaching its peak in the afternoon or evening), blood pressure rhythm, cardiac and renal functions, urinary excretion, and endocrine activity. Proteins are better utilized early in the day; alcohol, barbiturates, and X-rays can be fatal at one part of the circadian cycle, simply an annoyance at another. Hormones seem to be more effective if taken early in the day. Births and deaths cluster at night or early in the morning. Individuals learn more effectively at certain times of the day. Our bodies have many different pulses and respond differently at various times of the day: each activity seems to have its prime time on a daily cycle.[7]

Rhythms that occur in cycles of several days or weeks are called *infradian rhythms*, which include the cycles of sexual activity. *Selenian rhythms* (named for Selene, goddess of the full moon) are those that occur every 28 days, the most obvious of which is the menstrual cycle. That the human body's 80%-water/20%-mineral proportion is about the same as Earth's points to our intricate connection to the lunar tide cycles, especially those of the new and full moon. Some people experience, with the lunar cycle, neuromuscular irritability or excitement; some notice swelling or even eruptions of the skin that increase with the waxing of the moon and decrease with its waning. Our epidermis follows a selenian rhythm; shedding constantly, it takes about 28 days to renew itself.[8] Similarly, there are seasonal rhythms: our heart beats faster in the summer than winter; the basal metabolic rate, reflecting the activity of the thyroid, is lower in winter than in the spring or summer; and hair really does grow faster in summer than winter.[9] My mother, a wise woman of 87 years, is absolutely sure that our bodies experience significant transitions and change every seven years! Although her claims are not scientifically substantiated, who am I to question her observations?

The moon is a major regulator of seasonal cycles and individual body rhythms, so being in or out of balance with the moon naturally seems to be a determinant of our health and harmony. We modern women have no moon lodges, no menstrual huts to which we can retreat on the dark moon. We have lost the deep connection with the cycles of our bodies that our foremothers felt when they bled together, counted due-dates on lunar calendar sticks, and entrusted the moon goddess and their healer-midwives. PMS did not exist for them; pregnancy and delivery were not a disease; menopause was not a trauma.[10]

While we would be foolish to reject all we know about modern medicine, we are better served when we *participate* more *with* our bodies, take more notice of our cycles, and reclaim what has, on many levels, been taken from us. When we try to maintain power over our world rather than to honor the power within us, we collaborate with the patriarchy. When we reclaim our own lunar cycles, we reclaim our connection to our bodies and to our power as women! The beginning point must be from within ourselves, our own cycles.

One of the most obvious ways to increase the clarity of our individual rhythms is to chart those cycles. *Lunaception* is based on the belief that primitive women menstruated at the dark of the moon and ovulated at the full moon. It appears that the light of the full moon evolutionarily affected the human woman's body three nights out of the month. Studies have shown that temperature changes of a woman's hormonal cycle correlate with the night light cycle and that light stimulation of the pineal gland causes ovulation. Maintaining a daily chart of our body temperature allows us to measure many of our physical cycles, such as the rhythm of activity and the ovulation cycle, and to ascertain some of our emotional cycles, such as our self-image, moods, feelings, and coping abilities. Having a knowledge of how those cycles naturally tend to flow allows us to be engaged with our daily, monthly, seasonal cycles.[11]

Woman's biological rhythm *is* in some strange way related to her psychological rhythm, which is the real significance of the moon cycle for her. The interaction between the activity in these two realms is so close, so intimate, that it is almost impossible to determine, of the many emotional experiences, what part is biological and what part is psychological—and furthermore, which is cause and which effect.[12] Indeed, our internal rhythms, reflective of our deepest needs, often seem incongruent with our conscious thoughts and wishes.

Many women experience psychological and/or physiological distress during the waning moon phase of their menstrual cycle. Unless the physical pain commands attention, most women tend to disregard any body/mind change. We have much to learn (without marching back into history) from our foremothers, who were obliged to take time for themselves. Seclusion was required of primitive women during their menses; they did not have to be ill to go to the menstrual hut for their time of solitude. It has been suggested that in response to the discarding of the practice of isolation/solitude each month, the unconscious takes revenge. When we refuse to acknowledge our internal, psychological need for solitude, it is projected to the outer, external world in the form of depression and shame.[13] To dismiss the distress of menstruation as simply neurotic or imaginary, to discount this part of the cycle as the "curse"—something to be endured simply because of its inevitability—is not only to miss an opportunity to experience more deeply the essential part of our feminine nature but also to negate a valued aspect of ourselves as women, and when we do so, we experience dissonance within ourselves. These needs must be dealt with in a more constructive and intentional way.[14]

During that time of seclusion, ancient woman gained more awareness of those "instinctive forces" and, I suggest, a deepening awareness not only of her emotional life but of her spiritual aspect as well. Modern woman has lost touch with this value and it is quite possible that her menstrual distress may be related to this loss.

In moon-centered societies, woman's entire life focused around her physiological cycles. Periods of work in her home and community, her social and marital relationships all alternated with periods of seclusion. At regular intervals, she was *obliged* to go away alone: she could not cook, nor tend to tasks; she was compelled to be alone, to commune with herself. While other women were probably sharing this time, there is reason to believe that her focus was on herself. This must have had a profound effect on her relationship with life. Days were spent in the menstrual hut, fasting and performing other purification rites. While men and boys entering puberty performed initiation ceremonies and spiritual quests in order to deepen their spiritual connection with the Earth, women did this not once, but monthly, in a less formal manner, affirming the voice of nature that was ever close in them.[15]

Just as our foremothers had the opportunity at the dark of the moon to get in touch with the deeper layers of their psychic lives, so must we attend to those tasks throughout our cycles. An inner necessity calls us from time to time to introvert, to withdraw psychologically from the demands of our external life and to live for a little while in the secret places of our own heart, where we may be able to touch the deeper part of our own nature, thereby strengthening ourselves.[16]

There are many ways to "go to the menstrual hut." To be in the metaphorical menstrual hut may mean being in a bubble bath, meditating, or taking a walk in the woods. I recommend monthly *temple days*, during which time we live the day moment-to-moment—in process time: reading, listening to music, simply *being* with ourselves!

The complexity and intricacy of our individual cycles—emotional, physical, or psychological; internal or external—are to be honored. We wax, reach fullness, and wane; we increase and decrease; our energy heightens and it diminishes. What is critical is to be attuned to what our particular needs may be—on all those levels—in order to return to that place of balance and harmony . . . to reclaim the wholeness of ourselves as taught by our foremothers. When we honor our own individual rhythms, we are more willing and able to honor the rhythms of another person. Our internal resources then support us and prepare us to be in harmony with ourselves and with others.

DEVELOPMENTAL CYCLES

Every whole is an integral part of a greater whole; every cycle is a subcycle of a greater cycle. This creates a cause/effect relationship among all the cycles. Because of the multidimensional relatedness among all there is, all cycles are cycles between two or more dynamics, each of which is moving and is *forever changing*. Simultaneously, then, along with our internal cycles, we each participate in our developmental cycles.

Passage through the various phases of the developmental cycle is defined by an underlying impulse toward change from within, and each passage from one phase of development to the next means a *necessary loss*.[17] The necessary losses that occur along the way often evoke feelings of vulnerability, while at the same time freeing us to stretch into a new way of being in the world. Passage from one phase to another sometimes takes years, but we can know that we will eventually emerge into a more stable time and experience a sense of relative balance and equilibrium.

Personality development is influenced by many factors—culture, generation, and social change, as well as age and gender. In the fascinating video *You Are What You Were When,* the viewer is asked to look at what was going on in her life when she was 10 years old—culturally, politically, spiritually, and in her family system. My father was 10 years old in 1920: World War I had ended, the Roaring Twenties were beginning; and even though the Great Depression was to have a major influence on him throughout his life, he maintained a hopeful, anything-is-possible world view. He had an ardent (and sometimes annoying) flair for the flamboyant, and his deep belief in his—and everyone else's—ability to "pull themselves up by the boot straps" shaped his self-image: he was truly a self-made man, moving from an economically and emotionally impoverished family to become a financially successful and highly respected businessman. A passionate man, he often walked the edge of conventionality, seeming always to risk himself—not only in business, but in countless creative endeavors as well. He balanced his financial wizardry with his artistic talents in music and painting as well as his passion for carrot juicing—leading my more traditional mother to frequently and despairingly wonder, "Now, what is he into?"

One's personal evolution is based on both internal and external systems, and the internal relates to the meaning we attach to our participation in the external world—our family, society, work, social class. The internal reflects our values, goals, dreams, and how they are either nurtured or repressed in our lives.

Periodically, we feel thrown off balance in very crucial and usually disarming ways: we are being nudged into the next phase of development. Suddenly, the old rules—the familiar and comfortable ways of being in the world—no longer seem to fit. We experience a sense of disequilibrium and sometimes plunge into a state of ambiguity and confusion where what had been predictable now feels outdated and useless. We must surrender our comfortable security and let go of those cherished illusions: like it or not, we are in a growth spurt and moving to a new stage and/or a deeper level of knowing ourselves.

This is the rhythm: waxing into new learnings, we reach a comfortable fullness before we wane into the confusion and imbalance that precedes yet another cycle of development. Moving into increasing awareness, we begin to risk ourselves, tentatively at first, waxing with more and more energy into a fullness of ourselves, a sureness, a sense of well being. Then, a restlessness, an off-centeredness, perhaps a conflict inflicts itself into our reality and we plunge into a state of confusion, fear, darkness—into ourselves.

Throughout our cycles, we face the the ever-present challenge: to allow the rhythms to ebb, to flow—honoring the light and the darkness—to complete the cycle. This is growth—inevitable and disarming! The more we honor those rhythms, the more graceful will be our journey through those transitions and throughout the cycles of life. Psychoanalyst Erik Erikson used the word *crisis*—psycho social crisis—for the turning points during which we experience both an increased sense of vulnerability and often an exciting feeling of anticipation and potential.[18] Passing through each of these periods of ambiguity does seem like a crisis, but it is passing: we go on.

Traditional developmental theories, such as Erikson's *Eight Stages of Man* [sic], describe human development in a linear model and fail to include women in their accounts of adult development. A few theorists of psychology in the 1980s began to develop inclusive descriptions. Carol Gilligan, in her revolutionary book *In a Different Voice*, challenged the prevailing developmental theories: "The silence of women in the narrative of adult development distorts the conception of its stages and sequence."[19] All psychological theories depend on the perspective of the observer, and all represent an attempt to make sense of our journey through the life cycle. However, "implicitly adopting the male life as the norm, they have tried to fashion women out of a masculine cloth . . . [thus] in the life cycle, as in the Garden of Eden, the woman has been the deviant."[20] From Freud on, women's differences have been either disregarded or pointed to as demonstrating our developmental failure. "Thus, a problem in theory became cast as a problem in women's development, and the problem in women's development was located in their experience of relationships."[21] Paradoxically, and sadly, the very traits that have defined the goodness of women—our caring and sensitivity—are viewed as deficits in our moral development![22]

Moving away from the linear perspective of psychological development, Katheryn Rich adapted Erikson's "Eight Stages of Man" to her own "Seasons of a Woman's Life" and conceived a circular model of the life cycle—dividing the wheel of life into four seasons. In her system,

- *Birth* is equated to the Vernal Equinox, the season she names "Preparing for Life," which includes the first three of Erikson's psycho social crises: trust versus mistrust, autonomy versus shame, and initiative versus guilt.
- Summer Solstice brings *Menses* and the stage "Bearing Others," which includes Erikson's industry versus inferiority and identity versus confusion.
- *Midlife*, a time for "Bearing the World," commences with the Autumnal Equinox, which includes the challenges of intimacy versus isolation and generativity versus stagnation.
- With Winter Solstice, *Menopause*, the "Bearing of Self" resolves the dilemma of Erikson's integrity versus despair.

Integrating Rich's dynamic perspective with the cyclical one of *Coming Full Circle*, we can ascribe the New Moon Cycle to the Birth phase, the Waxing Moon Cycle to Menses, Full Moon Cycle to

the Seasons of a womans life

Midlife, and Waning Moon Cycle to Menopause. The phases of the moon do reflect the stages of women's lives. The New Moon is the dark of the moon, the time of preparation for life, of conception and birth; the Waxing Moon is the young girl, the Maiden, before menarche. She exudes innocence, aliveness, anticipation, and hope; her energy quickens in growth. The Full Moon is the Mother experiencing her empowering energy in the choices she makes. She is fertile—fertile with creativity, creating children, ideas, art. She's so full she may fear her "muchness." The time of the Crone, woman past menopause, is the time of the Waning Moon. She, who no longer gives birth nor bleeds, holds onto all her power, channeling this inward as she prepares for the years to follow. Her deep inner wisdom is powerful and foretelling.

Within and throughout each cycle, we experience a rhythm, an ever-changing flow as we struggle with the dilemmas of interconnectedness and separation, of oneness and individuation. We begin our lives, and our relationships, in a blissful state of symbiosis, but soon we are struggling to leave that oneness in order to search for our separate selves, waxing anew into that place of connection. We settle into a place of fullness only to have that serenity disturbed as we wane into yet another time of independence, affirming once more our intrinsic separateness. The degree to which we honor all levels of cycles is the degree to which we flow more easily and respectfully through the passages of our lives.

Individual Cycle 1: New Moon

We receive the gift of life—some of us more easily than others. We are transformed through the miraculous process of birthing from a mere seed of desire into a body of hope and possibilities. We in the cycle of the new moon are imbued with all that is possible. We are alive and ready to greet the world!

The New Moon Cycle, perceived to be the most powerful, symbolizes growth and infinite potentialities. A universe of possibilities awaits us. In preparation for the journey of life, we experience rapid and dramatic change during our first two years. Most significantly, the ways and kinds of social attachments that occur during our infancy have extensive implications for the development of our later interpersonal relationships. Inevitably, mother is our first primary relationship. "We shall have no greater need than this need for our mother. . . . In the early years of life we embark on the process of giving up what we have to give up to be separate human beings. But until we can learn to tolerate our physical and psychological separateness, our need for our mother's presence—our mother's literal, actual presence—is absolute."[23] This is safety. And the earliest and greatest terror we know is the fear of the loss of mother.

Our first time through the New Moon Cycle, as infants, we develop object permanence: we learn that objects do not cease to exist when they are out of reach or sight. We learn trust through an increasing confidence that our needs will be met and that we are valued. If our needs are not met, we experience the world as an untrustworthy place, and we may become withdrawn; symptoms of depression and grief may appear. As a matter of fact, the early loss of the mother (in the first six years) has been equated to a severe burn or a very deep wound . . . an unimaginable pain, the damage from which "although not fatal, may be permanent."[24]

During this time, mother (or other primary caregiver) and child establish a feeling of *mutuality*. This significant connection comes from the experience of gaining confidence in the belief that our basic needs will be met. As we grow in confidence, we become more willing to modify our own demands in order to maintain the continuing goodwill of the family. Through repeated interaction with mother, we begin to develop a well-differentiated concept of her as *both separate and permanent*. This process of social attachment is intimately bound to our recognition of our parents as separate beings. Once established, the trusting relationship between us—the infant and the caregiver—serves as a source of security for further explorations of our environment and as a model for future relationships.

> Nestling her infant daughter in the crook of her am, she gazed through blurred vision, as first one then another tear dropped onto her bared breast and crawled slowly across the full mound and into the corner of the tiny pink mouth suckling, tugging rhythmically on her nipple. Grace felt at once both humbled and empowered by the flood of unfathomable passion washing over her as she surrendered to the pull on her breast, tugging at her very soul.
>
> Her first born, Kathleen. The touch of the baby's little hand, her tiny fingers grasping in utter trust her mother's forefinger, melded into some very deep place in the new mother's soul, dropped petals of warm light in untouched corners, releasing feelings held too long in hostage by her fears.

The world is yours, my little one, to be discovered and explored. She struggled to push aside her fears, awed by the task of mothering this precious child. *May you always be safe in my guidance and love, and may I be open to your love and all you've come to teach me,* she whispered to the dozing child. She yielded to the infant's slowing rhythm, her tightly closed lids, thick lashes brushing plump cheeks as the tiny softness grew heavy in her mother's arm and the child slipped into a deep and gentle slumber. To the rhythm of the *cheeping, creaking* rocker, the young mother hummed the lullaby of her own childhood.

The process of social attachment and differentiation is the process of developing trust.

The initial parent/child bond teaches us we are lovable. It is in these very early years that we learn to be loved, to love, to fall in love. Unfortunately, this leaves us intensely vulnerable to the loss (or threat of loss) of that someone we love, and when that bond is broken, we experience shame and alienation: we cannot be whole. When we experience early separation and abandonment in that primary attachment, it is difficult to trust ourselves, to trust others, or to trust that we deserve to find someone to meet our needs. This has significant implications for our future relationships: we transfer early brokenness into later intimacies, expecting to be abandoned, betrayed, disappointed, and rejected. In these expectations, we cling to the other for dear life. Paradoxically, we set ourselves up for that which we least desire: to be rejected and left. We drive away those we love by our rage, our neediness, or our dependency, thus creating exactly what we have feared the most.

We may not consciously remember our early losses, but we do remember the feelings. Our bodies hold the memories. The disconnections often occur before we have the words to wrap around the experience, and our bodies become the vessels for that early pain.

Expecting disappointment and what we perceive to be inevitable loss, we avoid the pain by developing defenses against the anticipated pain of separation. We may develop the belief that no one will leave us if we don't care: we may remain emotionally detached and invest little or nothing in our relationships. Or we may avoid our own pain by becoming eminent caretakers: as long as we are compulsively taking care of others, we don't have to care for ourselves or tend to our own feelings and needs. We may become prematurely autonomous, armoring ourselves—becoming self-reliant little adults while still children.

Toddlerhood is the time when the expression of anger, very important to the child's developing autonomy, is being socialized. Relying heavily on our parents as models, we learn how to express anger. When we are able to find appropriate channels for our anger, we make tremendous gains in the development of autonomy. Inevitably, differences occur in the socialization of girls and boys with regard to the expression of anger, yet it is imperative that children begin to integrate both love and hate, happiness and anger: all must be embraced. There are no *bad* feelings. The prevailing assumption remains, even after decades of feminist activism, that little girls must not get angry. The truth, however, is that developing appropriate expressions of anger allows the child—boy or girl—to experience herself separately from her parents. Children who are severely punished or ridiculed for their anger are likely to experience shame and extreme self-doubt.

Discipline is necessary for setting limits and creating safety. When discipline is used to teach and to set limits, the child begins to learn to internalize self-defining boundaries; when discipline is used as punishment and is shaming, however, dependence on parents for validation and approval is instilled. Sometimes, due to extensive criticism or lack of encouragement, or because of repeated failure at attempted activities, or more likely because of both, we develop an overwhelming sense of shame and self-doubt. In order to avoid feeling shame, we may refrain from all kinds of new endeavors, thereby slowing—or making more painful—the process of acquiring new skills. In response to being overly criticized, we are likely to feel that we are innately bad and/or defective. We are inclined, then, to cling to what we already know, what is familiar, rather than risk the unknown, the untried.

The appropriate flow through this phase of the New Moon Cycle is one of waxing—increasing—into a delicious sense of well-being: we believe exuberantly in our powers and we are filled with wonder at all our universe holds for us. But, alas! Suddenly, we fall into a waning time when our efforts, our wishes, are thwarted by someone imposing limits. We hear No! and No! and angrily we learn that our explorations are restricted.

● ○ ●

As we approach early school age, we acquire gender-role identification, a task that we will revise and reintegrate throughout our childhood and into later adolescence. Newman and Newman note that "a strong, positive identification with the appropriate sex, regardless of the specific standards associated with that sex, is essential for the development of self-esteem and for the elaboration of peer group relationships."[25] This has implications for self-acceptance, relationships with our peers, and the development of gender-linked skills and interests. Because our moral development and sexual identity are evolving simultaneously, connections tend to be made between the two, and we may experience a moral obligation to maintain certain gender-role standards. We may feel moral guilt if these standards are violated. Imagine the feelings of confusion and guilt a child may experience should s/he experience her/himself as a tomboy or sissy; imagine the pain s/he may feel if s/he experiences being shamed for these feelings.

We've moved into another waxing phase of our first cycle as our focus turns to our external environment. We develop initiative. We begin an "active conceptual investigation of the world; autonomy is the active physical investigation of the world. . . . Initiative adds to autonomy the quality of undertaking, planning and 'attacking' a task for the sake of being active."[26]

Guilt, the internal signal when an area of prohibition has been violated, becomes an issue for the early school-age child. When our curiosity and experimentation are not supported, we are made to feel that our questions and/or doubts about the world are inappropriate. We begin to develop the ability to guide behavior by an internalized standard. But the more restrictions imposed on our thinking, the more difficult it becomes for us to distinguish between legitimate and inappropriate areas of investigation, which usually leads us toward a heavily moralistic and restrictive way of being in the world.

Guilt, beginning around age five, aids in developing a conscience. The external admonitions become internalized. According to Viorst, "true guilt, it can be argued, is not the fear of our parents' wrath or the loss of love. True guilt, it can be argued, is the fear of our *conscience's* wrath, the loss of *its* love."[27] We affirm our initiative but, thwarted, we feel guilt, turning once more within ourselves.

Of course, there is appropriate guilt and inappropriate guilt; there is insufficient guilt and excessive guilt. There is neurotic guilt, which acts like an internalized KGB, creating disproportionate self-punitiveness. Guilt can make life very interesting. Most of us are guilty of daily, thoughtless indiscretions that present us with important signals and thus opportunities for change and growth.

I have a friend who in her omnipotent way takes responsibility for *everything* and thus can feel guilty about *anything*! She feels guilty if she calls me too early or too late or when I'm writing or when I'm not—feels guilty for interrupting me or for not supporting me; she feels guilty when her children are unhappy, misbehaving, boisterous, or quiet; when her husband is successful in business and when he's not; she feels guilty when she wins a tennis match and when she loses a contract and *always* when she eats a hot fudge sundae! I have been known to prescribe 5-10 minutes per day for guilt, preferably early in the day, for the likes of my friend: if you need to feel guilty, do it, do it well, and be done with it. Unnecessary guilt is usually a distraction for other more "real" feelings. If I feel guilty, I don't have to feel angry or sad, or disappointed or scared.

Appropriate, healthy guilt occurs when we've done something truly wrong and we feel remorseful for that mistake. This is an opportunity for a lesson, not for self-flagellation. By contrast, shame occurs when we feel innately defective, when we feel we *are* a mistake, not when we've simply and humanly made a mistake: this is guilt.*

We emerge from the New Moon Cycle with our first relationship lessons. To the extent that our learnings have been healthy and nurturing, we are prepared to move into the cycles that follow. To the extent that our efforts have been thwarted, abused, or disturbed, we remain here, still needing to accomplish these tasks that are crucial for any relationship we may invite into our lives. The rhythm is created—waxing and waning: we connect; we separate. In the waxing, we surrender to our own vulnerability, trusting our beloved with our safety and our goodwill. We wane into letting go, trusting ourselves to be separate, to reach beyond the bounds so we may grow into the cycles that follow and into the lessons that await us. We learn from the beginning of our lives the challenges of waxing into connectedness, reaching an expansive fullness, and waning into separateness—the rhythm of relationships.

---

* When we are filled with shame, we are not free to be in a healthy relationship, for when we feel defective, we are unable to feel loved by another. See Lessons of the New Moon Cycle in chapter 4.

Individual Cycle 2: Waxing Moon

We move into the waxing moontime of our lives with an enthusiastic impatience for life beyond the family. We are eager to be part of a group apart from the family—the familiar. We yearn to reach beyond the limits, to explore our minds and our senses, and we do this as we develop intimate friendships—best friends—with our same-sex peers. We are entering into the summer of our lives, leaving, letting go of the first cycle.

To recall the time of the New Moon Cycle of our lives is difficult, often painful. Our memories may be dim, vague, or hurtful. In reflection, we tend to ascribe the feelings and wisdom of our older, more mature selves onto that young child-self. We are apt to have little compassion or patience for that younger, awkward part of ourselves—for the one who may have faced enormous odds in her struggle to survive and to grow.

With our greater cognitive skills, we'll successfully maneuver the transition into the wider world only if we have established some sense of separateness. If, however, we've been held too close to the family through emotional abuse, physical abuse, or incest, we will find it difficult to move along on our journey: we'll be distracted and less likely to perform the tasks that await us. The challenge of the Waxing Moon Cycle is to focus on work—whether reading and writing or skipping and skateboarding: it is through work that we feel competent, that we define our reality. We will certainly become, with this focus on work, preoccupied with self-evaluation, either from self-confidence or self-doubt. This self-evaluation is grounded in a need for approval and conformity.

Through the years of puberty and adolescence, we may have a special grown-up friend—a teacher, scout leader, neighbor—who is able to teach us things we wouldn't be caught dead discussing with our mom. Pat was such a person for me. She'd named her baby after me and when I turned 9, I was able to help her tend the sweet, curly-haired child. I loved Pat: she was so pretty, with her glorious auburn hair and smiling green eyes. She never scolded me, never told me to clean my room, do the dishes, wash the dog, pick up my toys, wash my hair, brush my teeth. She simply talked to me—I have no idea, now, about what, but talking with her made me feel "big." With her, I got to practice being grown-up. And as I grew older and she began leaving me alone with the baby, I felt quite capable and competent and adult.

Fundamental attitudes toward work are established during this stage: industry implies an eagerness for skill-building and performing meaningful work; inferiority occurs when we are unable to see ourselves as having the potential to be a contributing member of our chosen community, when we are excluded from any meaningful social group. Many of us occasionally relive the humiliation we felt by being *always* the last chosen for the softball team. My own short legs and awkward body simply couldn't move with the grace that Sally Lancer's could. No doubt, I'll have to wait till my next lifetime to be both jock and ballerina I so longed to be.

Through these years, we struggle with moral conflict. The differences in moral development between girls and boys have long been analyzed from a hierarchical perspective. In fact, "the contrasting images of hierarchy and network in children's thinking about moral conflict and choice illuminates two views of morality which are complementary rather than sequential or opposed. But this construction of differences goes against the bias of developmental theory toward ordering differences in a hierarchical mode."[28] Girls, it seems, tend to make choices from a contextual perspective; boys, from a legalistic or categorical one. This underscores the importance for women of viewing development and relationships as cyclical—dynamic, moving, nonlinear and nonhierarchical.

● ○ ●

The waxing of puberty is experienced with an excitement for learning, achieving, acquiring competency. As it wanes, we move into deep self-evaluation and self-consciousness as we shift, usually quite awkwardly, toward adolescence, the time of menses. We may acquire a group of friends that provides us with a sense of belonging; this is the positive resolution of adolescence. On the other hand, a negative resolution may leave us with a pervasive sense of alienation from our peers. We may have little or no feeling of belonging. In that case, we are continually ill at ease in the presence of peers. We may also perceive others' expectations to be in conflict with our own values or needs, thus we may feel alienated and estranged and unable to identify with social groups. As young adolescents, we engage in a process of self-evaluation within the context of our peer group. We are extremely conscious of others' opinions and preoccupied with our need for acceptance from friends. At this time, peers can be a resource for the building of self-confidence or a source of pressure for conformity and conflict of values. If we are not able to integrate those values, we will probably feel alienation and rejection and self-deprecation.

Consider the young woman or man who is becoming increasingly aware of feelings of attraction to same-sex friends. The conflict between the need to conform to values of peers and the need to value and honor the needs for a same-sex relationship in heterosexist culture is profoundly confusing and painful; it may lead to even greater alienation and despair. For some girls, the pressure to leave behind activities that are not only fun but that build confidence and competence—playing ball with the guys—for more feminine ways, is traumatic and confusing. For some boys, the pressure to abandon intellectual or artistic activities at which they excel and take up physical activities where they expect to fail is similarly burdensome.

All of us, in our attempt to discover "who am I?" may experience identity confusion. We may have problems with intimacy and struggle with feelings of estrangement. We may over-identify with a hero. We may fall in with the "wrong crowd." We would rather be *really* bad than be only slightly okay; we'd rather be part of a group—any group—than be isolated from peers.

We use our friends in adolescence—and then later our lovers—to discover and to validate who we are becoming. Our friends love us, no matter what; through and with them we get to experience empathy, loyalty, and commitment. Close friendships require at least a developing sense of self.

In the crazy time called adolescence, we need all the friends we can get. We worry about everything that is different about us: our hips are bigger than anyone's, our ankles are thicker than anyone's, our eyelashes are too sparse, our hair too curly or too straight, our legs too thin. To be *normal*, we think, is to be just like everyone else. What is *really* normal is change and utter disharmony—from moment to moment. In both our bodies and our heads, the conflicts and mood swings and extremes are problematic. For everyone.

Sara's body was surely betraying her. Always taut, lean, and limber, now she was rounding into hills and mounds that annoyed her. What was happening to her? She pondered the question as she lay among tall grasses in the meadow while finches lunched on prickly thistle and imagined herself flying on the hawk's wing high among the cottony clouds overhead. Waves of euphoric energy could vanish into awful feelings of weirdness at any moment.

Her body seemed strange and foreign to her, with its budding breasts and sprouting hairs. Having breasts was not at all useful for playing football, and her mother was becoming paranoid about her physical safety. Wasn't it bad enough she'd probably start having periods soon? She promised herself that when she did, she wouldn't be bitchy and depressed like her sister. Not that it mattered anyway. Kitty wasn't home much anymore—always out with her friends or mooning over Tom! Why anyone would want to have a boyfriend was beyond her comprehension. She'd *never* get married; she knew that much. And the thought of having babies was sickening! At least Jenny agreed with her. Jenny was her very best friend. They played together every day and talked about everything: school, their sisters, their moms and dads, and what they would be when they grew up. Imagine being a forest ranger or maybe a doctor, or a missionary to Africa. She just couldn't decide.

It was time to find Jenny in their secret grove and then they'd probably explore the woods, climb into the big old sycamore. In a flash, she was once again in motion—on to another adventure. Long legs running, unruly hair flying, off to see what the beavers had been up to down by the creek, collecting rocks and, along the way, if they were lucky they might even find another hawk's feather.

Adolescence is a manic, withdrawn, goofy, now-I'm-a-grown-up-and-now-I'm-7-again-time, when we're trying to fit into those outrageously changing bodies with scary exciting feelings, when the normal state is usually hard to discern from insanity, "when development—normal development—demands that we lose and leave and let go of . . . everything. Zapped by hormones, our body undertakes a massive revision—enlarging our sexual parts and our hair supply, demonstrating (by menstrual flows and seminal emissions) that we are joining the race of the baby-makers, changing our height and our weight and our shape and our skin and our voice and our odors, till we hardly know what to expect when we wake up in the morning."[29] No wonder this time is known as an identity *crisis*!

● ○ ●

In adolescence, we begin the lifelong process of distinguishing between our dreams and our possibilities and the distance between the two begins to lessen. "In early adolescence, we are preoccupied with puberty's bodily changes. By middle adolescence, we are struggling with 'who am I' and looking outside the home for sexual love. In late adolescence, we further mute our conscience's harshness and include . . . value commitments which are connected with our place in the wider world." All the while we mourn the loss of our childhood.[30]

For women, the concept of *identity* includes interconnectedness: it has more to do with intimacy than with separateness—which makes women the more vulnerable, but not the weaker, sex. Perhaps one of the reasons psychologists have been so baffled by women's experience is that imagery used by men and women differs considerably. Images of hierarchy and of web (drawn from fantasies and thoughts of men and women) reflect different ways of structuring relationships as well as different views of morality and self. These conflicting images create a problem between men and women in their understanding of each other because each image distorts the other's and, in fact, the images represent unsafe places to each other. The top of the hierarchy becomes the edge of the web, while the center web of connection becomes the middle of a hierarchical progression. "Thus the images of hierarchy and web inform different modes of assertion and response: the wish to be alone at the top and the consequent fear that others will get too close; the wish to be at the center of connection and the consequent fear of being too far out on the edge. These disparate fears of being stranded and being caught give rise to different portrayals of achievement and affiliation leading to different modes of action and different ways of assessing the consequences of choice."[31]

Perceiving relationships through this imagery of interconnection—not hierarchy, which inevitably is problematic and unstable—lends itself to resolution of differences and conflicts, revealing the truth of relationship: that the self and other are indeed interdependent and can, in the end, only be sustained by care and nurture in that relationship.[32] Currently in the field of psychology, there are no descriptors for structuring a woman's sense of self. Some have advocated a new psychological language—a language organized around being able to make and then to maintain affiliations and relationships.

Without such a language, women are impeded in fully and adequately describing their experience: "When the interconnections of the web are dissolved by the hierarchical ordering of relationships, when nets are portrayed as dangerous entrapments, impeding flight rather than protecting against a fall, women come to question whether what they have seen exists and whether what they know from their own experience is true."[33] Questioning our own reality, our own truth, becomes an issue of trusting ourselves and our willingness to take responsibility for those selves. There is no support for our knowing what we *know.*

Different voices are heard: males usually speak of separation as defining and empowering of the self, while females speak of attachment that creates and sustains community.[34]

Identity and intimacy are woven intricately throughout women's development. Young women, when asked to describe themselves, inevitably describe a relationship, identifying themselves in connection with another person. Their descriptions typically reflect an ethic of nurturance, responsibility, and care.[35] Although approached from different perspectives, the tasks for both women and men are the same: resolving the conflict between integrity and care—bringing into focus contrasting truths that are reflected in different moral ideologies; "separation is justified by an ethic of rights while attachment is supported by an ethic of care."[36]

● ○ ●

By later adolescence, we should be making a commitment to a personal integration of values, goals, and abilities; this identity that we choose reflects our own values, as well as those of our reference group. We may fall into expected roles without having sorted through our own values from external expectations. Or, unable to integrate those various roles, we may not make a commitment to a single self-perception or identity—thus creating a fear of losing hold of our selves and our futures. The implications of a lack of identity are profound when we begin to involve ourselves in intimate relationships.

As we grow into the young adult years, we tend to move toward tolerance and away from the absolutes of adolescence. We develop a greater capacity to believe in both truth and choice. In women's developmental process, the value of caring (which we typically define as not hurting anyone) becomes more complex as we recognize our need for personal integrity. This recognition challenges us to balance what is right for ourselves and what is right for our relationships; we must redefine just what care means. For men, the value of truth and fairness, in the context of equality and reciprocity, is questioned when differences between other and self are recognized.[37]

The challenge we face is to discover those characteristics essential for self-definition while not alienating ourselves from our social environment. This definition of self is achieved only after an extensive period of questioning, evaluation, and experimentation—essential strategies for coping with new information and new value orientations. Only when we know what we stand for can we participate fully in deep commitments with and to others.

Once again, the rhythm of the waxing and waning emerges, for the theme of the adolescent years is that of waxing into connectedness, exploring intimacy with others, and then waning into separateness and an individual definition of self. Waxing and waning: connecting and separating. Experienced and defined differently by women and men, the theme remains.

Individual Cycle 3: Full Moon

We wax into the Autumn of our lives. We grow up! Just as the moon grows into a fullness of being, so do we! During our young to middle adult years, we are busy, productive, energetic, and sometimes frenetic. Throughout the waxing of this third cycle, this increasing generativity, in our work, our parenting, and our countless commitments, we confront the challenge of deepening intimacies with those with whom we've chosen to share our lives. This is the full moon of our lives. Like the enormous, glorious, amber harvest moon, breathtaking in her prodigious beauty, we feel filled up; we are often overwhelmed by the demands of simply living our lives.

Everything that preceded this cycle can be seen as preparation for midlife and all the relationships we will develop and deepen in the Full Moon Cycle. All that follows may be perceived as actualization, for the developmental tasks of early adulthood are about developing intimacies—with our partner, our children, and our work. Our challenge throughout the fullness of adulthood is to refine the tasks of generativity and intimacy. Traditional, male-defined developmental theory would have us believe these to be separate stages through which we travel, but we women know that *generativity*—the concern in establishing and guiding the next generation[38]—is well integrated with our ability to be intimate.

Women know about cycles; our experience is not a linear one. Our intimacies are intricately woven into the texture of our lives—in our relationships with our friends, our lovers, our children, and our life's work. We know there are many cycles, and cycles within cycles. Within this, the cycle of the autumn of our lives, we wax, reach fullness, and then wane. At the same time, we are experiencing—or enduring—our unique individual cycles, which may be out of sync with those with whom we share our lives. Women often confront the challenges, the quest, of midlife earlier than men: attending to our biological rhythms is unavoidable.

In retrospect, Sara remained bewildered by the reluctance she'd felt just two days ago as she'd wound her way through this very forest on her way to the lake. The early autumn sun danced through the trees brushing her unruly hair with threads of red and gold. Feeling more invigorated than she had in months, she pushed her red Honda Prelude to its limits, taking the winding curves through the woods as fast as she dared. She laughed aloud at her earlier foolishness.

Jenny had convinced her to join the girls for their annual autumn gathering. Her hesitation confused her. Hadn't she known these women since high school—some from kindergarten! They were her oldest friends. They knew each other so well. Yet in that knowing, Sara felt vulnerable. What they knew, after all, was that wild, rebellious, restless kid who hated dating guys and who was forever enlisting her long-suffering friends in one cause or another. Although all of them had continued after high school to meet regularly, she, believing she had little in common with them, had distanced herself from the group. While her girlfriends were busy marrying their high school heroes, having babies and playing bridge, she'd been completing graduate school, paying off school loans, and trying in vain to convince 13-year-old girls not to have sex. As an overworked and underpaid social worker, she took her career very seriously and often felt overwhelmed by the poverty and disease, abuse and hopelessness she confronted each day at Concord Center. She was intensely passionate about her work and had little time for things less crucial.

She did treasure this group of women. She felt warmed in their affection and grateful for the unequivocal acceptance and respect most held for her as a feminist and a lesbian. In spite of the very different paths they walked, each of them struggled to find room in their love for the variegated threads they wove.

A chuckle escaped into the cool autumn air as scenes rushed across her mind. They might all be 15 years older now, but the weekend had seemed just like one of their many slumber parties—everyone talking and laughing at once, staying up until nearly dawn whispering and giggling until sleep could no longer be evaded and fell like a blanket upon everyone at once.

For the weekend, no one had worried about diapers or preschool, husbands or kids. Instead, they tackled major life issues such as who among them had the biggest breasts and who really was the tallest. They worried about their diets while consuming vast quantities of Pepsi, popcorn, hot fudge sundaes, pizza and beer, and anything chocolate. And into the mix was their deep concern for Jo whose father had died suddenly of heart failure and for Sandy whose son struggled so in school and for Janet whose mother—whom they all loved as their own—was becoming alarmingly forgetful. They knew one another's self-centered sisters and bratty brothers; they knew whose mothers they could confide in and whose fathers to avoid. They had been in one another's lives since they were children, and the fabric was woven securely with shared pleasures and pain. These women knew and cared for each other; they had nurtured a very special community. Sara was grateful to have these women in her life, these women who offered her the gifts of acceptance and continuity and courage. She vowed to set aside the fears that had separated her and to surrender to loving and taking in her girlfriends' love.

Our friendships are vital to us. They are the place where we learn to connect and to separate, yet our most significant relationship (or marriage—however that is defined) is the primary context within which the hard work of intimacy and mature social relationships takes place. Not unlike our first psychosocial crisis (trust versus mistrust), we set out on the path of relationships by measuring and testing one another. The differences we discover in this process will need to be named, affirmed, and celebrated.

Typically, women enter the fullness of our lives well equipped as nurturers and caretakers—weavers of the web of relationships, intricately woven into the fabric of our self-definition. Women tend to bring to this cycle not only distinct experiences and perspectives but also unique individual priorities. As Carol Gilligan points out, "The elusive mystery of woman's development lies in its recognition of the continuing importance of attachment in the human life cycle. Woman's place in man's cycle is to protect this recognition while the developmental litany intones the celebration of separation, autonomy [and] individuation."[39] For women, marriage, divorce, and childbearing tend to be the focal points of our life stories simply because this is who we *are*. Women's lives are almost completely organized around their commitments to other people.

We may ask ourselves: why, when we're doing *so* good, do we feel so bad? Is it "the problem that has no name"?[40] The answer, of course, is that the patriarchal culture has devalued that care that we feel and show toward others. Patriarchal psychological theories focus on individuation and achievement as the parameters by which maturity is measured. Concern with relationships continues to be seen, in patriarchy, as a weakness of women rather than as a strength.[41] When we grow up surrounded by disparagement—implicit or explicit—we carry those wounds, and upon reclaiming, the undiscovered self becomes an unexpected resource.[42]

The typical patriarchal conception of adulthood as favoring an autonomous life of work and achievement rather than an interdependent life of love and care and relating is out of balance. The norm in our male-dominated culture is one of *acting upon* rather than of *participating with* one another.[43] Sadly, this attitude pervades all levels of our culture. Our ailing planet is a tragic example of the imbalance in the devaluation of relationships.* As we learn to commit ourselves to a *relationship with* our Mother Earth, by nurturing, caring and healing Her, we utilize the very properties inherent in any healthy relationship.

A "new psychology of women," posited by Jean Baker Miller,[44] recognizes that women do enter into relationships at a different place.

---

* It is becoming alarmingly clear that our unwillingness to *participate with our Mother Earth* is rapidly and perhaps irrevocably taking us down a path of destruction—some say as early as the year 2040! We can no longer afford to try simply to "save" our planet, for that implies a separation from Her.

Women persist and develop in the context of relationships with others: our sense of self is organized around our ability to build and maintain relationships. When that is threatened or disrupted, women often experience a loss of self. A valid psychology must recognize that adult development cannot negate or exclude the value of attachment and affiliation; we can no longer afford to devalue the significance of nurturance and care in relationships—*all relationships.*

The reality is that women as yet have no substantive language; the challenge to listen, to trust our own inner knowings remains. Communication of our thoughts and feelings is difficult at best: we struggle to separate others' voices from our own and to find a language that expresses our experience of relationship and of our sense of self. As we learn to honor the rhythms inherent within ourselves *and* within our relationships, to remember that both different/nesses and commonalties can be enriching, we begin to value our relationship cycles and our individual cycles and thus to create our own story, our own journey.

In the meantime, we continue to struggle to define ourselves as at once *both* separate *and* connected. We need language to facilitate this knowing that we can be with others in ways that allow us to be with ourselves. We are on uncharted paths here, however. The dominant, patriarchal culture continues to view our experience in dichotomous terms: individual or in relationship; separate or together. So we continue to seek another way of defining intimacy: we struggle not to *react* to the expectations of others but rather to *respond* to others and to ourselves. We're seeking a path of responsibility in relating that arises from recognizing that others are counting on us, and we wish to respond, both to ourselves and to them. For women, responsibility has less to do with following the rules, as created by men, and more to do with the *ability to respond.*

Intimacy is the ability to respond to another in open, supportive, tender ways without fear of losing our own identity in the process of growing close. *Closeness, fear, vulnerability, honesty, sexuality, risk-taking* are all words that speak to us of intimacy. Intimacy is a rich and complex experience. The possibility of establishing intimacy depends on the confidence that each of us has in herself as a valuable, competent, and significant person. Intimacy implies the ability for mutual empathy and mutual regulation of needs. We must be able to give pleasure as well as to receive pleasure within the intimate relationship.[45] We must have the capacity for both giving and receiving tenderness, kindness and respect. We must have the capacity for compassion and understanding.

Learning of the progression of relationships toward a maturity of interdependence is key to our emotional health. In the traditional psychological paradigm, relationships take on a connotation of immaturity or insignificance. The men who created that prevailing view tend to use self-descriptive words such as *intelligent, logical, honest*—words of separation. So instead of attachment, individual achievement and activity define success for men, and that linear approach to development more aptly fits the adult male's transition from adolescence into adulthood. While women resonate with a cyclical perspective, power and separation define the man in an identity achieved through work, which, unfortunately, is more likely to leave him distanced from others. Thus intimacy is often experienced quite differently by women and men.

For both women and men, the positive resolution of this Full Moon Cycle is one of a deepening intimacy. The negative outcome, on the other hand, is isolation: for some of us, the possibility of closeness with another threatens our sense of self. Sensing a blurring of boundaries of our own identity, we cannot let ourselves engage in intimate relationships.[46]

Mutuality is the willingness to integrate the differences between us into the relationship. We increase our ability to meet each other's needs and to accept each other's shortcomings. The integrating process serves as a way of enhancing both partners. This is how intimacy is developed. Just as the baby learns to trust the ability of her caregiver to meet her needs, so each of us in a committed/married couple learns to trust the other's ability to anticipate and satisfy our needs.[47] In addition, our relationship with our work and the nurturing of other friendships are significant in staving off the isolation that threatens us, for we can easily become isolated even in busyness. Maintaining balance, particularly in the area of work, is challenging.

Growing up means more of those necessary losses. With each birth there is a death: with the birth of a new cycle, there is a letting go of those aspects of ourselves that no longer serve us. We must release if we are to have a rebirth. Growing up means letting go of those cherished childhood dreams of omnipotence; it means realizing we can't have it all, can't do it all. Growing up means achieving both skills and wisdom—acquiring resources that allow us to get what we can within realistic limitations—"a reality which consists of diminished powers, restricted freedoms and, with the people we love, imperfect connections . . . a reality built in part upon the acceptance of our necessary losses."[48]

We move into young adulthood—our crazy 20s: seeking a place in the adult world, we become focused on externals. This is a time of *shoulds*. At the same time that we are driven to do what we should do, we're creating a vision, a dream. This is a time of aliveness, energy, and hope. The challenge of the waxing time of this cycle is to become settled and simultaneously to explore and experiment. To get too settled too soon may mean getting prematurely locked in; to experiment too much too long may mean not ever really getting started.

By our late 20s and into our 30s, we should have developed enough experience living outside our parents' care that we've established ourselves as independent, self-reliant grown-ups. We can afford, now that we are less focused on becoming competent, to glimpse a deeper place wherein lie our passions: those desires that used to frighten us too much or for which we had no time or energy. We begin to explore those passions that promise to evolve into that which gives our lives meaning. Often motivated by a restlessness and dissatisfaction, we begin a spiritual awakening through which we clarify our values and ascertain what has significance for us.

If the 20s are about *I should,* then the late 20s into our 30s become *I can.* We become more focused on career and family—bearing and rearing children and establishing our home. We begin to feel more settled; life is busy but orderly. Our world view becomes more diverse and inclusive as we begin to affirm our interdependence with the world. Truly this is a time when our need for personal gratification becomes subordinated to our need for mutual satisfaction in relationships. The experiences of love and attachment, heretofore experienced in the context of our family of origin, are now transferred and transformed into a newly formed expression of affection that includes sexual maturity, cognitive perspective, personal identity, and mature moral thought. At the same time, many obstacles to successfully attaining an intimate relationship remain—unresolved issues including shame, guilt, inferiority, or alienation. These may undermine our successful definition of our self and thus limit our ability to experience intimacy.

The mutuality we experience as parents through childrearing most significantly contributes to an increasing capacity for intimacy. In fact, through our child's open expressions of affection, we learn about the expression of love and our capacity for demonstrating love.[49] Throughout our 30s, we begin to discover, often to our horror, many resemblances to our parents: we are just like mom—not externally, but our mother in ourselves. In our parenting, we may discover something else too: a gentler, less judgmental part of ourselves that is more forgiving of others and of ourselves. We now have the opportunity for transforming those hurtful, ineffective patterns that too often inhibit a healthy way of being in the world—with our peers, our partners, and our children.

Soon we enter into the midlife decade—another one to which *crisis* seems to apply, for change is the primary characteristic of midlife. We find ourselves—at age 35 to 45—undeniably in our middle years. The challenges of middle age are the greatest opportunity we may ever have to become most truly alive and ourselves.[50] Midlife can be a wonderful opportunity—a time for another reassessment. Finally, we need no one's permission but our own to live our lives fully. We move into the fullness of the cycle and we celebrate the richness of growth and change as we redefine old patterns and become the parents, the partner, the friend we envisioned for ourselves.

Women tend to do midlife revaluing earlier than do men. At 35, we may feel an urgency, a sense that this may be our last chance—to have a career, to marry, to have children. Indeed, the biological clock is ticking: old age looms. In our youth-obsessed culture, most—women and men alike—feel threatened by the lurking shadow of age. In actuality, more and more women are deferring childbearing to their middle years, electing to have children after age 35. This places them in a unique developmental phase: the woman whose menopause coincides with her daughter's menarche will have a different experience from one who at the same age is adjusting to letting go of her children as, one by one, they begin to leave home. An increasing dilemma of our time seems to be one of adult children needing to return home. Just when we begin to adjust to their absence, they—often for economic reasons—return.

As Gail Sheehy points out, "boomers having babies in their forties know they have departed from life-cycle norms when they have to put on reading glasses to breast feed."[51] The woman who postpones childbearing until her 40s in order to pursue a career often feels as if she is leading a compressed life: marriage at 43, motherhood at 45, and menopause at 46. Nevertheless, her passages, her inner knowings and nudgings are similar; her external circumstances are not. On the other hand, women and men who have pushed hard in their careers may feel, by 40, burdened, restless, and unappreciated. Midlife offers an opportunity to explore a second career and to become more ethically focused. For women, midlife often means claiming assertiveness and other inner resources heretofore lain dormant.

At the same time, we begin to face our finitude. Physically we may recognize certain limitations—a little arthritis here and there and a metabolism that stubbornly slows. Our neatly defined roles lose their luster, and we begin a recognition of mortality, thrusting us headlong into a spiritual crisis. Terrifying and dangerous as this feels, this is a time for redefining ourselves once more, for assessing our purpose, the meaning of our lives. We feel an urgency about our life and the I *should* of our 20s that became the I *can* of our 30s now, in our 40s, evolves into I *must*!

> Her fortieth year coincided—head-on with savage ferocity—with the Women's Movement. Lost as Kit was, she might never have noticed had it not been for Sara's loving persistence.
>
> In spite of their many differences, the two sisters had grown into close and loving friends. Geographical moves and emotional transitions had created numerous waxings and wanings between them, but there remained a connection that ran deep and strong between the two women, until the preceding summer.

Sara had arrived at the family cottage on Massachusetts Bay a few days earlier than her sister and her family. Happily and passionately in love, she was eager to share her story first with her parents and then with Kit. With surprisingly little bewilderment, her parents had received the news gracefully. Kit's reaction had been another story.

For years, they had spent the first night of the family gathering talking and giggling together through the night, then gleefully racing down to the beach as the huge red sun popped above the horizon.

As soon as the chaos of Kit's arrival with Tom and the kids had quieted and everyone seemed settled in for the night, the women nestled into the sofa for their marathon session. Heart pounding, Sara exclaimed, *I can't wait another minute, Kit. I'm in love!*

Oh, Sara, how wonderful! I'm so happy! Leaping from the sofa, she pulled Sara into a warm embrace. They danced and hopped around the room in happy celebration. When she caught her breath, Kit insisted on every detail.

Who is he? Do I know him? Tell me all!

First of all, Sara took a deep breath, *I don't believe you've met her.* She gently emphasized the pronoun. *Her name is Emily and she's a third grade teacher.*

But Kit's face had paled, her body stiffened. *I see . . .* Her voice came from a tight, hard place. *Well, I'm happy for you.* Her voice sounded forced, tense.

I love her very much, Kit. Disappointment washed through Sara. She didn't want to cry.

Well, I'm sure I'll get used to this, were the only words Kit could find.

Not only had the night ended early, so had Sara's visit. She'd left the following day and for the months that followed, Kit remained distant. Phone messages went unanswered; letters unacknowledged.

Winter Solstice brought the sisters together for the first time in months, and Sara's worst fears were confirmed. Her sister remained cool; yet Sara, who knew her sister better than anyone, sensed something was troubling Kit deeply—something that had nothing at all to do with Sara.

Kit, what's wrong? They stood in their familiar places at the kitchen sink, Kit carefully washing, Sara drying their grandmother's china and silver dulled to a burnished luster, just as they had for nearly 30 Yules.

Nothing, voice empty, distant.

*Kit, I know you. Behind that well-coifed hair and lovely
porcelain face, you seem so troubled. Please, talk to me.* Sara's
gentle tone held an urgency Kit couldn't ignore. One by one,
salty tears splashed into the dishwater as the faultline she'd
long ignored began to split wide. She remained silent, if not
stoic.

If you won't talk to me, Sara was speaking to Kit's stiffened
back, *then please, let's just spend some time together.* She
hesitated and then placed her arm around her sister's small,
tense shoulders. *I miss you, Kit, so much.*

So Kit had agreed—reluctantly—to join Sara at her women's
group. They were enlisting volunteers in the struggle to pass
the Equal Rights Amendment.

And Kit was hooked.

The ERA—the Women's Movement's political focus, became
her *raison d'être.* Given any opportunity, she, in
uncharacteristic outspokenness, was likely to expound on
issues of equality for women with a passion previously
unclaimed. Kit, the conservative, middle-class, Junior League
board member who just ten years before had not only voted
for Barry Goldwater but had volunteered for the Republican
Party as well was now participating in sit-ins and the Chicago
Mother's Day March for ERA! Her passions had been stirred
and were now unleashed and roaring! Finally, there was
purpose to her life.

As we finally see our lives more clearly, we feel excited, yes, but also
frightened—afraid that we're running out of time. We grieve the loss of
those sensible, stable years of our 30s when our whole lives stretched
before us and everything seemed possible; we grieve the loss of the
illusion that we would have plenty of time in which to do it all. Those
years are inevitably giving way to a relentless pressure to do it now! This
is our last chance and whatever it is that must be done, must be done
NOW. Our last remaining illusion of security is wrenched away and the
rushing of time makes existentialists of us all. "We stand naked and
exposed, toe to toe with life. Our naiveté is lost forever. The illusion of
our immortality is dying." We must face the reality that nothing will save
us from the inevitable—death![52] As our inner pendulum moves between
the denial and acceptance of our vulnerability, we evolve into a deeper
understanding of the meaning of our lives. The backdrop to the swinging
pendulum, however, is usually rage, despair, passivity or depression as
we confront our own finitude, "the repugnance of death."[53]

We come to see the honoring of the waning of the cycle as essential. Separating is a process, a necessary process. As parents, we must renegotiate our relationship with our children at each passage—as infants, children, adolescents, and again as adult women and men—just as we did with our parents as we passed through each age. We must continually be open to renegotiating within ourselves just what is required of us as parents—and as children. I'm certainly not the same parent to my 34-year-old daughter that I was when she was 24 much less when she was 14. Nor am I the same daughter to my 87-year-old mother that I was 10, 20 years ago. We're all growing up.

Each transition represents another letting go—another death—of the old as we wax into a new cycle; we define a new form: waxing and waning and waxing once more. Simultaneously, we must remind ourselves to give up the hope of being the perfect mother and to affirm that indeed we can be, and probably are, *good enough*. Our children will leave, to experience their own unique waxings and wanings. All relationships end—on some level; they must die in order to be rebirthed.

The midlife moments of reevaluation and reorganization occur with half a lifetime of creativity and productivity awaiting us. We stand on the threshold of the second half of our adulthood. Middle adulthood, potentially a very creative period, is characterized by our readiness and willingness to take responsibility for our own actions and decisions. While this can be disrupted by our fear of aging or an over-responsiveness to social expectations as we learn to balance the self and the social system, we have the capacity for directing the course of action in our own life and in the lives of others. We notice the consequences of our behavior on immediate situations and as we move toward fulfilling long-term goals. We are fine-tuning our ability to make decisions, to plan for the future, to anticipate the needs of others, and to conceptualize the developmental phases of the life cycle, thus allowing us to make a deliberate impact on the future.[54]

For women, this transition time is reflected in our relationships. Because woman's sense of integrity is experienced through the values of caring and connectedness, the midlife passage must involve significant changes in attachment and in the activities of caring. Women's psychological reactions in the middle years differ from men's; we face different realities and possibilities in both love and work. We make choices based on our knowledge that may lead us to an understanding of life that reflects the limits of autonomy and control. Women's experience provides a key to understanding central truths of adult life. Viewing our anatomy as a destiny leaves us scarred with inferiority. Instead, we can see glimpses of a truth common to both genders: "the fact that in life you never see it all, that things unseen undergo change through time, that there is more than one path to gratification, and that the boundaries between self and other are less clear than they sometimes seem."[55]

When we see ourselves in the context of relationships, we can appreciate the challenges that midlife holds for us as we face the challenges inherent in the waning of the cycle; menopause, changes in the family system, and work may alter our total definition of self.

The waning of the autumn cycle is marked by the onset of menopause.* A very significant passage, menopause remains in the shadows of ourselves. Although it's difficult to deny, few wish to talk about it: the sudden gushing of blood, the night sweats, the unpredictable moody blues, the fatigue, and then the flushing, dripping hot flashes—or as one young friend sweetly confirmed for me, "Well, you do look a little *dewy!*" In spite of a conspiracy of silence that engulfs a perfectly natural and normal—not to mention potentially empowering—process, menopause has an enormous impact on us and our relationships. Commonly called the *change of life*, menopause serves as a powerful metaphor for the waning of the Full Moon Cycle, for change is the theme for midlife.

Generativity, a concept that equates to productivity and creativity, is primarily the concern for establishing and guiding the next genera-

---

* While men have nothing comparable to our menstrual cycle and therefore have no corresponding hormonal change to mark their midlife, many do experience significant changes. Like midlife women, midlife men may have a new sense of strength along with an increasing vulnerability; they experience physical changes as well: pelvic muscles lose their tone and the testes decrease in size and become more flaccid. However, there is evidence that there is no change in the sex hormone level of men even into their later years, although they may experience a gradual slowing of the arousal process.[56]

tion.[57] This is our task throughout the Full Moon Cycle—our midlife. Many women experience generativity through childrearing; others choose alternative avenues for the expression of creativity. Most of us experience some renewed desire for creating. The two forces, birth and death, coexist and become more clearly integrated. We long to integrate the feminine with the masculine, the creative with the destructive, the separate self—that will inevitably be alone— with the self that desires connections and community.

In the autumn of our lives, the waning of the third cycle, we grieve the passing of our spring and summer. We grieve the loss of our younger selves as our past realities collapse; those earlier self-perceptions neces- sarily must be redefined yet again. *Is this all there is?* cries Peggy Lee in that sultry, throaty voice, echoing, for many of us, the limitations that must be confronted. For we in midlife are concerned with our own mortality—with death and endings—both our own and others. We undeniably stand on the threshold of the final cycle of our lives. At the same time, we are experiencing a strong need to create, to contribute to the generations that will follow. This "crisis of generativity versus stag- nation is a crisis in meaningfulness."[58] We strive to come to some philosophy of life that imparts significance to daily activities, including the actual attainment of creative efforts, and to establish a clear perspec- tive regarding our life's work.

We remember that the waning of the cycle is about deepening, diving into the underworld, meeting the shadow; for many of us everything in which we believed needs re/value-ating! We may meet our demons, our shadow. What we heretofore perceived to be our blessings may now be our nemesis. Indeed, the path narrows, the years shorten, the light wanes. We have the opportunity in the waning of midlife to confront all our illusions, to meet the shadow side of ourselves, to descend into the darkness of the soul. The acceptance of the darkness, paradoxically, allows us to discover the light. The descent allows us to ascend into the waxing of the next—our final—developmental cycle. The resolution of the waning acts as the catalyst, the impetus, to thrust us forward, renewed, ready for what lies ahead. That is the irony: the nature of the shadow is both the container of darkness and the beacon pointing into the light.[59]

Change is the primary characteristic of midlife. Without change, we cannot grow—there will be no transformation. We become stagnant and ultimately die—to ourselves and in our relationship. Fear is what makes midlife a crisis.

Individual Cycle 4: Waning Moon

As we move into our final cycle—the Waning Moon Cycle—we remember that all of the cycles of our lives ebb and flow, wax, reach fullness, and wane. All phases of each cycle are to be honored. As we experience the increasing energy, the connections inherent in the waxing of the cycle, we do well to flow into that rhythm which is natural and life-giving. Moving into the fullness of our cycle, we relish the sense of well-being, of serenity, of completeness that fills us; and when we proceed into the waning phase of our life cycle, we surrender to the separateness that leads us into darkness in which we deepen our sense of self. So it is—increasingly—through each of the four cycles of our life: ever growing toward more and more wholeness and integration.

We look retrospectively through our lives into the wholeness of a complete cycle in this Waning Moon Cycle. The new moon of our childhood grew into the waxing moon of our adolescence and young adulthood, and thence we flowed into the full moon of midlife; now we ebb into the waning moon of our elderhood. Each cycle must be sustained; each phase of each cycle must be honored. For no phase of any cycle is any less sacred than the other; the waning of the life cycle is no less venerable than the full, than the waxing. As a matter of fact, Mark Gerzon points out that "whenever a society collapses or dies, you will notice that the life cycle has been disrespected. . . . Conversely, when a society flourishes, you will find that the life cycle has been honored. Each stage has been cared for and provided with some kind of initiation [ritual] into the next. To bind the generations together, to nurture them all, and to enable them to rediscover the natural synergy in the human life cycle—this is a crucial part of our quest for wholeness."[60]

The life cycle, a series of interwoven, interdependent phases that all together weave the web of our lives, simply cannot be sustained without the elders of that society, and by respecting the elders, we sustain the cycles of life. Just as children need adults, so those in midlife need elders. In fact, what is required is a vision of elderhood, of how we wish our waning years to be. But, be warned: it is not possible to have this vision until we look at death.

Elderhood has been suggested as the term to be used for those of us in our final—our waning—cycle of life: the term "conveys a fundamental and forgotten tribal truth."[61] Elders hold the wisdom of the community; we know things from earlier cycles, from our life's experience, that others need to understand. Just as those in the New Moon Cycle embody hope and new beginnings, so do those in the Waning Moon Cycle symbolize wisdom and integration. *Elder* demands respect, connoting that no matter our frailties and limitations, we must maintain "our right and respected place within the tribal council" having an honored place—not out of pity or charity—but simply "because elderhood, like the other spokes on the wheel of life and death, is vital to its turning."[62]

Aging is not only a biological fact, it is a cultural one, and "existentially, aging changes our relationship with time and therefore our relationship with the world and with our own history"[63]—and certainly with each other. Old age must be understood as a whole, for if we don't know what we are becoming, then we can't know who we are. If we are to take upon ourselves the entirety of our humanness, then we must necessarily recognize ourselves in this old man or in that old woman.[64] More often than not in our youth-centric society, we are unwilling to look upon that old woman, for fear of seeing the inevitability of our own aging: old age is something that happens only to other people—until the moment it is absolutely upon us.

Old age brings more and more of those necessary losses—of health, loved ones, home, status, purpose, and often financial security. In the end, it is our own attitude toward aging—a particular challenge in the face of the societal ambivalence—and toward those concomitant losses that determine the quality of life through our waning years.

Our old age is more apparent to others than it is to ourselves. Unlike the adolescent who, tormented by the hormonal changes that rage through her body, is undeniably aware of her biological changes, the aging person adapts so gradually in the process that she fails to notice the changes that happen: "habit and compensatory attitude mean that psychomotor shortcomings can be alleviated for a long while."[65] So, as we age, we come to the realization that we are old through the perceptions of others without experiencing the changes in our bodies that are more obvious to the adolescent.

The waxing phase of the Waning Moon Cycle offers us the opportunity for resolving the last stage of development: whether—upon reflection of our lives and in anticipation of our remaining years—we will maintain a sense of integrity or surrender to the despair that envelops many of the elders of society.

We enter this phase with carefully honed values and intentionally refined attitudes. If we have respectfully honored the autumn of our lives, we have confronted the darkness within and have reclaimed the vibrancy that can, with fewer encumbrances, be ours. We can reorganize our lives, rededicate ourselves to new interests and relationships; we can renew our commitment to the nurturing of our bodies within whatever parameters are necessary. We may choose to become more focused, eliminating those activities about which we no longer have passion. Having served others for most of our lives, we may become more inner-directed, more contemplative, being content with quieter, more spiritual endeavors. Or we may channel our reclaimed passions into a social cause, remembering the Seven Generations.*

If we have emerged from the confrontation with the shadows in the underworld with a more pervasive awareness of both aging and death in our consciousness, then this awareness has for us negative or positive implications that will determine whether our life's meaning holds despair or enrichment for us. No matter how long it lasts, our primary theme through this cycle is our search for personal meaning. We begin to assert the competence and creativity attained during midlife as we enter this phase. There is a redirection of energy to new roles and activities— grandparenting (and surrogate grandparenting), mentoring, widowhood. There are inevitable physical limitations and/or adjustments to serious illness. The realization that we have lived more years than remain stimulates a process of self-assessment through which our earlier values and ideals are once again reviewed and evaluated. We may feel discouraged as we face these limitations, for concerted energy is required during this time of life acceptance, and we are, at the same time, developing a point of view about death that daily becomes more reality than not.

Our task as elders is one of attaining a sense of integrity or falling into despair. Integrity is an ability to accept the facts of our life and to face death without great fear. We view our past in an existential light. The achievement of integrity results from an ability to introspect about the gradual evolution of our life's events and to appreciate the significance

---

* Native American culture, very respectful of Mother Earth, honors the seventh generation, still unborn.

of each of those events in the formation of our personality. Resolving the conflict of integrity versus despair is a process of achieving an attitude of self-acceptance through private introspection, appreciating the cycles through which we have passed, and perceiving and accepting the process in its entirety. Integrity comes about only after extensive introspection and self-evaluation. Despair, on the other hand, is a sense of regret about our personal history. Given the culture's resistance against, and even hostility toward, aging, it is not difficult to understand why many of us resolve this final crisis in a negative direction. In fact, despair, in contrast to integrity, is the more common response to this crisis. It is significantly more likely that adults will experience a negative resolution of integrity versus despair than that infants will resolve the crisis of trust versus mistrust in the negative direction.[66] Furthermore, we might conclude that the relationship of adult integrity and infantile trust is such "that healthy children will not fear life if their elders have integrity enough not to fear death."[67]

Relationships often mirror this despair. Typically, children move away, often leaving a void the partnership is unable to fill, and then we are likely to be widowed and left alone. We have no community; our friends are all dying. We are too old and frail to fend for ourselves; we become utterly dependent on well-meaning relatives or, worse, institutions and bureaucracies. "Just when we need to be supported and held, we are isolated. Just when we most need the security of having a home, we are housed in a unit. Just when we most need to be known, we become a number. Just when we most need to be remembered, we are forgotten."[68]

Interdependence of the generations strengthens the entire society. We enter the last cycle of our lives in a crisis of despair or in quest for integrity, depending in large part on the social context of our lives. We are certainly more likely to move through this final cycle with integrity if

- we have women and men in our lives who serve as way/showers who inspire us
- we are nurtured by a support system of friends who accept us as we change while at the same time reminding us of our continuity
- we are honored and respected for our wisdom rather than being made invisible
- we are care/full, compassionate and nurturing of our bodies as they slow and ache and cease to function and if we have

community support—compassion and inclusion; information, facilities and incentive to become fit
- we remain committed to enriching and growing in our marriages and committed relationships and if the culture supports the special/ness of relationships that defy the stereotypes by remaining growthful, sexual, sensual, and caring
- we are able to continue to choose the work role that enables us to participate as fully as we desire, remaining productive and respected without the threat of dependency and impoverishment.[69]

Honoring the life cycle ultimately means honoring community—the intricate and lovely web of human connections in which all the waxings and wanings, all the phases of each of the cycles, are equally respected from birth through infancy into childhood and puberty, coming of age; from partnering into parenting and into midlife; thence into a graceful elderhood and death. The thread that weaves through the various stages and cycles of life is one of interdependence, for each needs the others. While this need for one another is clear during the cycles when we are young and must be nurtured, we elders need to be cared for as well—to be respected and ultimately to be mourned. Just as each of the phases of the moon must be honored, so must each cycle of life be nurtured to do the growing required during it.

As we move through this final cycle, we are particularly aware of the fabric of our lives. We yearn for all the threads to be woven firmly among the others, knowing that no thread is more significant than another: we need all the generations including us elders who hold the wisdom of the generations. We cannot sustain the cycles of life without elders, and we cannot respect elders without sustaining the whole life cycle: we need a vision of elderhood. When we as elders are not a visible and integral part of the community, when we are unacknowledged and discarded, the young are left without direction to finding their way from youth to adulthood.

Research findings demonstrate conclusively that social contact and support keep people healthy and alive longer. By contrast, isolation—not physical illness and not mental illness—is the key variable in the rising rates of suicide among elders. The loss of daily contact with others actually alters bodily rhythms and produces depression, which in turn can lead to suicide, while anything that promotes connectedness and intimacy will be healing and life-giving.

An important integrating factor in honoring the life cycle is the sense of community, and in the last cycle of life, community is not merely a luxury, it is an absolute necessity. This is how the whole life cycle is sustained. We need "elders who can create common ground where all the tribes can come together. So we cannot afford simply to walk in our fathers' and mothers' footsteps. Many of their footprints have already been washed away. We must look farther back . . . to the perennial wisdom of our ancestors, and to the future needs of our children's children. This is true elderhood."[70]

Look, Grandmama; how am I doing?
Grace set aside her own embroidery to examine her granddaughter's.
Why, honey, your work is quite lovely. Indeed, Jennifer's cross-stitches were neat and fine. She turned the sampler over. *And the stitches are just as nice on the reverse side—a sign of really good work.*
Jennifer grinned proudly. *Who taught you to embroider?* The words lurched awkwardly through her braces.
My grandmother.
Was she the schoolteacher who taught in the one-room school? Although hopelessly enraptured by her grandmother's stories, Jennifer had a terrible time keeping everyone in orderly places in her head.
No, that was my grandmother Laura. This grandmother, Beatrice, was a very wise woman, a crone. And they say she was a witch.
Oooh, Jennifer's face crinkled in alarm. *Like the wicked witch of the west?*
Oh, no, Grace chuckled, reassuringly. *Witches are healers, like doctors. They use herbs and flowers instead of pills to tend to the sick. People came from very far away for my grandmother's care and she delivered so many babies, she lost count.*
Grace retrieved her embroidery. She needed to stitch quickly while the light remained good. Her eyes just weren't what they once were, but she was eager to finish these pieces for her daughters' Solstice gifts. *Always my daughter. Now too my friend.* Muted blues, greens, and deep pinks sprawled across the ecru linen with graceful charm. She hoped Kit and Sara knew how very true the words were for her. She appraised her handiwork with a critical eye and felt warmed by

love and gratitude for her daughters, now grown into such lovely young women.

Grandmama, Jennifer had diligently completed the B on her sampler on which a rainbow of colors emerged. *What's a crone?* Tossing the embroidery aside, she was ready for another distraction. *Are you a crone?*

Well, yes, I guess I am. Grace smiled into the young, freckled face so like her own girlish self. *In ancient times, the crone was the elder of the tribe, the one to whom all others came for healing and guidance. The old women were deeply respected.*

Can I be a crone when I grow up?

Grace laid a soft gnarled hand upon her granddaughter's cheek. *Of course. You will be a fine old crone.* And her old eyes misted at the vision of Jennifer now a young maiden growing into mother then crone.

Through this, the final cycle, the winter of our lives, our greatest challenge is the inner struggle for a sense of integrity; we struggle between hope and despair. As our lives wane, we reflect on our losses and on what we've accomplished; we wonder about who we are and how we've loved. This struggle inevitably reveals a need to tie up the loose ends of the fabric of our lives, to finish old business. Completing unfinished business does not mean totaling old accounts and balancing out all those old resentments and angers. It does mean *releasing* those resentments and fears, releasing those yearnings, those "if-onlys."

Finishing the unfinished necessarily leads us through a process of forgiveness. As we search for integrity, we begin to see that the degree to which we judge another is the degree to which we judge ourselves. We begin to see that the degree to which we push away from ourselves is the degree to which we push others away from us. This process of forgiveness ultimately leads us to a place of compassion—for ourselves and for others. In forgiving, we let go of those resentments; we enter into our own heart, feeling the pain that lies within—ours and the other's, and then we release that pain.

Throughout our lifetime, we have touched and been touched by many; our relationships are abundant. None is as significant as the relationship we have with our planet. How we relate to the earth serves as a living metaphor for how we relate to one another. If we participate with the earth and all its inhabitants, we are more likely to participate with the humans with whom we share our lives. If, on the other hand, we come from a place of power over the planet, our relationships are likely to be fraught with power struggles.

Wisdomkeepers, an exquisite and priceless gift from our Native elders, makes abundantly clear that the law of nature prevails everywhere and our consistent and blatant disregard of The Law has much to do with the cultural and earthly despair that pervades our planet.

> This we know: the Earth does not belong to us; we belong to
> the Earth. All things are connected like to blood that
> connects us all. All things are connected. What e'er befalls
> the Earth befalls the children of the Earth. We did not weave
> the web of life; we are merely a strand in it. Whatever we do
> to the web, we do to ourselves. This we know.[71]

Integrity. Integration. Wholeness. Mindfulness. Community. Interdependence. These create the weft of the fabric, this tapestry of aging of the life we continue to weave. The warp of the fabric must be our spirituality—a most personal aspect of who we are and are ever becoming.

From the perspective of Goddess thealogy and magic, wholeness has to do with interconnections among the Maiden, the Mother, and the Crone. This is manifested in Goddess sociology as fluid interactions among women of all these age groups. Similarly, Goddess psychology can be understood as harmony and flow among these three aspects within each woman. Patriarchy has divided these aspects, forcing them into separate worlds. As a result, we are alienated from ourselves and from each other. Socially, women of different ages seldom interact with one another. Birth and Death are seen in opposition, rather than as a cyclical movement of Birth into Life into Death into Rebirth. And within ourselves, many of us have lost touch with and been wounded in one or more of these aspects.[72]

The Crone—the most powerful of the goddess's three aspects, seen in many myths as the old woman—is the part of ourselves that has indeed been most wounded. As we honor ourselves through this waning cycle, we remember that when the image of the Crone was recognized as a valid one, the elder woman commanded respect; her advice was sought; her community revered her. Reclamation of the image of Crone can serve contemporary women by symbolizing the kind of power that is desperately needed in our society as we do what is vital for the benefit of humankind and for our beautiful but ailing planet.

We re/member that the ancient Goddess had many names and many forms: she was as changeable as nature itself. Both beautiful and ugly, Virgin and Crone, darkness and light, winter and summer, birth giver and death bringer, she was a true image of the variety of the earth in all its cycles. The ancient ones knew that constant tending of the whole living system is required in order to maintain the constant and simultaneous creation and destruction of that system. Forms in life cannot exist without destroying other life forms. And every form is temporary, running through its own cycle from burgeoning growth to decline, death, and decay.[73]

As we open ourselves to this knowing, this remembering, we open ourselves to awareness itself: we can no longer be threatened by anything, we no longer need to withdraw from anything. Finally, we become one with life—flowing, moment to moment, life into death, growth into destruction, waxing and waning. We hear the echo of ancient voices reminding us that the *Goddess rules all cycles, therefore each phase of each cycle is no less sacred than the other.*[74]

Ultimately, integrity has everything to do with one's spirituality, for to be whole is to be fully integrated spiritually, emotionally, mentally, and physically. We are in pure relationship with ourselves. To be one with the Spirit may or may not have anything to do with Christianity, Judaism, or Buddhism; it may or may not have anything to do with Native American spirituality or Goddess thealogy. However the Spirit is re/claimed, almost certainly a commitment to serve emerges. When we and the Spirit merge, we honor more deeply all that is: we honor the Spirit in our daily lives: She is indeed everywhere.

Faced irrevocably with the waning of our lives, we move into a spiritual re/awakening or deepening, one that evolves from our own deep search into our soul. Deepening and honoring the sacred is an ongoing process, for some a constant act of becoming. Many are able to see that, in fact, we are not the body; rather we are consciousness in a continual state of creation.

Dreams were once seen as the gateway to the soul; our attending to them now can be an exciting aspect of our spiritual growth. While our quest for the sacred is grounded in our daily living as well as in our nightly dreaming, most people find some sort of particular discipline or spiritual practice. Remembering that ritual is about making the everyday sacred, we may participate in rituals of our own choosing or of our own design. These rituals may take the form of a walk by the sea, or in the woods; we may sit in the light of the moon. Listening to special music or reading poetry may be our focus. Some read tarot cards, go on retreat, participate in vision quests or sweat lodges. Meditation is a widely recognized method for both relaxation and spiritual growth. If nature is a way of communing externally, meditation is a way of communing with the self. Each of us must find her own path and there are many.

Because women tend to see ourselves in the context of the whole, this sense of connectedness has implications for our spirituality; we experience ourselves as being connected to something greater than ourselves. We look again to our foremothers—many, many generations past, for models to guide us through our aging and support our reclaiming of the sacred, and we remember. We remember the crones of the matriarchal community who were women past the age of menopause. Like their younger sisters whose magic blood was withheld during the making of the miraculous child, the old women, described as the wisest of the tribe, were seen to withhold their blood—the source of their wisdom. We remember the ancient times when to be an elder was to be wise and respected, to be revered, and to be a spiritual leader. We take these images with us, for having achieved a sense of integrity, we gracefully, if slowly, enter into the fullness of this last cycle. We realize, more and more clearly now, that none of us will live forever, so the issue becomes just how do we live now; how can we feel more free, alive, joy/filled; how do we maintain the love, compassion, and forgiveness that heals the isolation that could lead us into the darkness of stress and illness and suffering.

Being open to healing and preparing for death are the same.[75] To be open to healing is to be open to life—in this and every moment. This is natural and healthy. But alas, the challenge is to live life fully and consciously, without denying death—to live in the face of death!

Chapter 3

Cycles of Relationships

Coming Full Circle is about healthy relationships—relationships in which we are willing to honor the fullness of the rhythms, of both the birthing and dying, of the ebbing and flowing, of the waxing and waning. *Coming Full Circle* presents this alternative: an ideal, a place we can call home. What follows is a map of possibilities, of potentialities, so that we may each begin to enjoy healthy, rhythmic, respectful relationships which can not only be healing of ourselves, but of the world in which we live.

We have few models of healthy, life-giving relationships. As we search for a course to follow—one that thrives and grows—the examples around us in real life and in media demonstrate only entanglements, paths rough and strewn with obstacles. Television, a primary source of information, yields inane, pathological images and unrealistically romantic ideals. We feel utterly lost in our search. Our parents were unclear about how to create healthy marriages, and their parents' needs were as foreign to our parents as theirs are to us. I'm sure that even my grandmother, a committed suffragist who shocked her family and community by divorcing her husband in 1920, had very different ideas of marriage and family from mine. She chose to rear her six children alone—a single mom. Yet what was required of her and what she desired from marriage at the turn of the century was not at all what I faced 50 years later.

It is my belief that an intimate relationship with another person is only as harmonious as one's relationship with oneself. However, to truly extricate the study of the individual from that of the relationship is foolish—no, impossible—because women, especially, perceive ourselves, actually *define* ourselves, in our connectedness to, not separateness from, others.

Women not only seem to be more able to maintain intimate relationships, we tend to be more attuned than men to the cyclical nature of the universe and of ourselves. Therefore, in our search for healthy models for relationships, we might do well to look to lesbian relationships which, in fact, may provide a glimpse at the possibilities for life-giving relationships. Ironically, as members of an oppressed group, many lesbians have been able to escape the constraints of patriarchal economics and traditional roles by stepping outside the mainstream and quietly and invisibly going about the business of creating reciprocal partnering. I am not suggesting that lesbian relationships are free of challenges and problems; more often than not they are rooted in homophobia and suffer the shame of societal disdain and isolation. I am suggesting, however, that women in same-sex relationships are freer to avert the pitfalls of the patriarchal model, to explore alternative ways of being in partnership and to create that paradigm shift—moving toward a truly mutual, egalitarian relationship. The recognition of diversity—both between us and among our relationships—remains an important factor in healthy relating.

Given that we have few if any models to guide us in our search for a relevant ideal for healthy relationships, we need to explore a new paradigm, or to reclaim and reshape an ancient form into a new paradigm. In our search for that new model, let us consider that which is natural and universal and nonlinear—the lunar cycle.

The lunar cycle has to do with the *relationship* of the moon with the sun as seen from Earth. What the lunar cycle measures is not the changes in the moon itself, but changes in the solar/lunar relationship. The phases of the moon tell us nothing about the moon itself or the position of the moon in the sky; the phases are simply indicators of the *state of relationship* between the sun and moon; the moon reflects in its appearance to us the changes in that relationship.

The cycles and the phases of the moon become the archetype of all cycles of relationship: the lunar cycle is a cycle of transformation. The rapidly moving moon, rising as it does 51 minutes later each day, not only changes its place in the sky, it appears to change its shape, even seeming to vanish entirely from sight during a part of its cycle.[1] So the lunar cycle symbolizes the relationship between two people who have an emotional/sexual/affectional commitment.

The relationship, like the individuals within that context, has a cycle of its own. It is a dynamic entity—waxing, coming into fullness/maturity, and waning, evolving, potentially, into a new cycle. Alternatively, however, at the ending of one cycle, in the dark of the moon phase, we may choose to end the relationship prior to the waxing of the next cycle.

The relationship is not independent of the two partners as individuals, of course, but, as any lover will attest, once the relationship "takes off," the two individuals seem to be caught up in the momentum of the cycle of their relatedness and the evolving relationship takes on a life, a rhythm of its own. Relationships go through definable cycles:

- New Moon Cycle: the birth of the relationship; falling in love; differences are denied
- Waxing Moon Cycle: establishing the foundation; growing; differences are acknowledged
- Full Moon Cycle: midlife of relationship; creating, producing; differences are affirmed
- Waning Moon Cycle: elderhood of relationship; ebbing, deepening, separating; differences are celebrated

Moreover, within each cycle are definable phases that follow the same pattern:

- new moon phase: time for birthing, renewing of the cycle; preparing, reflecting, evaluating
- waxing moon phase: time for connecting and learning; energy is increasing
- full moon phase: time of abundance, celebration
- waning moon phase: time of restlessness, conflict, separation, introspection; affirming the self

These cyclical rhythms apply to all intimate relationships. While the issues may vary among different types of relationships—heterosexual marriage, cohabitation, multicultural, lesbian, gay—the rhythm is consistent. Furthermore, nonsexual relationships—mother/daughter, sibling, and friendships—are cyclical as well. The advantage of recognizing these rhythms is that with recognition comes understanding, and understanding diminishes fear.

It has been suggested that "every cycle of relationship divides itself into two hemi-cycles. The waxing hemi-cycle is a period of spirit-emanated . . . activity which witnesses the triumph of 'life.' The waning hemi-cycle is a period of individual and conscious [human]-controlled release of creative meaning—or else in a negative sense, of gradual disintegration."[2] While I resist the implication of dualism here, I agree that the early, waxing-into-fullness phase of the relationship, characterized by an abundance of energy, is a time of "spontaneous and instinctual action" while the fullness-into-waning phase is more about the "conscious growth in meaning and immortal selfhood." Our evolving self-awareness and growth is enhanced not in a static, isolated state but in the process of sharing increased meaning and value with another person. "No individual can gain real immortality (personal or social) except as a participant of an immortal whole. Thus understood, both the new and full moon constitute beginnings. The new moon is the starting point of the realm of life; the full moon opens up the realm of [our] spiritual identity, of [our] individual immortality."[3] To be in harmony with the moon—with its waxing and waning—is to have the opportunity for maximizing our own fluctuations in energy and creativity and in restfulness and reflection—to honor the wholeness of ourselves.

So it is with relationships.

A relationship between two people who love and care for one another takes on a rhythm of its own: its process is cyclical—waxing and waning in the flow and ebb of energy. Typically, the first cycle commences at the time of meeting. (At that moment of mutual attraction and response, some even report having been "moonstruck.") The cycle begins when two of us experience a focusing of energy on one another. For one or several of a multitude of reasons— that often defy even the pens of poets—we are attracted to one another and the dynamic of the relationship is set in motion.

In a growing, dynamic relationship, we experience a number of cycles. *Coming Full Circle* explores four cycles that occur in a lifelong relationship. Each cycle has unique characteristics, but there is a com-monality in the process or dynamic of the waxing and waning in each of these cycles that varies, to some degree, in intensity.

The dynamic of each cycle in the relationship begins at New Moon with a connection (or, in ensuing cycles, with a reconnection). Flowing into the waxing moon phase is a time of closeness, of sharing: a veritable high. In the first cycle, the two lovers are focused on one another; the energy between them is exhilarating and intense. This is the time of romance and intentionality in the relationship. Often people report feeling extremely excited *and* vulnerable *and* sexual *and* creative *and* tireless. This is the time of hope, of ecstasy, of intense erotic feelings. In the cycles that follow, the waxing phase will certainly be less intense, yet energy nonetheless increases into the fullness of each cycle.

While we can certainly have sex without love and love without sex, the waxing time is the time when romantic passion (especially in the New Moon Cycle of a relationship) is often at its peak. The waxing phase is the time of "organic and instinctual growth." Energies soar! Sensuality reigns! Life becomes poetry in action!

Anything is possible! Waxing, in the later cycles, is the time of re-newal, of reconnection; the power available here must not be underesti-mated. In the mature relationship, the waxing time, in subsequent cycles, is a time for new/renewed beginnings: undertaking dreamed-of projects together, practicing untried behaviors, exploring and deepening ways of *being* together. Because so much energy is available to the partnership, it behooves the couple to utilize this resource to enrich the relationship by taking risks with each other.

The New Moon Cycle has, for many, the most intense of the waxings; yet throughout the cycles, the flow of energy is ever-increasing into the fullness of the cycle. We resist relinquishing the utter deliciousness of the waxing: it can be addictive, this blissful flowing—indeed a time for creating visions and dreams and possibilities. Whether it be new or renewed, preparation for the fullness of the partnership is taking place. We are euphoric!

The full moon phase of each cycle of the relationship is the center and highest point of energy and brings with it a sense of wholeness. We feel one with the other and with the world. The seeds of thoughts and feelings sown during the new moon phase, having reached fruition during the waxing moon phase, are now being harvested. We pause in the full moon phase (celebrate the Sabbath—heart-rest) to take in the fullness of the expression of being with one another.

Although relatively short-lived, because no healthy relationship remains static, this full moontime is the time of creative release. The couple, experiencing a sense of fulfillment, is at the height of creativity. Metaphorically, the full moon is the time of ovulation, so the relationship is, again symbolically, pregnant, mature, at its peak in fertility and sexuality. Fully illuminated, the relationship is ripe for choice-making—to have children, buy a home, make a commitment to a joint venture, support one or the other in a dream of her own. The amount of energy for creating, accomplishing, for transforming dreams and ideas into reality is enormous and can be awe-inspiring. The couple is urged to take this power and channel it into ways that are truly enriching for the relationship. The creative release in the full moon phase often takes the form of a celebration, of a ritual.

Sometimes, in reaction to all the intensity of the full moon phase of the cycle or perhaps due to an outside force, the relationship becomes impacted by conflict: the waning moon phase begins.

Because the nature of the waning of any cycle connotes increasing darkness, most of us approach the waning time with feelings of dread and fear. And either in anticipation of or in response to the darkening, we tend to be more reactive than proactive. We respond to the decreasing light not by simply honoring the naturally rhythmic process but in ways that are based in fear and anger. We seem more easily able and willing to honor the increasing, the waxing, than we are able to honor the decreasing, the waning.

What is important to remember is that there are many opportunities available to us throughout the waning, the most significant of which is that this time allows us—if we choose—a deepening of ourselves. While we may, after careful reflection, in the waning, choose to end the relationship—and this certainly is the appropriate time for a healthy ending—what is most important to realize is that it is *the cycle that is waning, not necessarily the relationship.* Yet out of our fear of loss and abandonment, we are usually much too quick to react to the necessary separateness: we often withdraw, create a crisis, or stir up a conflict.

The waning moon phase is vital in the dynamic of any relationship. Without darkness, there is no light; without death, there can be no rebirth. The waning moon phase of a relationship is the phase of positive darkness, and the waning requires affirmation and honoring just as do the other aspects of the cycle.

Rub any two objects together and friction occurs. Inevitably, two people relating with one another will experience friction and conflict.

The waning moon phase is stimulated, primarily, by conflict, which may take one of two forms: internal conflict or external conflict, acted out in either covert or overt ways. Conflict, internal or external, is seldom welcome in any relationship—even if it does serve a vital function. Recognizing the difference between internal conflict and external conflict in the waning moon phase gives greater understanding and makes us more prepared to integrate healthy conflict into our relationship.

- *Internal conflict* is that which is evoked from within the relationship—coming from one of the two persons involved. Although sometimes generated covertly, this is an internal process. One, or both, in varying levels of intensity, may be needing some breathing room. We may feel simply and utterly overwhelmed by all the togetherness, the intensity of feelings, the abundance of energy experienced in the waxing and full moon phases: we need a rest, a break. Typically, an argument or withdrawal of energy ensues, resulting in an indirect "solution" to the issue at hand: getting some well-deserved and necessary distance.

  The waning time is often precipitated by one of us experiencing undefined anger, a feeling of depression or anxiety. This is simply a *cue* that it is time for the nurturing of ourselves and this is vital to the growth of both the self and the relationship. This has to do with the *internal* dynamic of the two people involved and their own individual cycles.

- *External conflict* is something caused by an outside force—an ex-lover returns to town, family members exert pressure for time together, one of us has unusual work demands, one becomes seriously ill. The source of pressure is external to, yet has an impact on, the relationship.

The very mention of *conflict*, a much maligned word, brings a negative response and even a visceral reaction in many people. A search through any thesaurus reveals words such as *struggle, battle, combat, fight, fray,* and *war* as synonyms for *conflict.* Is it any wonder that those who shy at the mere hint of confrontation will run and hide in abject terror when we dare to suggest conflict? But another synonym is *difference*—a much more relevant, not to mention more palatable, word. Indeed, different/ness is, as we shall see, the stuff with which any relationship is enriched. Without conflict, and without the *resolution* of conflict and the *integration* of inevitable differences, there can be no intimacy.

Whatever the impetus, internal or external, the conflict is an opportunity for the two to differentiate, for each to reaffirm her autonomy. There are, after all, two individuals in the relationship, each of whom is a growing, discrete entity, each of whom is experiencing her own individual cycle. The relationship should and can be a source of nurturance for each member as she goes through her individual cycles. *You are you, I am I, and we are this relationship.* The purpose of any relationship is to provide a place of nurturance for the learning, the deepening of each of the individuals involved—in order for each to be reaching for, and growing into, her greater good.

Although there is generally a third option available to us as we negotiate our differences, one of two outcomes usually occurs in a relationship during the waning phase, both of which are reactive positions:

- One or both of us, usually out of fear of abandonment/ rejection/conflict/anger will move into avoidance of the point of difference or of the other person, perhaps even to the extent of emotionally, if not physically, leaving the relationship. Or we may simply avoid the issue at hand by arguing or fighting about something completely irrelevant to the actual issue.
- The second option is avoidance with a different face, but avoidance nevertheless. One or both of us simply pretends the difference never occurred; we refuse to discuss the dispute, and we attempt to bury all feelings. We move back together and into a pseudo-waxing phase.

These behaviors do not lead to resolution or to renewal. In the first instance, if one physically and permanently leaves, the relationship ends immediately, although the feelings of hurt, mistrust, and anger will remain to be carried—or dragged—along into the next relationship. In the second example, the result of this altogether too common avoidance is a relationship that, rather than becoming a growing, dynamic one, becomes static. As in the first example, the feelings remain and become a source of bitterness, resentment, and toxicity. The cycle is repeated over and over with no resolution occurring, and the relationship gradually disintegrates and eventually suffers a slow, often tedious death. Whenever the difference/conflict has not been resolved, an opportunity has been missed to create flict has not been resolved, an opportunity has been missed to create intimacy and growth for the individuals involved as well as for the relationship.

What about that third option? Not all conflict can be neatly *resolved*. What is important is that feelings be expressed and heard. My experience is that often all any of us needs (and something most of us never receive) is *validation* of our feelings. We don't need to be "fixed"; we simply need to name our feelings, feel them, and be heard so that the energy of/in those feelings is allowed to move along. This option is the most important one if we are to have a healthy relationship. Intimacy is nurtured through the sharing of our feelings. We think and negotiate and plan and act, but the place where we truly *meet* one another, where we deeply connect with one another, is in that place where our feelings live. So the integrity of the relationship is achieved and then maintained through the mutual risking and sharing of our feelings. Herein lies the key to building trust within the relationship.

There must be room in the relationship for different/nesses: different feelings, rhythms, moods, cycles! If one of the rules in the relationship is that both parties must feel the same or that both must have the same rhythms (identical individual cycles—a rare species, indeed!), then one inevitably will feel threatened/scared/angry/terrified with her partner's different feeling or perception. In that case, any difference becomes a potential threat to the relationship. Yet, for the relationship to experience growth and healing, these differences must be shared.

Goethe wrote, "In a true marriage, we become the custodians of each other's solitude."[4] The waning time is the time for solitude, for going within. To experience solitude does not mean to become solitary. To support the deepening of both individuals and of the relationship, we must be willing to take intentional time apart—for an hour, an afternoon, a day, a week, a month, in order to allow room for healing, for reclamation, for reaffirmation, of our own sense of self. (Remember the menstrual hut!) The waning moontime becomes a time for completions—completion within the individuals and within the relationship. To prepare for the cycle that follows, old business must be finished. The learnings of the current cycle become the catalyst, the energy, that move us into the next cycle.

What seems to be most threatening about the darkness of the waning moon phase of any cycle is the feeling of ambiguity inherent in this time. Imagine the feelings upon first entering into a "haunted house" at Hallowe'en or even into a darkened theater. Those feelings range from disorientation and confusion to fear or even terror. We trust, however, that if we simply wait in the darkness, our vision almost magically will clear.

The waning is the time of magic and sorcery, of darkness and death, yes; but only with death comes rebirth. We must allow ourselves to sink into the darkness of ambiguity into the unknown, even though this discomfort/fear of the ambiguous/unknown feels scary—especially for those for whom maintaining the illusion of control is important. We are inclined toward controlling behaviors that promise to alleviate the discomfort, the darkness.* Our challenge in the face of increasing darkness is to honor the ambiguity of what lies before us, to breathe into those moments of darkness, and to trust ourselves as we walk into the darkness so that we may experience the magic of what follows.

Concurrent with the waxing and waning of the relationship cycles are our individual cycles. We each experience our own cyclical rhythms, and in a relationship, our individual rhythm is bound to collide with our partner's rhythm from time to time. Often conflict occurs when our need for separateness does not coincide with our partner's rhythm: she may be denying or unwilling to claim her own autonomy, or her needs may simply be different from ours. But we recall that when a woman at waning moontime experiences disharmony, inertia, irritability, or restlessness, she will probably be able to reclaim a sense of centeredness within by deliberately taking some time alone. As ancient woman submitted to the imposed taboo by going to the menstrual hut, we find that periods of seclusion and introversion are vital to maintaining balance and rhythm in our own lives.

This time of turning within is most effective when it is an intentional act, actively undertaken, not simply submitted to because of physical dis/ease. Many of us have learned "the hard way" that when we aren't purposefully caring of our body, our body will take revenge; it will get sick. In confronting ourselves, we may experience a darkness in our own

---

* It is usually true that the more out of control we feel, the more controlling we become.

heart; we may meet the shadow part of ourselves. Yet we can meet that conflict consciously rather than unconsciously. When we submit to the unconscious, we become captive to those unresolved conflicts and unreconciled projections.[5] Paradoxically, in our own "captivity," we often hold the other hostage by blaming and shaming, by creating conflict and crisis. This only serves to distract us from our own darkness—and our own growth.

Because each of us is moving through her own individual cycle, rarely are both partners in a couple in the same place at the same time. The challenge is for each of us to honor her own rhythm, where *she* is on the wheel, while respecting her partner's need as well. This time of separateness can be eased by maintaining a *connection with a dotted line*, claiming alone time or some distance without totally disconnecting from our beloved. Each of us can take separate time *and* be intentional about reconnecting. There are many creative ways to maintain our own integrity—to honor our own rhythm and, at the same time, to respect our partner's rhythm. We can articulate our needs and establish mutually agreed upon times for checking in with one another—with a phone call, a planned date, taking a meal together. The process of separation and reconnection (the waning and the waxing) begins with each of us clearly stating her needs, conflicting though they may be, recognizing we may not get exactly what we want exactly when we want it. This is the time of individual growth and hence growth in the relationship. Every relationship, if it is to be a healthy, dynamic one, must have room for closeness *and* separateness: waxing and waning. We must become the "custodians of each other's solitude."

In this regard, there are necessary distinctions to be made between *differentiation* and *disconnection*, between *detachment* and *disengagement*. The fear that often surfaces during the waning phase of the cycle is usually based in the terror of our being abandoned, our fear of an existential aloneness; therefore, it is important to articulate more precisely this process of differentiating and detaching that is the basic challenge of the waning phase and that, to a greater or lesser degree, recurs with each of the cycles. Because in the first cycle we have as yet no basis of trust in the rhythm of the relationship, the process of separation is most sharply experienced in the first cycle.

Recalling that the waxing-into-fullness aspect is about creating—re/creating life—and that the waning-into-new phase is about deepening within ourselves, it becomes clear that we must make room in our lives, in our relationships, for respecting what is natural—to deepen, to introspect, to honor and empower ourselves from within. To *differentiate*, then, is to "serve to make a distinction between, to show *difference* in or between."[6] A healthy relationship consists of two individuals each of whom invites the other into her life in order to learn from and with each other—through differences *and* connectedness. To *disconnect*, however, is to sever, to interrupt, and this aborts the natural rhythm of the cyclical flow. To ebb does not mean to discontinue; waning does not have to be disconnecting. Rather, the waning aspect of the relationship provides an opportunity for each to affirm the differentiation of her self and the other while maintaining a connection with a dotted line.

Detachment, a term frequently used in Twelve-Step recovery programs such as Al-Anon, has a different connotation from *disengagement*. *Disengaging*—freeing oneself or getting loose—becomes necessary in a seriously enmeshed relationship where there is no demarcation of boundaries, where there is no clarity about where one person ends and the other begins. This model of relationship is reflected in nearly every Top-40 song, "I'm Addicted To You, Baby" being one of my all-time favorites! The traditional lighting of the "unity candle," a ritual performed in many marriage ceremonies, also symbolizes this model of enmeshed relationships. To extinguish the individual candles following the lighting of the unity candle symbolizes how, too often, the individuals (the *you* and *I*) become indistinguishable from each other and from the relationship.* In true linear, either/or, patriarchal style, the relationship takes precedence over the two individuals. As the candle is extinguished, so, often, are the two individuals as separate human beings.

A healthy relationship is one in which there is room for the *both/ands*, not the *either/ors*. We are inclusive of all aspects while remaining differentiated as individuals. Just as we learn to honor all aspects of the cycle, so we learn to honor all aspects of each other. The risk, however, is that we may realize that we are unable or unwilling to live with some of these aspects of the other; for, in honoring her, we give up our need to change or to control her.

Detachment occurs when one is responsible *to*, not *for*, another person. The process of learning to detach has to do with being empathic with the other while remaining cognizant of our own feelings, thoughts, wants, and needs. While it is often more common and usually easier to

---

*   Couples often mirror each other's gestures, behaviors, and philosophies, and many even begin to look alike!

focus on what the other person wants, feels, should do, and think, this leads to an enmeshed relationship and prevents us as individuals from taking responsibility for our own feelings and needs. As long as each is focused on the other, individual growth, which is basic to any healthy relationship, cannot occur. This does not preclude *caring for* the other; nor does it mean not, selectively, taking care of the other. It does mean experiencing our world from the inside of oneself and moving outward—not the more familiar process of first assessing how the outside world will react to our feelings, thoughts, and behaviors and reacting to that external assessment with little or no regard to our own integrity. When we notice first our own wants and needs, our world view becomes one of beginning from the inside and moving out, not the outside in. We are no longer externally referenced; our beginning point is simply an awareness of our internal space. We begin with an awareness of what our needs, wants, feelings and choices are and then name them, so that together we can begin to be intentional in our choices.

Disengaging, like disconnecting, becomes necessary only when the differentiation process is not respected. Detachment is simply a way of honoring those differences by staying present, remaining empathic with the other, without being *attached* to or overly-invested in the other's feelings or in a specific outcome.

Being intentional about those needs for separateness, for quiet and alone time in the waning aspect of the cycle, eases the pain of separation and deepens our relationship with the self and ultimately with our partner. It is useful to remember that our need for time alone is our own need and is not about the other person. It is not about getting away *from* the other but about being *with* ourselves.

The waning time is the time for letting go: letting go of the old, of that which is not useful; it is a time for trusting in our creativity and trusting in the light that will soon reappear. This is a time of resting, of letting go of the past and preparing for the next cycle. The waning phase of the cycle is as valuable as all other aspects and offers us significant opportunities for our individual growth which ultimately serve to nourish and enrich the relationship.

The waning of the cycle does not necessarily imply that the relationship is waning. It is important, however, to remember that while our intention may be *forever*, after honest reflection we may realize that the relationship is not a life-giving one. Our needs are not being met; we are not thriving nor are we able, or perhaps willing, to accept and support the other. Respectful termination is, in fact, a viable choice. It should not be simply a reaction. Endings can and should be honest, thoughtful, and respectful. Most, unfortunately, are angry, but there are other options for separating.

● ○ ●

The process, the dynamic, of each cycle of the relationship—as with the phases of the moon—is predictable; each cycle has a waxing time, a time of fullness, and a waning. Concurrently with the cycles of the relationship, each of the two individuals in the relationship is experiencing her own cycles. Typically, the waxing phases of the relationship will be in synchronization with both our waxing rhythms. Conflict in the waning phases, however, often occurs when the two individuals' cycles conflict or, more likely, when one experiences her own waning differently from her partner's. Similarly, when one of us denies or ignores her waning—thus creating conflict within—those unacknowledged feelings, wants, needs surface in indirect or subversive ways.

Throughout each cycle, certain developmental tasks are being undertaken in the relationship. For example, the primary task through the first cycle is a developing of trust while, at the same time, each of us is affirming her own autonomy and learning about—while establishing—the boundaries defining us within the relationship.

The Waxing Moon Cycle of a relationship, in all its intensity, feels the most terrifying in its waning phase. We have no history of having moved through the cycles with this person before; we don't yet know how to do this. We are still building trust within ourselves and each other.

In the Waxing Moon Cycle, our differences begin to emerge, needing to be acknowledged and clearly named. Rules and boundaries within the relationship are being established; the identity of the relationship is being formulated. There's much tough work to be accomplished in the Waxing Moon Cycle. The Full Moon Cycle offers us the opportunity to affirm those differences and by affirming them, to integrate them and thereby deepen the intimacy between us—into a full, life-giving relationship. As we let go of old resentments, as we release the if-onlys, as we forgive the other and ourselves, assimilating the realities of our lives, of our own mortality, we are free in the Waning Moon Cycle to face the struggle between integrity and despair. Together we can savor the bittersweetness of our final years.

That we often think of the waxing and waning phases as two antagonistic and irreconcilable experiences is an outgrowth of the linear, polarized mentality of patriarchy. It is the illusion of separateness, bred in a culture of dualism, that sets the mind against the body and the ego against the spiritual self. This illusion of separateness destroys the vital essence of relationship and extinguishes the power of integration that *naturally* moves us toward the fullest possible inclusiveness of all. The true essence of a life-giving relationship involves the integration and the inclusion of the waxing, full, and waning aspects of all there is. The more dualistic view destroys the very essence of the relationship, which ultimately sets one person against the other, while at the same time setting one aspect of the self against another. Similarly, it is the denial of the relatedness of cycles and all phases of cycles that constitutes the first step on the path of destruction and disintegration where hate comes to supersede love, where the ego overpowers the spirit.

A more growthful approach emphasizes the relationship between the ego and the spirit; the waxing, the full, and the waning; the mind and the body, all of which allows for an enhancement of the development of creativity within the individual and the relationship, becoming a *creationship*.[7] When the waning time is experienced in a positive way, creativity deepens. The waxing moon brings new vision and revelation, and the full moon promises a sense of fulfillment and renewed purpose. The new realizations are not ends in themselves, but rather a climax of the process: the *process* of waxing, full, and waning is only a means to an end—a creative end. Thus, it is the responsibility of each individual to make the moon image, in all aspects, her own—integrating the spirit with the ego, the body with the mind: ebbing *and* flowing, waxing *and* waning.

Musician, composer, and political activist Kay Gardner, in her *Sounding the Inner Landscape*, warns that "when large corporations persist in dumping toxic wastes into the atmosphere, they are not working in harmony with nature." Individuals in conflict, she tells us, are not in harmony with the group. Within ourselves, we feel inharmonious when the body and soul are at odds. "The basic concept of harmony is the same as that of healing. It is the *relationship of contrasting elements* working in balance with each other" [emphasis mine]. Further,

Sufi teacher Hazrat Inayat Khan describes harmony as three-fold: (1) The harmony of consciousness, or one's surrender to the will of the Divine, both infinite and manifest; (2) universal harmony, or Nature's law determining the interdependent relationships of all living things, as well as the cycling of the seasons, the movement of tides, of birth and death, the cycles of the sun, moon, stars, and planets in the cosmos; and (3) individual harmony, both the harmony of relationships between individuals and the harmony of the relationships of one's own body and soul.[8]

Just as it is imperative that each of us experience all aspects of ourselves—the waxing moon, the full moon and the waning moon phases—so must a relationship move through all these aspects in order to be whole and in harmony. For, as with the moon, when we honor the cycles of ourselves, in our relationship, we begin to see and to appreciate that for all our changeability, there is predictability, vitality, harmony, and renewal.

The lunar cycle, our model for the cyclical nature of relationships, is a cycle of two entities, the sun and moon, moving at different speeds on different planes whose relationship impacts a third factor, the earth. "Any relationship which would not be for the purpose of fulfilling the need of some third factor would have no meaning at all."[9] The effect, then, is what we perceive from our earthly perspective: the process of the new moon waxing into a full moon, then waning once more into a new moon. The dark, or new moon, phase is a time for introspection, meditation, and quiet, for preparing the seeds of creativity; the full moon phase is for far-reaching psychic and creative activity; both waxing and waning phases are preparation for the new and full aspects.

A relationship begins with a connection between two individuals. When this contact is of a sexual nature, all rational determinism of objective time seems to disappear, and the process of creative unfolding between us commences (or *potentially* occurs). No relationship is truly static, so the relationship, as it unfolds from one to the next cycle, will be either progressive or regressive—the latter becoming stagnant and eventually disintegrating and dying.

The cycles in a healthy relationship, following a progressive path, each come to an end just as a new conjunction occurs, and each new conjunction or beginning will occur in a different place from the previous cycle. We remain, as individuals or in relationship, in any one cycle for as long as is necessary in order to accomplish the developmental tasks related to that particular cycle. We may wax and wane many times through the cycle, and as with the individual life cycle, the relationship cycles tend to be more expanded through the later years than in the earlier stages of the life of the relationship. For instance, we tend to stay longer in the Full Moon Cycle (the middle years) of a relationship than we do in the New Moon Cycle; the waxings and wanings in the Full Moon Cycle seem more expanded in the later cycles. Furthermore, as in our individual life cycle, our learnings may need to be refreshed and earlier cycles revisited as we confront significant transitional issues.

Each new cycle retains some residual of former cycles, requiring a renewed integration and evoking the creative energy characterized in the waxing phase, while the waning phase disseminates what has been brought to fruition in the full moon phase. This creative energy is the spiritual component or foundation inherent in any healthy, life-giving relationship. Any relationship whose sole purpose is to be *in* relationship—focusing only on each other—without some greater purpose, without an altruistic or spiritual aspect, would have no meaning at all. While this external dimension may not fully evolve until the relationship matures, the spiritual component is essential for the relationship's creative flow and unfolding.

Spirituality is simply the honoring of the sacred within every living thing while honoring the existence of an entity greater than ourselves. With this in mind, we turn now to the life cycle of relationships in which we will explore the characteristics of the four cycles. Through the New Moon Cycle, trust is the primary theme, for this is the preparation of the life of the relationship, the birth of our journey together. Differences are acknowledged and issues emerge and are named during the Waxing Moon Cycle, as the energy quickens and growth accelerates. The Full Moon Cycle, during which time those differences are affirmed and issues are more intentionally confronted, is the time of manifestation. The Waning Moon Cycle is when those differences are celebrated and spirituality is deepened. We shall explore the four cycles, first considering the process of each of the cycles and then examining the developmental tasks

as well as possible outcomes for each cycle—both healthy and negative—relevant to each of these four cycles. Because one of the primary
internal supports for the rhythmic flow through the cycles is the integration of ritual—making our transitions more intentional and meaningful—rituals are suggested for the various passages.

As we journey through the relationship cycles, it is important to resist
the tendency toward linear thinking so pervasive in our culture. While
generally we move from the New Moon Cycle into the Waxing Moon
Cycle, and so on, during any significant life transition—career change,
birthing children, children leaving home, significant losses—we may
return to earlier cycles, if only for a brief time, in order to redefine the
relationship, to clarify values, and to reinterpret the rules of the relationship. The relationship is always in flux, ebbing and flowing. With any
significant life change, the relationship will experience stress and require
intentional redefining. In failing to purposefully redefine our relationship throughout these transitions, we miss opportunities for nurturing
the relationship into renewed growth and vitality.

To assist us along the path toward wholeness in our relationships, we
return often to Native American teachings, which have much to teach
us about the cycles and the rhythm of the universe. One such teacher is
Jamie Sams, whose *Sacred Path Cards* provide meditative focal points.
She speaks of the Drum, which "allows us to access the patterns of
life-force inside and outside of ourselves so that we may come to the
understanding that all exists simultaneously." She then reminds us that
"all life has rhythm whether in the physical or Spirit Worlds. . . . Rhythm
is a personal thing. To honor your own rhythm is to come back into
harmony with the Self. . . . If it feels right, you become the music and the
dance you are dancing becomes a celebration of life."[10]

So as we continue down this path, listen to the drum echoing the
heart throb, reminding us of the rhythm of the cycles:

> Drum that marks the heartbeat
>   Of our Mother Earth,
> Constantly reminding us
>   Who gave us birth.
> The rhythm of connection
>   Pulse of flame and Fire,
> The perfect reflection
>   Of our heart's desire.[11]

Our challenge through the cycles is to be both intentional in our actions while at the same time to honor the natural rhythm inherent in those cycles—to allow for the ebbing and flowing, and to remember always our Grandmother Moon, who in lightness and darkness reminds us that in all things there is birth and life and death and rebirth: there is waxing and waning and waxing once more.

Chapter 4

New Moon Cycle

Birth   **Spring Equinox**   **Trust**

Ah! My young ones . . .
I bless you in the birthing of your love
May you grow in trust as the light grows from darkness
And may your blending be like the beech
    whose delicate branches gently dance in the strong arms of the
        oak
May you know that all deeds of beauty and pleasure are sacred
when performed in my name.

Poets throughout the ages have been inspired to celebrate the birthing of relationships. Countless love songs and sonnets have been written and sung about the New Moon Cycle—the delicious time of falling in love. Never is the waxing phase of a cycle as exquisite, as lust-filled, as intensely compelling and passionate as in the birthing of a new relationship. Nor is the waning phase ever as terror-filled, as threatening to our very core. In the New Moon Cycle, our whole being is alive as never before. We hear sounds as no one, surely, has heard them—sweet, lilting songs resonate through the universe that resides suddenly within us. We see hues and colors as no one, surely, has ever seen before—brilliant tones are vividly awash over the whole canvas of our being. What was once mere touch melds into a blissful merging with the whole of life. Our taste for life, for love, for all there is, is ravenous. All our senses are alive; we are life! We feel one with every aspect of the cosmos.

We are transformed; we shall never again be quite the same as we were before we fell in love. We may truly experience "birth trauma," for our world seems suddenly and utterly in upheaval. Upon falling in love—for whatever mysterious reason—our life has a new focus, new meaning. We are reborn.

Symbolically, the new moon phase is imbued with great power. The ancient ones knew this: they planted their crops and bore their babies in the new moon phase which holds within all possibilities. So it is in the New Moon Cycle that we plant the seeds of our loving. And in the planting, we begin a journey of metamorphosis through which we will learn of the rhythms of life and love. With one another, we will learn of the emerging cycles of the journey we're choosing to share with another.

The New Moon Cycle promises us adventure. In the transformation that evolves when we invite another to join us, our lives are touched in ways we cannot possibly imagine. We see ourselves in new—sometimes startling—ways; we behave in exciting—sometimes alarming—ways that push the edges of our perceptions—of ourselves, of our life, of our world. In fact, we invite another into our lives to do just that (though we aren't usually conscious of the reason): to learn lessons we need in order that we may move along on our path toward wholeness. Healthy, life-giving choices will nurture us on our journey; and while unhealthy choices will certainly inhibit our growth, all provide lessons that are available to us—if only we will attend to them.

While we experience only once that bittersweetness of the first blush of love, the first journey through the New Moon Cycle—when passion exceeds all bounds, when our feelings soar to the greatest heights and plunge into the darkest depths—we remain in the first cycle for as long as we need in order to achieve the tasks confronting us. Eventually, life's challenges inevitably encroach on our impassioned romance, and we must confront the realities of sharing our life with another. In doing so, we face the most significant challenge of all—the honoring of the rhythm of the cycles of our individual lives *and* of our evolving relationship.

We will have many opportunities to forsake the present-centeredness of our loving and relating. We will be tempted to ask "how long will she be here?" "Can this exquisite ecstasy last forever?" "How long do I have to tolerate this separation?" In a culture that thrives on the future—on what happens next—we are sorely tempted to dishonor where we are *now* and to leap ahead. But if we are to create—purposefully and respectfully—a healthy, life-giving relationship, one that can become the arena where each of us can grow into our individual and collective potential, then our intention must be to honor our own rhythms.

The natural process of a healthy relationship is one in which we wax creatively and energetically, we reach the fullness of our fertility and productivity, and then we separately wane into the gathering darkness in order to prepare for the stillness of the new moon. We wax, reach fullness, and wane. We initiate and connect with another in the waxing phase; we reach the optimum of creativity in the full of the moon; and in the waning phase, we separate and attend to the integration of our learnings. In the dark of the moon, we rest in the stillness and allow for the transforming visions that rebirth us into the cycle that follows.

Each cycle presents distinctive tasks for us to undertake and lessons for us to learn, and there is no right or wrong flow. Out task is simply to honor our own rhythm and the developing rhythm of our relationship. Dis/ease will occur only when we abort the natural rhythm of ourselves and of our partner. Most couples move all too quickly through the New Moon Cycle, and each subsequent cycle grows more expansive as our lives move toward greater fullness. The wondrous first waxing phase of the New Moon Cycle is a singular event, but we may remain in the first cycle for several turns. This is because our task—that of learning to trust—is a challenging one.[*]

WAXING MOON PHASE

Ah! the waxing: the heart flutters like a butterfly's wing hovering and savoring the violet's nectar; the breath shortens and catches in the breast, holding, embracing each delicious moment; and the belly churns and turns into rollercoaster loops, even as those lovely images tickle our rememberings of the New Moon Cycle of a relationship. Passion! Lust! Romance! Sexuality! Rapture! We cannot sleep; we cannot eat—such mundane bodily functions have no place in the lives of the falling-in-lovers! We can't breathe. We lose ourselves in

---

[*] Similarly, our lessons are many in the Waxing Moon Cycle as we begin the work of living our lives together. We know we have much to learn as we honor our own rhythm while we discover our lover's. For now, however, we have only to honor the deliciousness of falling in love. Indeed, in this, the New Moon Cycle, we are preparing the ground and planting the seeds of our love.

the exciting discovery of the other and in the poetic revelations of ourselves. The beloved becomes our focus as we lavish hours and hours, loving and talking together through the night—immersed in the process of waxing into love. Life becomes timeless: we ride the spaces between—filling each moment with such purity of being.

This state of ecstasy, this delicious feeling of being in love is known as the state of *limerence*. Limerence is our virgin passage out of the new moon of our meeting and into the waxing of the New Moon Cycle, and "when limerence is in full force, it eclipses other relationships."[1] Sometimes limerence happens quite suddenly, like a bolt out of the blue, when we least expect it: there's no way to conjure it! Have we, indeed, been *moonstruck*? We are suddenly and magically pulled into the tide of love. We feel bewitched! Perhaps it's an instant, almost mystical connection with someone we've just met. Other times limerence rather sneaks up on us. Surprise! Here's an old friend we're suddenly seeing in a new way! How could we not have noticed? And now, suddenly, we do and our whole world turns upside down! However *it* happens, the beginning of a relationship is a time of transformation.

> When had it happened? When had their lovely, warm friendship become transformed into this hot, spiral dance into ecstasy? Surely, it was magic. Surely they'd been bewitched by the meteors showering, falling from a darkened sky, enchanted in stardust brushing the heavens and sprinkled from the Goddess's own hand.
>
> How could it be she'd never noticed the mischievous twinkle in those deep brown eyes, bottomless dark pools of warmth, inviting, reassuring, drawing her into places and spaces untraveled? How could she not have known the wild passion held in check, barely restrained in a body lean and muscular, yielding and sensual?
>
> Ah, but now she noticed! She knew the instant of their merging, a single magical moment when on the night of the new moon, the star-filled heavens illuminated in celebration of their love, newly born. Their friendship deepened, transformed, became a sigh of mystical, magical falling stars and tropical sea breezes.
>
> Swimming in sensation, moment flows into moment, each an exquisite jewel. No thought to past or future. The now of loving fills their days with song and laughter, exploring each other's stories and bodies and dreams. Wide-eyed innocents, children who know the tastes of everything they see and hear and touch. Souls meet, merge, surrender to the other's rhythm.

The heartbeat of time becomes irrelevant, each instant expanding, pregnant with hope and imaginings born into the magic of tender love.

Limerence is not mere sexual attraction, although we may name those early feelings sexual. In limerence, we desire more than mere sex, even though the sexual act comes to symbolize the highest achievement of reciprocal connection. That physical union creates an ecstatic and blissful condition called the "greatest happiness."[2] This state of limerence has certain characteristics: intrusive thinking about the object of our passionate desire; acute longing for reciprocation; dependence of mood on the other's actions; anticipation of the other's reciprocation. Most people report an inability to fall in love with more than one person at a time, a fear of rejection, and an unsettling shyness in the other's presence, especially early in the attraction. When we are in limerence, we experience an intensification of feeling during adversity; an acute sensitivity to any act, thought, or condition that could be interpreted favorably; and a rationalization for any disinterest or apathy. We may feel an aching in the heart during uncertainty and euphoria during reciprocation, a general intensity of feeling discounting all other concerns, and an ability to focus on all admirable qualities of the love object, while minimizing or denying any negative ones.[3] We create a magic mirror that allows us to see only what we wish to see and to ignore any blemishes we wish to ignore. At this time in a relationship, we view any distraction in the mirror of magic as simply a reflection of our own.

This is the waxing moon phase of the first time around the New Moon Cycle. Is it any wonder we call this state of limerence *falling* in love? More rational folks may claim that we don't *fall* in love—we may fall into a cauldron of chocolate!—but that we don't *fall* so passively into love. I'm not willing to relinquish the image of falling in love. Oh, I know, there is choice here; it's not just something that happens *to* us, but, romantic that I am, there is such delight in surrendering, just for a while, to the blissful, bewitching illusion of *falling* in love.

We can fall in love over and over with our lover. With luck, and attentiveness to our rhythms, we continue, in subsequent cycles, to feel that delicious and exciting rush of emotions when our eyes meet those of our beloved, to notice an exhilarating high when we reconnect with each other after an absence, to surrender to her, to lose ourselves in times of utter bliss. But no matter how we may try to replicate the feelings of lustful abandon, there is only one virginal experiencing of limerence.

While life transitions and passages may evoke a return to the New Moon Cycle, there is only one first trip through the deliciousness and fear, the ecstasy and terror characteristic of this time.

The intensity of the New Moon Cycle is due, in large part, of course, to this "virginal" quality; there is no history between the two lovers—every experience is a first. Neither of us has been in this place with the other before—every meeting is an unfolding adventure imbued with a freshness and newness that is both exciting and frightening. This is a time of revelation, as we each discover ourselves in relation to the other, as we explore the other's story and body and being and all the nooks and crannies of our lives.

Into this new relationship we each bring our own history, our own life's experiences, our unresolved issues—our own definition and expectations of what a relationship is and what we hope it will be. Oh, but we won't talk of that . . . not yet. For now, we just want to play and laugh and love and dance the dreams of lovers.

In this waxing of the New Moon Cycle, woven into the web of our falling in love, our limerence, we are filled with hope and possibilities and the ecstasy of blissful energy. Yet the old patriarchal rules remain in effect; we've only known about the dualistic—the black/white, right/wrong, good/bad, power over/overpowered—perspective in which we've both been completely socialized. We know nothing about trusting ourselves in the face of all this delightful rapture; we certainly know little of surrendering to the waxing—and we know nothing of yielding to the waning that surely lurks on the other side of the wheel. We want to risk and freely give of ourselves, but we don't know how; we don't yet trust—ourselves or the other—enough to do that. So we minimize the risk; we play it safe. We emphasize all the ways we're alike. We play at engaging at the many places where we connect: *We have so much in common . . . don't we? After all, don't I often finish her sentences? We dream the same dreams. And, he always knows exactly what I'm thinking. Surely those differences aren't really that important, are they?* So any differences are minimized; those dissimilarities are simply intriguing at this point. The bond is still too fragile to tolerate many differences; instead, we focus on all the ways in which we blend. We focus on how we are similar; our connectedness is paramount.

The waxing of the New Moon Cycle is truly and simply utter bliss and joy and exquisite aliveness which, as in the increasing light of the moon, swells and fills us with possibilities and hope and promise.

FULL MOON PHASE

As we share our stories, and perhaps our bodies, we slowly begin to experience the creation of trust in one another. And as we move into the process of learning to trust each other, we begin to try on this new relationship; we begin to emerge from the intensity of the cocoon of our new love and to look at ourselves in relation to our world. Shyly, at first, we begin to hint that, yes, the silly grin and that radiant glow, about which our friends persistently inquire, is, well, uh, yes . . . it's true, we're in love.

This is the full moon phase of the New Moon Cycle. While it is premature to talk about *forever* (except, perhaps, for those sweet mumblings uttered in the heat of passion), we begin to celebrate the fullness of this relationship and may even begin to acknowledge that this is becoming a relationship with a capital R. We begin—tentatively—to make public our evolving relationship; we begin to acknowledge to friends and family our feelings for our new love. We begin to share with others what feels like a very special, even sacred, secret. In this first fullness, we feel pregnant with desire and hope and the promise of what might be. In celebration, we want to shout our joy to the world. At the same time, we yearn to hold this treasure, so precious, still fragile, close to our hearts. Our feelings are intense in this time of fullness, and to name them often creates fear that they may, like a dream, evaporate with the morning light. Naming the relationship confirms the experience, thus making more real this new creation.

We are, after all, still in the process of acknowledging to ourselves these feelings, so full, so unfamiliar. *Am I truly sure enough of myself to merge with another? Can I trust myself enough to really trust someone else? Remember all those past hurts? Am I really ready to try again?* Questions flood us as we anticipate and begin to actually name our relationship to our family and friends. In our eagerness to share our delicious secret, we push aside any hint of doubt, of difference. To name publicly this emerging relationship raises ambivalent feelings, for that naming has serious implications—even though we are just dating, after all! The naming pulls us from the lovely soft hue of our private loving and suddenly places the relationship in full, bright light for all to see.

Magnificent frigatebirds, riding thermals of desire, sun catching majestic wings as they fly higher and higher into the heavens, encircling the moon. Sensation dissolving into feeling with astonishing awareness: tastes most delectable, smells most fragrant, sounds most melodious, sights most exquisite. Wild desire flows into quiet passion. At last, *I love you. I love you!* Words whispered into the night and hung on a crescent moon, grinning, laughing in celebration of young love. Replete with pleasure, pregnant with life, feeling suspended in timelessness, whirling, twirling together into spaciousness, opening to the wonder of the moment, this moment and no other. Holding close the seeds of love, protecting them, shielding them from harm. Shy in the glow of passion, unwilling to share their treasure, yet wanting to shout for all the world to hear, *I love you! I love you!*

Only the voluptuous full moon, hanging high above a canopy of trees in the hidden grove, witnessed their pledge; its brilliant light cast a lacy mantle through leaves, lighting their promise, blessing their promise to honor a love bursting into full flower. *I want to grow in fullness through the waxing and waning of many moons,* they said.

We must take responsibility for examining our own feelings as honestly as we are able, to look at the implications in naming our relationship. This is our first chance to define the relationship; to name it to the outside world means we must name it for ourselves. We begin to ask more questions: *Are we dating? Are we ready to be exclusive? Monogamous? What does this mean to each of us?* For bicultural couples, for lesbians and gays, this coming out, this public naming, may, in fact, have complex implications. Such couples do not have the same societal support that more traditional couples enjoy, which means that defining the relationship—"coming out" as a couple—requires not only more risk but more purposefulness.

The public recognition and affirmation of the relationship in this first cycle is significant. For some couples, this may not occur for months into the process, and others may not feel compelled intentionally to name it at all. However, I suggest that this is probably the first opportunity for a purposeful action, and the more intentional we can be in our relating, the healthier the relationship will continue to be. As a matter of fact, the more direct we can be with one another, the more we can share all our feelings, the healthier this passage will be. This is, no doubt, our first chance to risk directness with each other. Too often I hear folks, sometimes years into the relationship, still puzzling over how they got where they are. "The relationship just sort of happened," they say. "One day we just started living together. I know I wasn't ready, but . . . "

I propose that in preparation for this "coming out" a ritual be planned—a private ritual, of course. Keeping in mind that the *planning* of the ritual is as important as the enactment, we have the opportunity to clearly communicate with each other what our intentions and our perceptions are about what is happening here. This is not to imply that we are ready for a *forever* commitment. Rather, this is an opportunity to identify what our current wants and needs are. For instance, we may choose to date one another exclusively but to limit our time in order to have freedom for our friends and family. On the other hand, we may not be willing, yet, to commit to exclusivity, but we may affirm that we want to focus on our friendship with one another by having specific playtimes as we continue to explore the possibilities of our deepening the relationship. We may choose to share some reading together, in order to more specifically explore our spirituality, for each to learn more of the other's passion, whatever that may be. We may choose a symbol that represents the birthing of this relationship, such as a seed or a young plant. What is important is that ritualmaking gives us an opportunity to clearly name with one another our perceptions of the fullness of the cycle. Because there is enormous pressure in our culture to "couple," we must work to be clear about what it is we want from and with each other in this evolving relationship.

WANING MOON PHASE

Just as we comfortably settle into the fullness of the New Moon Cycle, we begin to notice some restlessness. Some gurglings of doubt begin to bubble to the surface of our minds. Just as the full moon in the night sky graces us with its brilliant illumination for too brief a time, so the full moon phase of this first cycle gives way too soon to the waning. As with the full moon, this phase may be short-lived. The intensity may be too much, the feelings overwhelming, making us fearful. The merging, the experience of loss of self, inherent in the first cycle's waxing, simply cannot be tolerated for an extended period of time, and the waning begins.

Along with these inner proddings, the realities of life begin to insist their way—unwelcome though they may be—into our lovely isle of bliss. Bills must be paid; our pet critters, as patient as they've been, must be tended; careers must be managed. It is time for us to come up for air; there is, after all, life beyond the rumpled sheets!

Long, lazy summer days, vibrant with colors of secrets shared, passion unleashed, yielded reluctantly to the waning of the year. Lengthening shadows of autumn brought restless stirrings, nudging the lovers out of their magical dream. What happens when the spell falls away, when we awaken to demands of the world? What do we do with the intrusive realities? these demands for immediate attention to overdue bills? an ex-lover's need for still more to a connection long severed? to leaking pipes and knocking pistons? Must we awaken? Must we stir? Must we leave behind the lovely hue of sunlight that warmed our bodies, our desire, and tickled and teased us in warm, summer breezes? Must we feel these darkening feelings, the edgy, unwanted naggings? Let's push them away, ignore them, for sure; shun them, forget them, beware!

But these nagging, dark feelings turn into bickering, and who left the cap off the toothpaste becomes reason to declare war and Sara's tardiness of a mere 15 minutes is cause for an all-night debate and Emily's ex-lover Mary's demands become reason to doubt, reason to wonder if this has been as good as it seemed, reason to disbelieve in magic.

Into these questions falls an awful void, a hollowness that fills the bellies and turns separation into terror. Where does Emily put the darkness, the fear of being abandoned to the night? Where does Sara find courage to face her dragon of jealousy? How do they cover the nakedness of terror?

Sara flails and she rages at the audacity of the world's intrusion. And Emily, practical Emily, pushes away. Not knowing how to extricate herself from the tangled web of desire, she complains of toothpaste left uncapped, dishes left unwashed, hearts left untended.

So they separate. *Poof!* the magic has ended . . . maybe never was. Their passion was just an illusion, a fragment of an elusive dream they foolishly wished would come true. Now they stand naked, exposed by their loving, grabbing for whatever might cover, protecting threatening frailties.

But, no. *NO!* They wanted, they promised to do this differently. They remember their pledge to walk together through this waning time, too. They talk, they cry, and they trust. Their moments of laughter and bliss mingle and blend into this time of darkness and fear. And they remind each other, *Believe in our magic!*

Reluctantly, but necessarily, we begin to pull away from one another; begrudgingly, we remember the time *before*—before we fell in love. Those necessities of life demand our attention: a friend is in need; family commitments can no longer be ignored; the phone company threatens to disconnect service; an ex-lover demands still more closure. In the face of those pressures, we may find ourselves bickering or actually arguing! In reaction to the increasing intensity and energy through the waxing and full moon phases, or due to some outside pressure thrusting itself into our sanctuary of happiness, the relationship must change.

In the waning phase of the New Moon Cycle, we begin to glimpse some dissimilarities; we realize that we have some differences between us, although we probably aren't prepared to discuss those areas where we differ. *Why can't she ever be punctual? Isn't he just a bit compulsive about his jogging? She actually reads the* National Enquirer*???? Must the TV be on all the time? Does she have to talk to me when she can see I'm reading?*

We find ourselves feeling edgy or restless or angry or depressed. These are cues that the time has come for individuating, for affirming that ultimately *You are you; I am I.* It is time for the nurturing of oneself, a process vital to the growth of both the self and the relationship. Moving into the increasing darkness of the waning is, after all, our opportunity for returning to the self, for examining and honoring our individual feelings. We acknowledge that it is through the affirmation of the self— of the two selves in the relationship—that we revitalize the relationship. *You are you and I am I and then there is us.*

The waning phase has to do with individually nurturing ourselves, of honoring our separateness in the context of the relationship. Without disconnecting, we simply notice and begin to allow those different/nesses that, of course, exist between any two people in a healthy life-giving relationship. Unfortunately, most of us are more inclined to focus on the other—what's wrong with her, how odd some of those idiosyncratic behaviors are—than we are to simply notice and to honor the places where we differ. Too quick to judge the wrongness of another's behavior and the rightness of our own, we miss important opportunities to evaluate our own willingness to learn through diversity.

● ○ ●

In this first passage into the waning phase, we often experience a great amount of discomfort. We've not been in this place with this person before. As we peer into the gathering darkness, we feel afraid. After all, we have no history of just how we might navigate this phase that appears so foreign and fear/filled. We approach the phase of decreasing light with great apprehension, and out of this fear, out of the anticipation of the eventual distancing that inevitably emerges, conflict in some form is likely to occur. We are probably still reluctant to state *directly* our needs for time, for space for ourselves. We may be unable to articulate our feelings. We may, in fact, be unable even to identify those needs and feelings. We have yet to trust the rhythm of the waxing *and* the waning *and* the return to the waxing because we have yet to experience the full cycle. We may trust the flow, but not the ebb—at least, not yet.

We are reminded that the life cycle of the relationship replicates the pattern of the individual life cycle: the waxing of any cycle is a time of connecting; the waning is the time for separating. In honoring the natural rhythm of the cycle, individuation is the process through which we move in the waning phase of the New Moon Cycle. We experienced the waxing phase of this cycle with profound feelings and move through the waning with equal intensity. Reluctant as we are to relinquish the lovely ecstasy of our falling-in-love time, we must, in the waning, make room in the relationship for the two individuals. In this afterglow, we must *detach*; we must *distance*—remembering the distinction between distancing and disconnection, between detachment and disengagement. Both to distance and to detach require proactive behaviors; to disconnect and to disengage is to be reactive in our choices.

When we proactively identify for ourselves and then name our need to be separate, to take time *for* oneself (which does not mean taking *away* from the other), we simply decrease the closeness by taking some distance. This may be in another chair, another room, another house; it may be by becoming immersed in a novel, spending the evening with a friend, taking a day of silence, or taking a vacation alone. The *key* is the intentionality of the choice: we choose, for the time being, to be separate from the other and to be involved in a separate activity. When we respect these choices, our own and our new beloved's, we offer ourselves the opportunity we deserve, to grow.

When we do not respect these feelings, pressure mounts and eventually, and inevitably, we react by disconnecting. This may happen in various ways: we may passively and quietly refuse to interact, we may pick a fight, we may get depressed, or we may engage in our addiction of choice—food, drugs, alcohol, work, or sex.*

We *choose* to detach when we can listen to and hear the other's feelings, when we can empathize with her discomfort and honor her ability to move through her own feelings without the benefit of our interference—whether that be in the form of advice, solutions or caretaking. When we are unable to detach, we become enmeshed—overly attached: we take charge of each other's thoughts and feelings. This leaves us only the option completely to disconnect, to break apart, maybe to leave.

Unfortunately, the challenges in the first waning, more often than not, create so much uncertainty that most of us are likely to *react* in this time of darkness. Out of our fear of change, fear of the ambiguity inherent in the waning—fear of the dark—we tend to be less proactive than reactive.

To separate respectfully is the challenge of the waning phase of the cycle—of all cycles. Having no previous practice in this process, we are particularly uncomfortable in the waning of the New Moon Cycle. To separate while maintaining the integrity of the relationship can be done by clearly distancing and detaching, and staying *connected with a dotted line*. We can create ways to reconnect by having selective time with one another, while honoring our alone time as well. But during the waning, the priority must be on each of us having private time.

The *process* of the New Moon Cycle is characterized by intense feelings and sensitivity to one another; it is a time of transformation. This first cycle is, no doubt, one of the most challenging. Just as infancy is the period of most rapid change and growth of the developing child, so is the first cycle of a relationship a time of intensely accelerated energy—both in the time of increasing and decreasing, of connecting and separating. And the waning is merely preparation for the next cycle—a time of rest as we prepare for renewal.

---

* Affairs inevitably occur during the waning phase of a cycle and serve as just another distraction from the issue at hand: to be with the self.

NEW MOON PHASE

The new moon phase of the New Moon Cycle may be the most challenging to honor. Having moved through the waning phase—usually with awkward, halting resistance—we are less than eager to simply sit in the dark stillness of the new moon and listen to who-knows-what! We are most eager to move right along, thank you!

Yet we must honor the quiet! It is in the dark of the moon that we integrate our knowings; in honoring the silence, we listen and we hear. Questions flood over us from the waning phase: questions of trust and boundaries and separation. We immerse ourselves in the silent darkness in order that we may hear the responses to our nudging inquiries, our doubts.

We know that learning to trust is a process requiring vigilant commitment; we know that trusting another and ourselves—yes, first ourselves—comes with time. So, how can we trust in the darkness of our first cycle? Can I trust myself to recognize the truth, *my truth,* as it emerges from the stillness? Can I trust my feelings? Her words? Is her interior congruent with what I see and hear? Do her words match her feelings? Her actions? Do mine? How do I know? Ahhh! But I *love* her, we say! Yes, and how do we *know* that?

Listen! *Listen, listen, listen to my heartsong:* the words of a lilting chant float out of the silence. We must surrender to our own truth.

Sara had claimed time for herself. She and Emily had talked their way through those difficult days when the threads of their weaving had become frayed with fear and doubt and jealousy. Yet she yearned for time to herself. She'd feared Emily's reaction to her need and, in fact, Emily had seemed hurt, scared when Sara had spoken of her wish to spend a week in her own home—alone. But she'd honored herself.

Now she missed Emily's presence. She'd become accustomed to the easy rhythm they'd established, sharing nearly all their time together in each other's homes. She thought lovingly of the woman who'd gently nestled her way into her life—this woman of easy grace and sweet humor. She mused over the many gestures which had already become familiar and dear to her. Sara treasured this friend, now lover, deeply.

And yet she was happy to be in her own home. Her little gray cat, Isis, pleased not to have to share her mother, had claimed a spot of sun on a cushioned chair near the oak table Sara diligently polished with lemon oil. Few leaves remained on the trees outside the leaded glass window and bright sunrays streamed in creating a dance of rainbows throughout the room.

She'd planned this time alone—her retreat—carefully, had wanted time, needed solitude to be in her own home, to meditate, to think about these past months when she'd fallen completely in love with Emily, with herself, and with life. She savored the moments, the beauty, the exhilaration of what had been and how she'd gotten here, to this very moment, sitting on the floor polishing her grandmother's caned rocker, dressed in her oldest sweatshirt and favorite tattered jeans, wild curly hair barely contained in an elastic band.

Sara liked who she was with Emily. She enjoyed watching herself—as she might a favored child—becoming the kind of passionate, vibrant woman she'd hoped to be, stretching, expanding within herself. She'd found herself yearning to reclaim her artwork, had already retrieved chalks and drawing paper from the attic. She was comforted in her recommitment to the morning routine she'd established long ago. A walking meditation followed by three pages of journaling inevitably renewed her spirit, affirmed a connection with herself. She needed to be mindful of her inclination to immerse, to lose herself in relationships, never to be seen or heard from again. She didn't want to do that with Emily. She vowed to do this differently. Isis yawned, stretched and shifted to another sunspot as if to say, *Oh yeah? Well, we'll just wait and see.*

Our lessons are many in this first New Moon Cycle. We learn of boundaries—defining our own, honoring another's. Feeling separate is very important, yes! But setting those boundaries is the real challenge! We learn—slowly and certainly—to trust—or not. We even begin to consider differences. We struggle in the darkness. So much to learn, to take in, to know in this budding relationship. Is it worth it? Can we do it? Can we do what is required to move forward?

And we remember . . . we remember that, indeed, we have successfully maneuvered through our first challenge. We actually resolved a disagreement. We've had a success, we're reminded. The world did not end! The universe did not stop, and—more is the wonder—she didn't leave when we challenged our differences, when we named our feelings, our needs for separate time and space!

We search within ourselves, considering the value of this relationship. We wonder exactly why we've invited this person into our lives. Do we seem to complement each other or are we seeking completion to ourselves? Does this relationship enrich our life together, separately? The questions are many, and while the answers may remain obscured in the darkness and the afterglow of this new love, we must listen . . . listen to our own truth.

In the stillness of the dark of the moon, we feel renewed. Hope embraces us as we surrender to the knowing that yes, we can do this! We can trust ourselves to honor the rhythm that is becoming clearer. We've waxed into delicious and exhilarating loving; we've become filled with glorious creative joy, and then we've waned into a time of separateness when the bond—fragile, yes—was stretched so thin.

And now, the darkness begins to lighten with a hint of dawning. We feel renewed. The promise of rebirth beckons.

Lessons of the New Moon Cycle

This first passage through the New Moon Cycle is usually experienced most intensely. Having no history of success, we tread very cautiously and often fearfully through our virginal voyage through the New Moon Cycle. And, as through the first cycle of life, we have many lessons to learn. The learnings of the New Moon Cycle are vital to the future of the relationship: we are laying the foundation for the relationship.

Our primary tasks in this first cycle have to do with developing trust—affirming and strengthening our autonomy, in the context of the growing relationship.* Corresponding to the individual developmental cycle, we are also developing initiative as we establish boundaries. In our evolving relationship, these themes replicate the developmental issues we confront as individuals. It is often said that the early years (Cycle 1) of a child's development are the most crucial; the same can be said of the

---

* The waning phase of each cycle seems to be when the relevant developmental tasks come most clearly into focus, but in healthy relationships we engage in the process of developing and learning through the various challenges each cycle offers throughout each phase of the cycle.

first cycle of a relationship. As the developing child is struggling with trust and mistrust, autonomy and shame, risk-taking and limiting behaviors, so are the falling-in-lovers. The extent to which each of us honors her own life cycle issues, in a respectful and rhythmic manner, is the extent to which the developmental stages in the relationship will be honored. As each of us honors her own need for growth, her own rhythm, so each of us will be respectful of the rhythm of the relationship and the healthier all the entities, the *you*, the *I*, the *us*, will be.

Failure to negotiate the relevant tasks in this formative cycle will inhibit the growth and movement into and through subsequent cycles. Simply stated, without trust, without respect for boundaries, we are simply unable to have a healthy, life-giving relationship in which each of us can thrive.

Trust

The developmental theme of the New Moon Cycle in the life of a relationship is trust. Trust is not a single event: we are in the process of developing an increasing confidence that, as each of us begins to feel valued by the other, our relationship needs will be met, for the most part. This is a process that gradually grows and increases as each risk is taken, each challenge is confronted, and each issue is respectfully resolved. Just as the infant develops a well-differentiated concept of the parent as both separate and permanent, so each participant in the newly developing relationship begins to trust this sense of separateness *and* continuity, of connectedness *and* individuation. While the waxing phase of a developing relationship seems to be about learning to trust the other, the waning phase is about affirming the trust in oneself—trusting the self to be separate, autonomous, *and* in relationship. Throughout the cycle, we are learning to trust the rhythm of the developing relationship—the waxing into connectedness and waning into separateness.

Only if we are able to trust ourselves in the separateness of waning will we be able to surrender to the closeness of the waxing. In fact, the extent to which we are able to trust the waning will be reflected in the extent to which we are able to trust the waxing. Similarly, as we learn to honor the increasing intimacy of the waxing, we learn to trust the distance of the waning. In the beginning, we simply invest our trust in the possibilities that we hope will grow between us. We can only sense that the object of our attraction is trustworthy. As we each take greater and greater risks, we see that our investment begins to reap the benefits of increasing trust. And as the cycles progress, we increasingly learn to honor the process of surrendering to the true intimacy of the waxing as we trust ourselves to be still in the darkness of the ambiguous waning.

Trust is a growing entity. As I invest a little of myself and you invest some of yourself, then I risk a little more and you take some more risks and, gradually, we come to a place of mutual sharing, where we believe we can say anything and trust that the other will do the same. But in the waning time, when we face the darkness, the separateness, the mutual trust is put to the test; suddenly, we question whether we can trust ourselves and the other—really trust enough to say honestly what we want and need in the face of hard choices.

Throughout the infancy of this new relationship, we may often feel very young, and we certainly feel vulnerable. In this time of testing and trusting, we may feel exposed in our vulnerability. For some, these feelings may be a manifestation of unresolved childhood issues of shame. We are reminded that shame is the experience of feeling innately defective and bad and often is evoked when we feel left, rejected, or abandoned. During those necessary separations—in the waning phase of the cycle—we may *react* to the required separation by plummeting into a pit of shame. In fact, if we are filled with shame, we may feel utterly crazy being in a healthy relationship; an unhealthy relationship, which explains our feelings of shame, makes much more sense. To feel cared about when we hate ourselves is incongruent and confusing. Finding ourselves in that place, we may respond by setting up circumstances that will reenact the shame in order to maintain the familiar dynamics in which we feel at home. Clearly, this kind of feeling/response situation demonstrates just how necessary it is for us to do our own individual healing before we can participate in a healthy relationship. Only if we have a self, can we bring that self to a relationship.

As we begin the process of trusting ourselves and the other, most of us are able to share confidences of our story with someone we are learning to love, but we are less inclined to be honest about our feelings, our needs, and our wants. The process of developing trust requires above all else that we be scrupulously honest and truthful—and trustworthy ourselves. Whether or not I tell you (unless you ask) how much I dislike your beloved, tacky, faded orange sweatshirt that makes you look as though you've been ill for six months is not really an issue; my letting you know that I want to go to the museum with a friend on Sunday *without you*—even though I'm afraid you may be hurt and angry—this is being scrupulously honest. That I'm feeling angry and sad when you fail to keep your promise to call—this is being scrupulously honest. Trust begins with our being vulnerable to our own truth.

Many couples never seem to move beyond the *Where do you want to go for dinner?—Oh, I don't care, where do you want to go?* stage: neither is willing to *risk* identifying a preference! Yet this is the stuff of which trust is made. If we can trust the other to be truthful with regard to these kinds of preferences, then we're more likely to trust ourselves to stipulate our own. Further, if we can trust on this basic level of honesty, then we can trust on deeper levels of feelings and differences. Being consistently and unrelentingly truthful about the smallest *and* the greatest of issues is an absolute requisite in the process of forming the foundation of a healthy, life-giving relationship.

Trust is the basis on which all else is built. Trust has everything to do with maintaining our sense of self and our own autonomy in the context of our relationship. It is inevitable that we will experience moments of losing ourselves in the other, moments when we surrender ourselves totally and completely to the other. This is part of intimacy. Ironically, in order to be free to risk the loss of self, we must trust our own wholeness, our ability to remain intact: we trust ourselves in order to maintain a sense of autonomy so that we can trust ourselves to surrender to the other.

Unlike the infant whose very survival depends on the caregiver, the lovers cannot expect that *all* individual needs will be met in the relationship. The relationship becomes a safe environment for needs and feelings to be expressed and named, for relational needs to be asserted and met. To name our needs does not guarantee their being met, of course. However, the naming is the first step toward negotiating our way to mutual satisfaction. What this entails is the learning/relearning about defining and setting *boundaries*. In the developing trusting relationship, each should be asserting her values and asking herself and her partner some hard questions: *Do we want to be sexually monogamous? What do we mean by commitment? fidelity? Is there room in this relationship*

*for full expression of feelings? all feelings? Can I be sad and mad and
scared, or only glad? Can I just share my fears or are you going to have
to rescue me? What are our intimacy needs? our sexual needs? How are
these felt? expressed? Can we honor our individual styles and rhythms?
Can we be different and be respected in that uniqueness?* The fundamental question is this: can each of us trust herself and the other to assert her
wants, needs, feelings, thoughts?

Learning to trust the rhythm of the growing relationship is our primary challenge. This aspect of trust—perhaps the most powerful of
all—may be the most difficult to achieve. Yet this is actually what
Coming Full Circle is all about: trusting the rhythm, the flow, and the
process of moving through the passages and cycles—our own and those
of the relationship.

Ultimately, our foremost task is to step out of our own way and allow
for what is the greater good. This is a spiritual issue—the knowing that,
in fact, we are not in control. Our unwillingness to surrender to that
which is greater than ourselves aborts the natural rhythm of *being* and
we attempt to maintain the *illusion* of controlling our lives and those in
our lives. Of course, we make choices—in every moment—as we, in each
moment, die and are reborn. Yet we have no control over what the next
moment might present to us. We can only trust ourselves to make the
choice that is best in that moment. To attempt to control the future (or
to change the past) is a lesson in futility: what is *is!* Our challenge, then,
is to develop trust in ourselves, in our Higher Power, our Goddess, our
God, the Universe—however we choose to name that which is greater
than ourselves.

Now and then, most of us let go of our need for control—for maintaining that illusion of control—for a moment, and then, inevitably, we
take it back. We surrender to our Goddess, knowing that all is as it is,
and then, out of fear, we take it all back. *Trusting* in the process that all
is and will be . . . is truly an ongoing challenge for most of us. This is our
humanness. This ambivalence we have for trusting is manifested in all
of our relationships. We are unwilling to trust—*really* trust—in the
rhythm of the ebb and flow, of the waxing and waning. We try to control
our own and/or the other's rhythm—her behavior, feelings, even her
thoughts, her time, her money, and on and on. Our challenge, always, is
to return to ourselves—to our own feelings and knowings, to our own
spiritual connection.

The waxing time of this first cycle, so intensely passion-filled, is a time of blending and merging. For many this first cycle is addictive. We seem to lose ourselves in the other and we feel utterly delicious as we surrender to this immersion, this *falling* in love. In all our bliss, we must still remember the primary lesson of the New Moon Cycle: trust. That trust implies a trust in oneself and one's own vulnerability as well as trust in the other. We need to be vigilant of and vulnerable to our own truth and willing to assert our needs, wants, feelings, experiences, choices, and values.

It has been said that the first time something happens, it's an accident; the second time it happens, it's coincidence; and by the third time that happens, it's a rule. An example: June accepts Henry's invitation to have a dinner date; they agree to meet at Enrico's at 7:30 p.m. on Saturday. Henry is 15 minutes late because he'd misplaced his car keys. June smiles, accepts his profuse apology, denies her own feelings; they hurry through dinner. Two weeks later, they agree to a movie date; Henry is to pick June up at her home at 6:45 on Friday. Henry is 30 minutes late because his car had a flat tire. June smiles, accepts his profuse apology, denies her own feelings; they choose another movie. Ten days later, June invites Henry to a gallery opening on Sunday afternoon; they're to meet at 4 p.m. for tea. Henry is 45 minutes late because he had car trouble. June smiles, accepts his profuse apology, denies her own feelings; they hurry through tea, arrive at the opening fashionably late. Five years later, Henry and June are in marriage counseling on the verge of divorce. June is furious at Henry's consistently thoughtless lateness, and Henry can't understand where all her anger is suddenly coming from! Neither realizes that in the early days of their dating, they collaborated in establishing the rule that Henry could be as late as he pleased (he didn't do it on purpose, after all!) and June would not get mad; in fact, she'd say nothing! The first time Henry was late it was an accident; the second time he was late it was a coincidence; but by the third time, it had become a rule in the relationship, albeit unstated, that Henry could be as late as he wished and June would smile and say nothing. The first cycle of the relationship, then, is a most crucial one. In the midst of intense passion and bliss, rules are beginning to be established.

Rules such as these are the stuff of which trust is made. Rules become more clearly identified and formulated in the second cycle of the relationship, yet in the very early phases of a relationship, rules are being established—even during the time of limerence, of our blissful falling in love, even in our starry-eyed state!

In a weaving, the *warp* consists of the threads that run lengthwise and give the fabric its definition, its form, its base. The *weft* are those threads that are woven horizontally, giving the weaving substance and beauty, bringing the fabric to completion. Any weaving or fabric requires both warp and weft. Trust is the warp we need as we weave the fabric of our relationship; each person's unique autonomy, her individuality, and her willingness to risk naming and setting boundaries—all of this is the weft of our strong and beautiful evolving tapestry. As we learn to trust ourselves and the other, we are more willing and able to set boundaries, a prerequisite for later cycles when we are more and more clearly defining ourselves and the relationship.

Boundaries

Setting boundaries, implicit in the process of trusting, is about defining the self and the relationship; boundary setting is also about asserting one's autonomy. When the toddler angrily stomps her foot and says No! she's asserting herself—pushing, testing the limits. The lovers in a healthy relationship also explore ways of appropriately expressing anger and dealing with conflict. This is one way of establishing boundaries.

Boundaries help us set limits, and limits help us feel safe. Growth has to do with pushing those boundaries. Boundaries are what separate me from you—what defines me, what defines you. A boundary is an invisible line that defines us—physically, emotionally psychologically, spiritually. Boundaries are not walls. Boundaries are firm yet flexible.

Every time we say *I want . . . , I need . . . , I think . . . , I feel . . . ,* we are setting a boundary: we are saying *I AM!* Without boundaries, the two of us are not separate—ever. We become one; we have an enmeshed relationship, one in which neither of us knows where one ends and the other begins.

Boundaries are simply limits—both internal and external—and are established through a process of self-empowerment and self-definition. Internal boundaries define us. Boundaries define where I end and you begin; internal boundaries separate my feelings from yours; they are emotional, intellectual, and spiritual definitions.

When I have good *internal boundaries*, I know that when you come into the room scowling and grumbling, you have had a bad day, and I don't automatically assume that I'm at fault or that I'm responsible for making you feel happy. Your anger is none of my business! Likewise, my feelings are my responsibility: you cannot make me happy—or sad or angry.

External boundaries are spatial. The fences around my land spatially define the property. To take time alone is setting an external boundary.

We come to each other with our own stories, our own expectations— much of which we learned in our own families. As we prepare to create a new "family," it is important to explore whence we came. Knowledge—or the lack thereof—of boundaries, as with most of life's lessons, has its roots in the family system. The word *family* is a boundary: it defines the unit of people who live together and support one another—in varying degrees. To name how and when we wish to be touched is setting a boundary.

Clarifying boundaries within a family is a good measure for evaluating the functionality of a family and helps us determine what it is we take with us into our new relationship. There are at least three kinds of family boundaries:

- The *system boundary* marks the family as an entity. In ascertaining the system boundary of the family, we look at how open or closed the family system is. An *open system* is an inclusive one; members are free to bring in friends and ultimately their partners. Similarly, family members are free to leave, to establish their own family system. We are welcomed into the extended family for gatherings; our separateness is acknowledged and honored. There is respectful freedom of movement in an open system.

  A *closed system*, by contrast, defines *family* in very strict terms: family members are either IN or they're OUT, and the inclusion of members' partners depends on strictly defined qualifications. For instance, a woman's successful, "straight" husband may be IN, but her sister's female partner is OUT. A son who chooses someone perceived to be better than or beneath the family's self-defined status may also be OUT.

  The system boundary affects the information coming into and leaving the family system. Typically, the more rigid the boundaries, the less information flows into and out of the family, creating a closed system. Family secrets are the norm. How people move into and out of the family defines whether the family is an inclusive system or an exclusive system. To welcome into the family friends and in-laws, for instance, would be perceived as a threat to a closed system. The absence of diversity fostered in a closed system perpetuates the status quo; in a closed system, we learn that it is definitely not okay to be different.

In a closed system, members have great difficulty leaving the family; we're never allowed to grow up, to be separate and establish our own family. In the rural Midwest, it is not uncommon to see large farm houses surrounded by similar smaller or mobile homes on the land. In these families, no one leaves. As adults, they are still quite attached to their family of origin, unable to establish their own, autonomous family units. The reality is that we can't really be free to be in a healthy adult relationship until we've left home, emotionally as well as physically.

- *Structural boundaries* within our families define who's close to whom and how rigid or diffuse the defining boundaries are within a family on the continuum of *disengaged* to *enmeshed*. In every relationship, there must be some structure, some definition. The two individuals in an intimate relationship do not become one: we retain some sense of separateness as well as connectedness. Similarly, in the family, there must exist a boundary between the parents and their children. When children are used to meet the physical or emotional needs of parents, we name this incest—sexual and/or emotional. Furthermore, children must have boundaries between each other. Excessive fighting, for instance, is often a manifestation of unexpressed anger in other parts of the system. Sexual abuse between siblings is an indication of serious lack of boundaries.

A family whose transactions are considered disengaged has inappropriately rigid boundaries and will tolerate a wide range of behaviors but is unlikely to respond to the needs of family members. In a disengaged family, there are no connections; there is no sense of one's place in the family. We have no sense of belonging. On the other end of that continuum is the enmeshed family whose boundaries are diffuse and ill-defined. The behaviors of one person in an enmeshed family affect all other members, creating excessive responses to that family member's need. We have no sense of identity.[4]

- *Ego boundaries* have to do with the definition of the self. Although internal themselves, ego boundaries are learned by setting external limits. How family members honored one another's privacy is one of the ways we are most clearly able to see what we learned of boundaries in our family of origin. Were there doors on bedrooms? Were we allowed to close them? What about bathroom privacy? Was our bedroom private? Were we allowed to have a secret diary? Was our diary read by a family member?

  Learning to establish physical boundaries strengthens our ego boundaries. We can choose what thoughts and feelings to let in and out; we develop a sense of self as separate and unique. We recognize who we are, what we need, what we feel, think, and value. We are aware of how much closeness we want and how much distance we need. Without a strong sense of self, we are unable to set these boundaries; and without boundaries we cannot know our wants and needs.

Within the context of a relationship—or without—our goal is to be fully integrated—physically, emotionally, intellectually, and spiritually. When these aspects of ourselves are violated, we feel off-center, disintegrated, and unsafe. Unfortunately, learning about boundaries often doesn't occur until those boundaries have been violated. Feeling anger or disappointment is often a clue that, in fact, our boundaries have been dishonored and we're losing our sense of self. Because many of us are alarmingly unaware when we have been so disrespected, let's further explore some specific ways in which these various aspects of ourselves are typically violated.

Physical and sexual boundaries are abused when our bodies or our spatial limits are ignored. Spatial violations negate our physical space. We experience these when others do not honor closed doors, when they enter without knocking or without waiting for permission—particularly in private space such as the bedroom and bathroom. Hitting, kicking, shoving, or restraining in any way are most obvious expressions of physical abuse. Paradoxically, each time the abuse occurs, we become further bonded to the abuser: our sense of self becomes increasingly eroded. Violations of physical/sexual boundaries affect our body image, which significantly contributes toward our having a poor self-image.

Sexual abuse is the most profound boundary violation: the most vulnerable part of oneself has been desecrated. Sexual abuse can be covert or overt. Any nonconsensual sexual overture or gesture, including unwanted touch, comments, teasing, and tickling, is abuse.

As adults, what we notice about ourselves when our physical boundaries have been violated is that we are likely to be sexually and/or physically abusive to ourselves and/or to others; we may abuse substances and/or food. We find ourselves being sexual on our partner's terms, not our own. We are not sensitive to touching: we touch another too freely and allow ourselves to be touched too freely—often without noticing. We tend to fall in love frequently—often with anyone who reaches out to us, who shows us the least bit of interest. We allow others too close in our physical field.

Emotional boundary violation is manifested through the keeping of family secrets. Often we have a felt sense of having to withhold information in our families of origin, especially around issues of relationships and sexuality. We participate in the wrong-doing by having to hold a family secret. Inappropriate bonding creates boundary abuse. For instance, if mom is alcoholic or chronically ill, an older daughter may become dad's emotional "wife." Denial, a familiar theme in many families, frequently exacerbates the absence of boundaries: we can't set boundaries around what's not being talked about. Other forms of emotional boundary violation include excessive pressure to perform, "guilt-tripping," withdrawal of affection, and lack of affirmation of our feelings, of our competency, and of our resources—both internal and external.

What we notice when our emotional boundaries have been abused is that we let others define who we are, which keeps us in a reactive state. We also tend to tell too much too soon about ourselves, thus fostering a "pseudo-intimacy." We don't notice when someone is being intrusive, and at the same time we play victim and passively expect others to anticipate our needs.

The dishonoring of *intellectual boundaries* is characterized by mind-reading, interrupting, and criticizing. Phrases such as "You don't want to do that" or "What you really need is (whatever)" or "Why would you do a dumb thing like that?" become familiar proscriptions. Negating any creative ventures, continuous correcting, prying, and lecturing are all typical behaviors in the ill-defined family system. What we notice in ourselves if our intellectual boundaries have been consistently violated is that we tend to speak for others and to allow others to speak for us, because we have no opinion on issues. On the other hand we tend to be overly self-disclosing and very self-critical!

Virtually all of the violations just described are also violations of our *spiritual boundaries*: our spirit has been negated, diminished, left to fallow. These various forms of intrusion keep us from being all that we can be—whole, healthy children of the Universe. What we notice about ourselves is that we violate our own values in order to please others. Because we have no firm beliefs, we either feel utter spiritual alienation or, conversely, we become involved in strict, rigidly judgmental religions or cult-like groups—both of which tell us what to believe and neither of which has the slightest resemblance to spirituality.

When our boundaries are ill-defined or have been violated, we are likely to become enmeshed with another or unable to make connections with another at all. We have no sense of self; we feel powerless and amorphous. We are like a tumbleweed, blowing aimlessly about in the wind, unable to take root, but becoming attached to whatever we happen to blow up against.

Healing and learning to set boundaries is about claiming—*re/claiming*—the empowerment of ourselves. The typical defense mechanisms, such as dissociation, denial, and intrusive behaviors are simply our distorted attempts to set limits. They are efforts in the extreme. These ineffective ways of boundary-setting are not limits; they are walls and they leave us with no choices, for they wall us in, isolate us and prevent us from experiencing healthy reciprocal relationships.

Healthy boundaries are flexible and permeable and are grounded in *choice-making*. As we gradually go about the business of learning to set boundaries, it is useful to recognize and accept our human limits and to know that ultimately boundary-setting is simply about making healthy choices for ourselves. We develop our own list of shoulds by sorting those out from the old messages still rattling around in our head—those that sound very much like dad's or mom's or grandma's voice—and we begin to delineate our own responsibilities, our own priorities. There is no denying that learning to set our own rules is difficult; it is hard to change life-long habits, to interrupt those old patterns. But if we are to have healthy, whole relationships, we must be healthy, whole individuals. Without a sense of self, we can't afford to be separate and different, so most of us, certainly in the early phases of our relationship, tend to minimize our differences and to maximize our similarities. Yet accepting and even celebrating ways in which we are different is the key to setting boundaries and thus to healthy, life-giving relationships.

We must recognize our ability and response/ability* to stop ourselves and to stop others from becoming enmeshed. We begin when we allow ourselves to explore, to "try on" new behaviors; we begin by saying, *I'm not sure what I feel, yet. I just know I'm not comfortable about that* or *I don't know what I feel, but I'll let you know when I do,* or *I'm feeling afraid to say this to you,* and we learn to say *NO!*

We learn what we can/cannot control. Control in and of itself is not bad. Controlling others or the illusion that we control others and life's events is what gets us in trouble. We can control, make choices, and take responsibility for our own behavior, our own feelings. We can learn to have little or no attachment to a specific outcome: to trust that we can be open and responsive to whatever presents itself to us and to make the healthy choice for ourselves in the face of that.

In learning about boundaries, it is helpful to begin with the physical limits. In the beginning, it is often easier to step back from someone, to leave the room or to physically stay away, than it is to name our feelings. We need to let this be a first step on the path to reclaiming ourselves, thence proceeding to the naming of our feelings.

There are specific ways we can, in each of the four aspects—physical, emotional, intellectual, and spiritual—strengthen our boundaries. Paradoxically, strong, healthy boundaries are also supple and flexible. We're not building walls here. For those of us for whom this is new behavior, it may seem, at first, that we are putting up—brick by brick— a wall ten feet high and six feet thick. In fact, extreme circumstances may require extreme measures. However, I invite you to give yourself permission to *learn.* Learning to establish boundaries is learning to trust and to empower oneself, and this is a *process.* It has been said that it requires our doing a new behavior 22 times before that behavior becomes a habit. We must begin with trying it once!

Strengthening our physical and sexual boundaries begins when we affirm/reclaim our own physical body: regular physical exercise, such as

---

* our ability to respond

a daily walk, is probably the best place to start. In addition, choose a time and a physical space that is yours. Virginia Woolf's *A Room of One's Own* has been a wonderful image for many of us. Whether we claim a room or a corner of our own, private space is crucial to our honoring our autonomy and privacy. Each of us needs a corner of her world where she can just *be!*

We need to learn to be touched appropriately; if this is uncomfortable, we must choose someone safe with whom to experiment with simple hugs. We need to learn to be sexual—with ourselves and with others, to make our own sexual choices about when, how often, and what feels pleasurable. We need to remember that our sexuality is not just about "having sex"; it's about being playful, having fun, and flirting! It is about re/claiming the temple that is our body. What is most important is that *we choose!* Setting physical boundaries is the place to begin.

As we begin to achieve some comfort about setting limits for ourselves, we begin to get some good feelings from our increasingly healthy behaviors. In fortifying our emotional boundaries, we affirm these changes: we can write something each day we feel successful about—yes, at least one thing each day! We can choose our feelings and we can choose what we do with those feelings, how we express them.

We need to surround ourselves with people who will support and affirm our feelings and our changes as we learn to have our own feelings and not others'. Certainly we can care for others; we just don't have to feel their feelings. When I'm inclined toward losing myself in another, when I'm overly attached to another's feelings or behaviors, I like to think of the process of detachment as putting the person and/or the situation up on a movie screen. Certainly, if it's a good movie, I have feelings about what I'm seeing on the movie screen, but I know that what is happening is not, in this moment, happening to me! I'm not attached to the outcome of the movie; I simply watch the story unfold. I am neither the movie's star nor am I the director; I am the observer.

Many of us have been shamed for our anger, our fears, our wants, needs, our sexuality—our *muchness.* We've been told that we are bad when we feel sexual, angry, needy, and so on. But in reality, feelings are not good or bad, and neither are we for having them. Feelings just *are!* What is important is what we do with those feelings! In learning about boundaries, we need to become aware of the areas in which we experience shame. When the violation or invasion of our boundaries goes unnoticed, we experience this as shame. Just because we have been shamed is no reason for us to continue the shaming of ourselves. Forgiveness of ourselves becomes a significant piece of the boundary-setting process.

Our intellectual boundaries are strengthened when we learn to think and speak for ourselves, and we need to choose friends who will support us in this. We need to learn to ask questions and to validate what we do know as well as what we want to know more about. And we must be free to make mistakes.

It is important in reclaiming our intellectual self that we have some privacy. There is an important distinction between secrets and privacy. Secrets are unhealthy when they affect the system, but having privacy is about setting boundaries. Many of us keep a journal in which we can "talk with ourselves"—about anything! Our feelings, our dreams, our fears, our hates. A journal must be private, unless we choose to share it.

In strengthening our intellectual boundaries, we need to develop some preferences. Even if we don't care whether we eat Italian or Chinese, we need to say something; make a choice! And we need to develop beliefs about some issues, whether it's concern for the extinction of the whales, ecofeminism, gays in the military, or organic gardening.

The healing of ourselves by learning to establish boundaries is ultimately a spiritual issue. We need to make a commitment to some kind of spiritual program—not necessarily a church, but some commitment to reading or sharing about our spirituality is important. We are becoming who we are meant to be, in all of our richness and fullness, claiming our unique place in the universe.

Our discussion on boundaries has been an extensive one. It can't be emphasized enough just how important this issue is in a healthy relationship. When we don't set limits and boundaries for ourselves, we set ourselves up to be rejected: someone else must set our boundary for us. Similarly, when our partner is unwilling to take responsibility for herself, to set her own boundaries, we are left to define them for both of us, which ultimately leads to resentment—on both parts—and sets up an unequal, parent-child dynamic.

The New Moon Cycle is where we begin to set those boundaries: the first time something happens is an accident, second time a coincidence, and the third time a rule in the relationship. We are, in the New Moon

Cycle, establishing the foundation for the relationship, and a healthy partnership must be one in which boundaries are clearly delineated. Paradoxically, the clearer the boundaries, the more freedom we have to move, to grow, to flourish, to trust, and to love.

Organizing Conflict

When boundaries are violated, ill-defined, or simply not honored, conflict inevitably follows. Hence, the waning phase of the New Moon Cycle is often characterized by conflict. Because we are still in the process of establishing boundaries and building trust, we experience the conflict of the first waning in a reactive way. Because we have no history yet of successfully moving through the ambiguity of separateness, of successfully resolving our differences, this is a scary time! What is important here is to maintain some connection (as with a dotted line!) while at the same time we make room for separateness. This is the challenge of the waning phase.

Unfortunately, conflict often is used indirectly to set boundaries. If we're not willing to say we want some time alone, we will probably start a fight. A common means for achieving the need for space in which to nurture oneself, to affirm our own separateness, is to have conflict of some kind. Conflict also serves the purpose of distracting ourselves from our own needs; most of us have little experience in genuinely caring for ourselves, so in the context of a relationship, our partner serves to divert the focus from our own needs.

Healthy conflict has a viable place in any relationship, and it is in the waning phases of cycles where conflict is most likely to emerge. Our varying styles for handling conflict come into focus during the New Moon Cycle. We each come to the other with our own story, our own life's experience, which is likely to be in direct contrast to the other's. Our different styles of "doing" conflict and our various feelings about confrontation are typically the areas in which we become all too clear about our differences.

Within our families of origin, we have often been exposed to at least two different models. For example, mom may have been passive and dad violent—both to varying degrees—neither of which teaches us workable and appropriate ways of dealing with our own anger and conflict. Furthermore, young boys typically learn to express their anger more directly than do girls. So most of us come into a new configuration, a new relationship, with ambivalent feelings about anger and conflict and with few skills for resolving the inevitable conflict in healthy and healing ways. No wonder we avoid the darkness of the waning and shudder at the prospect of any dissimilarity. We have few or no skills with which to move through conflict with grace and respect—for ourselves much less the other.

The two of us will flow through the waning time with more or less ease depending on the extent to which each of us as individuals is comfortable with ourselves and with our own willingness to be with ourselves. The more comfortable each of us is with her own company, and the more we have resolved our own trust and autonomy issues and are able to affirm our own boundaries, the more likely we are to honor our partner's. From a solid grounding, in this time of ambiguity, we are less likely to react out of fear to our own and our partner's need for separateness and introspection.

External pressure on the relationship may have different implications for the two lovers. On one hand, there is the potential for us to join forces, working together to reach a mutually beneficial solution. This is most likely to occur when each of us is clear about our own needs and feelings relevant to the external issue. On the other hand, the external demand can act as a point of triangulation, creating a wedge between us. This is especially likely if the need for separateness, implicit in the waning phase of the cycle, has not been explicitly honored.

As we have seen in our discussion of the New Moon Cycle, the waning phase is characterized by conflict, either internal or external, covert or overt, and is experienced as either a distancing, on one end of the continuum, or as overt arguing, on the other end of that continuum. Having no previous experience in dealing with conflict and differentness, the first waning of the New Moon Cycle is especially threatening and often evokes intense reactions on the part of one or both partners.

The process by which we resolve our individual differences, along with those pressures that impinge on the relationship, has everything to do with the manner in which the relationship moves into the subsequent cycle and, of course, with whether the relationship continues. The resolution of the conflict and the integration of those individual differences determines the relative harmony with which the two lovers move through this cycle.

We know that conflict is not only inevitable, it is a vital aspect of any healthy, intimate relationship. The process of conflict will be further explored in the Waxing Moon Cycle; it is important to be aware here that the role conflict plays not only in the waning phase of a cycle but in the convergence into the cycle that follows is very significant. Just as rules are being put in place in other aspects of our relationship, so are they being established in the area of conflict and the articulation of our differences. No doubt, our styles are quite different from one another's, so it is useful to be open to creating rules that work for the two of us.

It is true that there is no neat and tidy resolution to many differences, which means that many fights never get resolved at all; they get recycled over and over and we end up virtually fighting the same fight. By "agreeing to disagree," we risk not ever resolving any issues. What is important here, however, is the commitment to meet at a specified time in order to complete the discussion. This is an example of learning to stay *connected with a dotted line* even in the face of conflict. Most conflict can be handled when we are feeling clear and centered and rested: we are able to proactively state our thoughts and feelings, to hear the other's, and then begin to look at options—many options—that are possible resolutions. In the face of addiction, Twelve-step Program members use an acronym that can be useful for all of us: HALT. When we are Hungry, Angry, Lonely, or Tired, we need to halt, to stop, to interrupt our ineffective or inappropriate behavior and take care of ourselves. Only after we have done that will we have the resources to handle the issue at hand.

Most conflict becomes threatening when one or both partners becomes attached to a right/wrong outcome. Too often our need to be right supersedes our need to be respectful and caring. Unhealthy conflict is nearly always based in the patriarchal good/bad, right/wrong, power-over/overpowered dualism that keeps us in a win/lose dynamic. Inevitably, there are no winners in win/lose conflict; everyone loses. When we are faced with a win/lose situation, we need to *halt* and listen—first to ourselves then to the other.

There are some of us for whom "trauma drama" is the norm: we thrive on crisis. This is familiar to many of us: it is what we grew up with. Living from one crisis to the next and conflict resolution meant we simply "kiss and make up"—until the next crisis. Unfortunately, many need crises in order to feel alive. On the other hand, some of us are so fearful that any conflict may erupt into a crisis that we become phobic about all differences. We avoid conflict at all cost. The healthiest option, of course, is to stay current with any differences as they arise, thus preventing either denial or crisis.

Conflict serves very significant purposes in our relationships, and it is useful to ascertain just what purposes those might be. For some, conflict simply for the sake of conflict is a way of setting boundaries, of getting the desired distance in the relationship. For others, conflict is the only way of making contact. Like the kid who's always getting into trouble, negative attention is better than no attention at all. So, for some, contact through conflict may be better than no contact—or, on the other hand, too much true intimacy. For this is another purpose conflict serves: diluting growing intimacy between us. We are afraid of our own vulnerability in intimacy.

Healthy conflict is an important part of any relationship committed to growth and wholeness, although it is true that not all differences are going to be neatly resolved. As we move through the process of learning to trust, to honor our own and one another's boundaries, we also must have room for those differences—some of which will be resolved, some of which will be integrated through compromise, and others of which will necessarily simply be accepted.

Known as *symbiosis* in the mother/child relationship, *fusion* or *merging* is characteristic of any newly developing intimate relationship. However, this blending, two-become-one, model in our culture tends to be extraordinarily destructive, and while there is a sense of oneness known as the *relationship*, there are also *you* and *I*—three entities. Honoring all three is what boundary setting is about. This requires a great amount of intentionality and care. Just when the lovers are deliciously and happily intoxicated with one another and with love—in a state of limerence—we are confronted with having to acknowledge some differences. How we as a couple approach these differences—indeed, the fact that there are differences—has much to do with how and if we move into the cycle that follows, how and if we stay for a while in the New Moon Cycle while we continue to learn our lessons.

Resolution of New Moon Cycle

We have waxed into the euphoria of falling in love; we have moved into the brilliant abundance of the fullness of hope and all the possibilities this new relationship holds; then, reluctantly, yet stubbornly, we have surrendered to the waning phase of the New Moon Cycle of this relationship. Finally, cautiously, we slip into the new moon phase—the dark of the moontime to which we now surrender. In the darkest of dark, we must confront the knowing of what awaits us in the convergence into the waxing that surely will appear once more.

In this phase of the dark of the moon, we peer into the darkness and we may feel safe and comforted, as though wrapped in a heavy protective cloak that warms us and protects us from harm. Or, perhaps, the darkness looms and threatens, filled with terror and unknown monsters lurking in the shadows. If we take time for our eyes to adjust to the blackness that envelops us, we may see a number of possibilities emerge. Quietly and peacefully as we await for the stillness to embrace us, we can, in the darkness, see our truth. The resolution of this cycle becomes clear to us as the cycles converge, leaving the old one, as we move ahead into the new. Let us look—carefully now—into the darkness for what lies ahead.

We recognize that this New Moon Cycle is coming to an end—or are we, rather, at a point of beginning? Is this the death of the cycle or the birth of the new cycle?

To answer those questions, we turn within and we hear the whispers of even more questions. *How am I feeling? Am I feeling renewed? Am I growing? Do I feel respected? loved? What does that mean for me? Do I feel loving and understanding of this person whom I've invited into my life? Are we good for each other? Are we both truly honest with one another? Am I committed to exploring this relationship, to trusting the rhythm? What exactly do I value? Just why have I invited this person into my life? and why has she invited me?*

In the dark of the moon, we must honestly examine our own integrity about just what it is we value in relation with another. My assumption, my bias, is that we invite another into our lives to support and nurture ourselves, to accompany us and nudge us along the path to our greater good. Why else invite another to join us if not to aid us in achieving our own—and the other's—greatness? What greater gift to give ourselves and another than to journey together toward our potentiality?

This ideal is not shared by everyone. Many choose another to complete them, not to complement them. And many choose not at all; they wait to be chosen. Some choose not to have a partner who participates in the journey, but rather prefer to "add-on" a mate simply to secure the status quo. I believe that this is an impossible state to maintain. We are always waxing and waning, ebbing and flowing, birthing and dying and being reborn. To remain static is to die. Often security is mistaken for fear of change. To grow within ourselves and thus within the relationship is too frightening, too risky: we desperately cling to what is secure, thus failing to honor the rhythm inherent to all that is alive and thriving.

The dark of the moon offers us the opportunity to confront ourselves, to acknowledge our own values, to know whether we are willing to *grow* into the next cycle or if we cling to the illusion of security that nongrowth offers and that ultimately leads to death. If our choice is the security of what is known and secure, then one of several alternatives will occur out of the darkness of the new moon. Typically what happens is that we repeat the cycle over and over and over. Our commitment to security inevitably results in nongrowth, in the ultimate death of the relationship.

On the other hand, should we choose to follow the more challenging and life-giving path, should we choose to grow into the cycle that follows, we may still remain in the New Moon Cycle for several turns, recognizing there are many important tasks at which we need to become proficient before we can proceed. This is, after all, the foundation of the relationship; we cannot afford to rush. We must honor the rhythm—the rhythm of the relationship.

Sometimes we ignore the challenges of the waning of the cycle: the differences have been too frightening; the threat of conflict has been too intimidating to risk our own vulnerability. We cannot go on. For those of us who thrive on chaos, the waning will have been, no doubt, an enormous crisis providing us an excuse for another waxing—a time for "kissing and making up." This unhealthy resolution of the New Moon Cycle feeds our addiction to excitement and intensity and evokes a pseudo-waxing. The relationship becomes static and will eventually die. It is not a life-giving relationship. Sooner or later, all life will be sucked out, and the relationship will remain on this suicidal path until its death.

Many of us assume that just because we love someone, we're meant to be in a *forever* relationship with her. I suggest that we are capable of loving many in our lifetime and that we will probably be blessed with many opportunities to love. It is ludicrous to assume there is only one Ms. or Mr. Right. Love is not a finite entity. There are many choices we can make with respect to what we do with those whom we love. Choosing not to continue a relationship may, in fact, be a loving act and need not negate the joy, the learning, the loving we have shared with one another.

How do we know when a relationship is over? How does a songwriter know when the music is finished? How does the artist know when the painting is complete? We know when there is nothing to be added and nothing to be taken away. We know when the present is empty and we have simply a reflection of our past and only illusions and promises fill the future. If we are willing, we know when we *know.*

In this dark of the moon, we have listened to the hard questions and now our answer has to be that this simply is not working. We make a choice—a healthy choice—to terminate the relationship, and we can do this by bringing about a respectful closure. We may have had a lovely falling-in-love time, and yet, for one or many reasons—maybe we're simply in the right place at the wrong time—we must make the choice not to go on.

If we are committed to healthy beginnings, so we must be committed to healthy endings. And if we are committed to our own growth, to being scrupulously honest, then, we must be honest with ourselves and honest with the other—even if we want to leave the relationship. To respectfully bring closure (now or later) may mean celebrating what was good between us, what we each learned from the other, the gifts we each take from our time together. We may name what didn't work, what we each needed and were unable to get, or unwilling to receive or to give. Partings are sorrowful and the sadness need not be disguised in anger.

If, on the other hand, after purposeful reflection, we emerge from the waning with a deep, knowing assent, and if out of the darkness of the new moon we each choose to continue together on this path of exploration of the evocative cycles, the energy of the resolution of the waning time acts as a catalyst for moving into the Waxing Moon Cycle. Of course, all our differences are not neatly and tidily resolved; we've barely named them. And of course we have no guarantees that we are to live happily ever after. Yet we trust ourselves—and the other—enough, now, that we have a felt sense of wanting to continue growing and exploring together. And we choose this person in the context of this relationship as a partner for learning more of the rhythm of living and growing and being.

Naming is clearly a primary theme in the New Moon Cycle. We are learning to name our feelings, our thoughts, our wants and needs. We are, perhaps, naming our very selves in ways we've never done before. And as we name what we are to each other, and then to those in our lives who really matter to us, we create a *ritual of naming.*

A Ritual of Naming

The day is gray and blustery: the cold north wind howls through the door, reluctant to yield to the warmth of spring which the emerging crocuses and budding tulips promise is on its way. It is Spring Equinox, the season of birth and youth, beginnings and renewal. We have chosen this day to celebrate our budding relationship and the newness and joy that we share.

Each of us has spent the morning alone—in quiet—an unusual occurrence, indeed. We always have so much to say, so many touches to share. But we have each taken a solitary walk in the woods, absorbing the wonders of this early spring morning. And as we walked we contemplated the past months, savoring this rapturous, delicious falling-in-love time, days of joy and ecstasy, of sharing and laughing and loving. And as we walked, each of us has chosen tokens of our loving, symbols of ourselves for our altar.

Now we've transformed the entire room into our altar: incense burns on the east, inviting the spirit of air, of inspiration and hope; to the south is the fireplace, ablaze with a roaring fire, symbolizing the energy and passion that moves between the two of us; out of the west windows, through the still barren trees, we see the waters of the merry stream as it ripples over the rocks and stones, creating lovely miniature waterfalls; this reminds us of the depth of emotions flowing within us and between us; and in the north, we have each placed a special geode that glistens and catches the light of the fire. We borrowed them from the earth near the stream this morning to symbolize the solid connection each of us feels to the Universe, to our Mother Earth and to each other. Between the two rocks is a small tree, a redbud sapling, that we rescued from a crowded garden spot—a symbol of our commitment to growing with one another—soon to be replanted in the spaciousness of the grove.

Near the fireplace, we have, like two youngsters playing house, made a pallet on the floor—thick blankets and a down comforter beckon us. And alongside our "nest" is a picnic basket filled with delicious morsels—all delectable and sensual finger foods. Adjacent to the basket is a bound book of blank pages, soon to become Our Journal.

We have each taken time, following our walk through the woods, to quietly reflect and to write in our individual journals of our own dreams, our hopes, our wants and needs, our feelings about ourselves and each other.

Together we enter our lovely sanctuary, and, circling the room sunwise, we light the many candles—white for purity, green for growth and abundance. Finally, we light the large white candle by the hearth, honoring Aphrodite, goddess of love. It is our intention that this candle will always be a part of our rituals of celebrating our love.

We move to our pallet and quietly share our journalings which, together, we record in Our Journal—our commitment to one another's and to our own growing, to honesty, to exploring the possibilities of sharing our lives, to being sexually exclusive, while inviting our friends and family to share our lives.

Bathed in the candlelight and warmed by the fire, we are embraced in the music that fills the room. We surrender to one another, to our loving.

The fire is low but the candles burn bravely on as we, in the afterglow of our loving, feed one another the delicacies of our picnic and toast to each other's health and love and to the Goddess in whose name we honor the pleasures of our loving.

Blessed be.

Chapter 5

Waxing Moon Cycle

Menses Summer Solstice Differences Acknowledged

Catch hold of the moonbeam, my children,
and with Artemis, ascend into the heavens.
The light of the waxing moon guides you, lovers still.
So may your love ripen and grow as the Moon waxes into
    fullness
and plays with you among the stars.

We have given birth to our relationship. We have grown through the waxing, the fullness, and the waning of the New Moon Cycle . . . perhaps several times. We have left behind the exhilaration of the waxing and the challenges of the waning of our first cycle together. We now hold in our possession many lovely souvenirs—blessings of our learnings. Now, as we venture into the cycle of the waxing moon, we pause to reflect on whence we came, reluctantly acknowledging that we shall never be able to recapture—not really—the ecstasy, the rapture of the cycle of the new moon when everything was new and fresh, when each experience was filled with wonder and enchantment. We delighted in exploring each other—our stories, our bodies, and our dreams. We waxed through time that seemed endless as the days melded into night and twilight and dawn merged in the glow of our loving. We grew expectant with our passion and imbued with our hopes. We became inspired with desire and bathed in promise, reaching a crescendo of fullness that surpassed all our dreams, most wild.

And then, oh, we surrendered. Reluctantly, yes, but we surrendered to the gradually decreasing light of the waning moon that threatened to extinguish our loving, to dash our dreams. Yet, through all our resistance, we honored the loosening clasp of one another's body as we each found our own place—alone again in the darkening night. In that place so dark, we had only ourselves to comfort through the unknown, to be comforted by our own reflections, to ponder those shadowy thoughts. Yet we grieve what was and can no longer be. Sadly, we mourn the loss of our birthing time, the delicious time of the infancy of our love: we grieve the death—the letting go—of our falling-in-love cycle.

As the dark of the moon phase of the New Moon Cycle blended and then vanished, into the new moon of the Waxing Moon Cycle, we honored the stillness and we knew our love, our trust, to be true. And out of the blackness an assuring glow promised rebirth—the Waxing Moon Cycle beckons us and we—our *us*—are born once more.

Now we dare to be reborn into loving anew. We venture into a new cycle—through the lovely bliss of waxing, the rich abundance of fullness, and the deep shadows of the waning; flowing and ebbing, connecting and separating, increasing and decreasing—waxing and waning: the tempo becomes more distinct and we surrender—more willingly, now—to the rhythm of our loving.

Throughout this, the second cycle, the Waxing Moon Cycle, we are confronted with more dilemmas, more issues to be explored. Increasingly, these are viewed as challenges, as opportunities for learning about ourselves and the other; less and less do they seem threatening. We have had, now, the experience of moving all the way through a cycle. We have waxed, reached fullness, and waned—and we survived! We are now in cycle two, and we affirm our growth—individually and collectively.

We glimpsed those eccentricities of each other, but now we are ready to actually acknowledge, to name those inevitable differences between us: the time has come. We can see that diversity may be a source of enrichment for the relationship; we are not so afraid that our differentnesses will divide us.

If cycle one was about building the foundation for the relationship, then cycle two is about fashioning the structure; for indeed this cycle, not unlike the first, is significant for the future of the relationship. The foundation has already been laid, but the supports must yet be put firmly in place. The tasks are many as we confront the significant issues in our developing relationship. Those issues that challenged us in the New Moon Cycle—at which we were only prepared to glimpse—need to be confronted more significantly and more practically now.

Just as the adolescent needs support and encouragement as she tries on adult behaviors, so does the young relationship require tender intentionality. In the Waxing Moon Cycle, we are becoming more serious about the business of "doing" this relationship as we not only explore the issues at hand but we begin to problem solve as well. We develop rituals both to sustain and to celebrate our efforts.

Significant lifestyle differences come into focus in the Waxing Moon Cycle. During the falling-in-love cycle, we were not very willing to confront questions about ethnic and cultural differences or potential problems stemming from any economic disparity—particularly in heterosexual relationships. Age differences are, potentially, increasingly problematic as our own developmental issues become more clearly defined, and we see that, in fact, there may be crucial variations in our priorities, our rhythms, and our interests and goals. And in same-sex relationships, we are now confronted with the serious implications that homophobia, both internalized and externalized, has for our evolving partnership.

These lifestyle issues are rooted in our families of origin. While we usually prefer to believe that we're all grown up and have truly left our families behind, the reality is that each of us does bring to the relationship a whole bag full of family stuff—history, experiences, values, expectations, and rules. Unless we're willing to look at that *baggage*, we have no choice about what to do with it. Many of us, reluctant to explore the implications of our past, just "do" our parents' marriage: we "do" Mom in our relationship or we "do" Dad. Lacking awareness, we are able only to replicate what was modeled for us. Sometimes, it seems as though we become "possessed," actually *become* Mom or Dad, in our relationships—our behaviors echo the past so resoundingly. But we must become aware of this before we can find our own way and establish our own relationship.

We bring into our love relationships all our unfinished business, all those unresolved issues of our past along with all the unconscious yearnings of childhood. We want so much; our dreams have no bounds. If we are to have a healthy relationship, we must continue to be vigilant of our own individual issues. As the relationship grows and differences come more clearly into focus, each of us will be personally challenged to confront those unresolved issues. We simply must be committed to our own individual journey if we are to come fully prepared to travel with our partner in healthy life-giving ways.

● ○ ●

As we journey into the Waxing Moon Cycle, we pause to prepare ourselves for the adventure that awaits us. As we wax into this growing relationship, we are mindful of the differences between us. Being more trusting of ourselves and of each other, we need not continue to maximize our similarities and minimize those ways in which we differ. We are more ready now to name just how we are different, in order that we may explore our options for integrating those differentnesses into our relationship. If, however, we come from families in which diversity was devalued, we will be even more challenged as we attempt to come to terms with the inevitable differ- ences between us. For where there is an absence or devaluing of diversity, the status quo—sameness—is perpetuated. We are not allowed to be different, nor can we allow for differentness. We find ourselves in the debilitating win/lose dynamic in which everyone loses.

An absence of diversity and a fullness of creativity are mutually exclusive, and if a relationship is to be a growthful and healthy one, creativity must be nurtured. Are we not creating together this relation- ship? At the same time, we remember that the waxing of the moon is reminiscent of the *Maiden aspect* of the Goddess who symbolizes new- ness and adventure. Seen as the virgin who is whole unto herself, the Maiden is playful and enchanting, willing to risk herself through this time of beginnings.

So as we move through the Waxing Moon Cycle, we retain that sense of empowerment in which we dare to discover, dare to risk! We believe in magic, for anything is possible—isn't it?

WAXING MOON PHASE

We emerge from the darkness of the new moon phase into the Waxing Moon Cycle; we move into the increasing light. The tiny sliver of the waxing moon holds promise and hope for us, and we flow out of our separateness into the deliciousness of reconnecting.

We feel both exhilarated and shy as we anticipate the waxing of the cycle: we remember the ecstasy of our blending when we seemed able to know the other's thoughts, to anticipate her needs, to feel her feelings intermingling with our own. We gaze once more upon our beloved and we remember: this is the one in whom we do have trust; this is the one who knows our dreams, who has heard those secret whisperings we've shared for the first time—ever.

Once more we feel the energy swell, throbbing, pulsating through us as the passion for each other, for life, for *being* consumes us.

Waxing is the time for initiating, for creating. Feeling renewed, we are energized and inspired to risk ourselves, to journey into new frontiers of loving. The Maiden playfully beckons us, urging us to abandon our fears, to trust Her and to join Her on this new phase of the great adventure.

More and more we trust the other and ourselves—growing and increasing as the tiny sliver waxes toward fullness. More and more we trust to be more fully ourselves with the other, trust enough to further divulge those dark shadowy knowings of ourselves. And we trust enough to be more fully autonomous, risking our preferences and our eccentricities.

We even begin to push against some of our neatly defined boundaries. We begin to reclaim some of our self-nurturing rituals, those that seemed to get lost in the intensity of our first cycle together. Now we begin to trust that, in fact, there *will* be enough time for us *and* for journaling and walking and even time with friends. So it is that we nudge those external boundaries and push against some internal ones as well as we become more willing to risk even more feelings and opinions.

We truly are able to be more vulnerable, reaching into depths of ourselves we didn't know existed. And as we are more open with ourselves, we find ourselves being more open to our loved one. We are still foolishly happy and delighted as we continue to discover utterly endearing qualities about the object of our adoration. *She is so adorable as she talks with a friend, unaware of my noticing. . . . How I melt when he grins at me with that look! . . . Oh, I love our candle-lit dinners and our talks that just go on and on and on. . . . How I thrill at catching a glimpse of him across a room crowded with strangers. . . . What a delicious treat to answer the phone and hear her soft, breathy voice "calling just to tell you how much I love you."*

● ○ ●

The waxing of the second cycle is distinguished by trusting ourselves and each other enough to validate our autonomy within the context of the relationship. We are learning to be with ourselves *and* with the other. We feel freer to explore some of our internal boundaries, being increasingly vulnerable to our own truth and naming those knowings to our beloved. Likewise, we are freer to expand some of the external ones as well as we individually and together extend ourselves to old and new friends, and we accomplish these risky tasks by sharing more and more of ourselves with the other. We are deepening and strengthening the connection between us as we trust our own—and the other's—humanness and vulnerabilities. Out of this increasing trust, we are able to look more closely at our differing needs, our idiosyncratic habits, and our varying rhythms.

The two women, mother and daughter, knelt in the garden, nourished by the moist earthy aroma of young, fragrant herbs and rich black soil. It was Beltane, celebration of flowers and fires and fertility, of the earth's passion to birth and bloom and bear fruit. As long as Sara could remember, she and her mother had honored this ancient and glorious rite of spring. No matter their inevitable separations through the year, Sara could relax into the warmth of the Beltane ritual she and her mother shared. Long before her tiny, pudgy fingers had been able to maneuver among the delicate emerging plants, her special task had been to harvest young dandelions for the annual feast of greens. How many times had they culled and cultivated, mulched and tilled the damp cool earth, ceremoniously preparing the gardens.

A potpourri of fragrances—tarragon and dill, rosemary and lovage, tansy and yarrow embraced the two women. Grace, her signature straw hat shielding her fair Celtic skin, raked her gloved hands through the soil, removing winter's debris while Sara, fingers unencumbered by gloves placed basil into ground cultivated and waiting to receive the tender sweet plants. Her hands, no longer pudgy yet blackened by the fertile soil, worked deftly.

Sun drenched the still cool air, and on this May Day, magic was afoot. Anything seemed possible. The sprawling garden was already rich with promise, promise of steaming fresh vegetables laced with ticklish tarragon and pungent oregano; open-faced cheese sandwiches, a scarlet tomato slice made elegant by a sprig of purple basil; and curly green hats atop baby pink stems a mere hint of Grandmother's bittersweet rhubarb pies.

Are you happy, Sara? Sara warmed in her mother's uncanny sensitivity. She always seemed to sense what was on her daughter's mind.

Oh, Mom, she knew she could trust herself to say anything to her mother. *I really do love Emily, and I feel happy and safe in her love for me,* she paused. *Most of the time. But why do I sometimes feel afraid to be close to her and at the same time afraid to be apart? Am I crazy? It's just not as easy as it was at first,* she sighed.

Grace smiled gently at this young woman whose spirit so reflected her own. *No, of course it's not. You're into the hard work of cultivating your relationship.* She moved to the bed of oregano, snipped a soft round leaf from its stem, rubbing it between her fingers, savoring its tangy fragrance. Thoughtfully, she replied, *I remember when your father and I first married.* Was that sorrow casting a shadow across those soft hazel eyes? *Sometimes, it seemed as though we'd come from different worlds. His was a world I both longed for and feared.* Then she smiled. *Why, I remember our first Thanksgiving dinner with the Barnes family. I was shocked to find neither sweet potatoes nor pumpkin pie on the table! Can you imagine?* She laughed. *Clearly, they had very different rules from my family's about how to do Thanksgiving dinner. That's when I realized he'd learned a dance quite different from the one I knew. So, we just had to learn to dance together.* She retreated to a place of long ago. *But it took a lot of stubbed toes and missteps before we were able to create our own dance.* She laughed again. *At first I insisted my way of dancing was the right way, and, of course, Dad was certain his was the only way. After all, this was what his parents did.*

Grace raked the clawed hoe through the earth, composting the already lush comfrey plants.

It wasn't hard for Sara to imagine her father's stubborn insistence that he was right. *How did you and Dad manage?*

We didn't, always, her voice soft and full. *Yet as I look back, I can see that eventually we were able to make up our own steps. Once we each let go of having to do it the way our parents did it, we seemed to begin to dance our own rhythm.* Sara loved to dance, so this made sense to her.

Oh, Mom, I really want to do this right!

Grace smiled at this lovely young woman, her daughter, sitting on a bale of straw, long legs stretched in front of her. Sara surrendered her slender body to warm spring breezes that ruffled her golden brown hair, tugged unruly curls from beneath the purple bandanna. A waxing moon was barely visible in the sunny blue afternoon sky.

You will, my dear. However you dance together, let it be what the two of you create. And then, just be kind to one another. Her soft words floated into the sweet fragrances of the Beltane afternoon.

While the waxing phase of the Waxing Moon Cycle is just as delicious, our bliss seems less intense than in the New Moon Cycle: our waxing has a gentler quality. The limerence of our falling in love is maturing into a deeper loving strengthened now by the threads of trust and reinforced by the appreciation that in our diversity there are depths that both entice and support our explorations and discoveries.

FULL MOON PHASE

Unlike our journey through the New Moon Cycle, when we seemed to career through the waxing and into the full moon phase, we move with more grace and gentleness into the full moon phase of the Waxing Moon Cycle. Our falling in love has evolved into an *in-love* state; we acknowledge that we truly *love* one another.

Countless people—from poets to psychologists—have attempted to wrap words around *love*. What *it* is—this thing we call love—is even debatable: a feeling? an experience? an action? Whatever *love* is, I prefer Scott Peck's definition: Love is "the will to extend one's self for the purpose of nurturing one's own or another's spiritual growth."[1] To truly contemplate what love is, gives us pause. And I invite you, dear reader, to ponder just what love means to you.

We may have, in earlier phases and in the heat of passion, uttered *I love you,* but now in the lumination of the full moon phase, it is time to be clear about just what we mean when we say *I love you*. When one of us says "I love you," does the other automatically respond? Let us hope not. Rather, let us be as purposeful with our words of endearment and the proclamation of our love as we are with all other expressions of ourselves.

Having proclaimed our love, now in the Full Moon Cycle of our relationship, we yearn to define the relationship more clearly. It is likely we are anticipating a more enduring commitment. Out of a deepening comfort with one another, through the trust that strengthens our unity and increasingly fortifies the integrity of our relationship, we contemplate formalizing our relationship, defining the form for ourselves and to those who are important in our lives.

Language becomes problematic for some. Are we dating, still? Are we going steady? betrothed? engaged? Do we want to live together? marry? For same-sex couples, the traditional heterosexist terminology is even more limiting. We may choose a union ceremony or a trysting to celebrate the commitment we make to one another. What is important here is that we define—for ourselves—just what our relationship means to us: we are ready to ascribe to our loving some ritualized form.

As we move to yet another level of definition, let us examine some benchmarks for assessing the new and growing relationship:

- Honest and open discussion of feelings—all feelings—and of differences
- Direct and honest communication
- Realistic expectations that allow for one another's humanness, vulnerabilities, and imperfections
- Trust in ourselves and in each other
- Playfulness and having fun together
- Willingness to confront issues, to "rock the boat," in order to move toward shifts and change
- Honoring of our individual rhythms and the rhythm of the relationship[2]

In the illumination of the full moon phase, we are willing to explore the differences that come to light as we evaluate our relationship. Once we have examined these criteria, we may wish to use them as a means for evaluating where we are in our ongoing commitment to achieving a life-giving relationship. We have much work to do in this cycle; we are, after all, creating the structure, and there are many issues to be confronted. It is time now to unpack our baggage, to examine the dowry of rules we have brought with us into this relationship and, in our probing, to make choices about what we wish to keep and what we shall discard. Keeping these things in mind, let us explore the various aspects relevant to most relationships. Throughout our exploration, let us be honest; let us be bold!

Decision Making

Many of us, women in particular, have little experience making decisions. In our efforts to please others, we forget to start from within ourselves. Then, once a decision is made—an arduous task, indeed—we are inclined to carve that decision in stone, unwilling as we are to make another. So let's begin our analysis of how the relationship is working by clarifying the way decisions are currently being made by each of us. No doubt the two of us will have at least two different styles: one of us may just *feel* when something is right; we may gather information by *hearing* and/or *seeing*.

Many of us, however, unwilling to tolerate the ambiguity of indecisiveness, are inclined toward rushing into a decision: *Just make a decision, any decision!* we're admonished. What is very important to remember is the option of *not deciding:* to choose to make no decision is, in fact, a decision—and often a viable one.

Whatever our styles, and both can be honored, we need to spend some time considering all our feelings and our perceptions. Decision making is a process that requires care and time. To more clearly understand our own style, let's imagine we are about to purchase a new automobile. Some of us might do extensive research, check out *Consumer Reports, talk* with friends, *talk* to ourselves about all possible options; we test drive the car *listening* to how it sounds and then we *talk* some more. Others might *look* at various cars, *see* what is most appealing, create in our minds an *image* of our dream car: we *imagine* the color, the style, the interior and exterior; we *see* ourselves in the car of our dreams. When we *see* the one, we know it's right. Others of us rely on our *intuition.* We try on various cars, sit in them, *touch* them. We test drive—checking out how the car *feels* to us, how we *feel* in the car—until we *feel* right about a car.

Some of us make decisions auditorily—how things *sound*, what we *hear*, what we *tell* ourselves. Others of us are more visual—we rely on *pictures*—internal and external—to provide the information necessary for making a decision. And some of us are primarily kinesthetic: we need to *touch* and *feel* right about our decision. There is no right or wrong mode, of course, although we each may have a preference—which, more than likely, will be different from our partner's. What is important is that we honor both our own and our partner's styles, making room for both in the process of making decisions.

Communication

We cannot not communicate! True, we may not communicate effectively, but it is not possible not to communicate: silence, averting the eyes, walking away—all are ways of making a statement, and a strong one, at that. What follows are a few basics to communicating effectively. These are simple rules and they're hard to do—at first:

- Learn to use *I-statements*: I feel . . . , I want . . . , I need . . . , I think . . . . For those of us who grew up being told we were "egotistical" when we used "I," who were taught never to begin a sentence with "I," this may be a difficult transition. But how else can we begin if I don't know where you are and you don't know where I am?

  "I think you should . . . " is *not* an I-statement; it is a thinly disguised *you-statement*. This leads us to the second rule: Avoid you-statements! You think . . . , you feel . . . , you should . . . statements place the other in a defensive position and will either abort communication or set up a reactive win–lose pattern—neither of which works!
- Several words can be deleted from our vocabularies for now: *should, must, ought to,* and certainly, *never* and *always,* especially when preceded by *you!*
- Avoid questions except to honestly solicit information. To ask our partner if she's taken the trash to be recycled when we are both stumbling over the over-flowing bin is not an honest inquiry. Again, question-asking inevitably causes the other to feel defensive and sets up a win/lose, good/bad, parent/child dynamic.
- Stay current; avoid history. There is absolutely nothing to be done about what happened last month, last year. If there are unfinished, unresolved feelings, express them, forgive—yourself

and the other, if necessary—and then, let go! Carrying around past hurts and old history is deadly—and deadening! It is vital to the health of any relationship that our feelings be expressed and problems discussed as currently as possible. To sit on issues, to withhold feelings, inevitably leads to resentment and ultimately to the stagnation of the relationship.

- Reflective listening goes a long way. To be truly heard is to receive the greatest of all gifts—and often the rarest. To empathically listen to someone is to give a precious gift. So we need to learn to listen! To begin, there are several criteria on which we must agree. First, we must want to hear the other and we must want to be cooperative. Additionally, we must be able to speak the language of feelings: to accept our own feelings and at the same time to accept the other's feelings as well as to accept her capacity to handle her own feelings. Her way may not be our choice, but we must trust that her choice is best for her! And we must be able to trust that feelings are transitory.

Learning any new skill (it requires doing it 22 times!) often means our *over*-doing. In learning to listen, we must be purposeful and reflect back (begin by parroting) what is heard. What we *think* we hear has often gone through many filters and usually has absolutely no resemblance to what was actually said. We respond not to what was said but to what we *assume* we heard. This results in distorted communication and gross misunderstandings—and neither of us receives the gift of being heard.

To practice, one person begins with an I-statement; the other responds with: "What I hear you saying is_____" (repeating the exact words). Once I receive validation from you, I then say: "What I feel is_____" (name the feelings regarding what was said), and then I say: "My assumption is _____."

For example, what typically happens is this:

Kathleen: Mother's coming for dinner on Sunday.

Tom: How could you invite her when you know it's Super Bowl Sunday and I just want to be left alone. You'll want me to be polite and even do the cleaning up!!!!

Or we can more reflectively listen:

Kathleen: I've invited Mother for dinner on Sunday.

Tom: You've invited your mother on Sunday.

Kathleen: Yes, I have.

Tom: I'm feeling really angry about that, and I feel left out of the decision. I'm assuming you forgot that it's Super Bowl Sunday and that you expect me to help with dinner.

At this point Kathleen who is less likely to feel defensive, has the opportunity to clarify with another I-statement, such as:

Kathleen: I want to have Mother for company while you watch the game with no distractions.

There is much to be said about communication, for how we talk with one another—with our voices (both in tone and words), our bodies, and our intent—symbolizes all our interactions. But this is a good place to begin. Effective communication requires intentionality, commitment to self-honesty, and practice.

Conflict Management and Problem Solving

We have already discussed conflict and some of its many facets; in this section, we examine conflict more from the perspective of problem solving. To begin, problem solving is usually done prematurely. Often, if we simply listen to one another, problems take care of themselves, and if not, we certainly are in a clearer position to create a solution, for problem solving is, like solving a puzzle, a creative process. However, frequently one of us becomes invested in a specific outcome or solution, which causes us to abort the possibilities for creating an even more effective solution—and we continue doing the old win/lose dance. So, let's back up about five steps.

We begin by focusing on just what the issue or problem is and *who has the problem.*

You have the problem when you have a need that is not being met but that is not tangibly affecting me. So while you own the problem, we begin by my listening reflectively.

When your needs are being met as are mine, we have no problem. We may have different perspectives on the issue and will simply need to spend time talking together; hearing one another.

When your needs are being met but your behavior is tangibly inter-fering with the satisfaction of my needs, then I own the problem, where-upon I have some options. One option is for me to try to modify your behavior by making a direct statement specifically identifying the behav-ior, stating my feelings, and requesting a change.

For example, as we negotiate for behavior change, we can take three simple steps:

1. When you _____ (identify, specifically, the present behavior).
2. I feel _____ (identify the resulting feeling).
3. And I want _____ (specify desired behavior).

When you drive fast, I feel scared, and I want you to slow down to the speed limit.

Another option is to modify the environment. In the above example, I can drive the car myself or I can drive separately.

A third option is to modify myself; I reevaluate my need.

After we've decided who has the problem and specifically what the issue is, it is vital to keep things clear with ourselves and with our partner.[3] Reminding ourselves that this is a creative process, we proceed to generate all possible alternatives. And this is the fun part! It is impor-tant to simply brainstorm—no holds barred! Be imaginative; be boda-cious! Play with all the possibilities—no matter how outrageous. Don't stop to evaluate or judge—not yet: just continue creating until all the possibilities are exhausted—aiming for an odd number, in order to avoid the either/or, right/wrong dualism.

Once all options have been identified, it's time to evaluate. We exam-ine all of the options we've generated. In our exploration, we must be honest—scrupulously so, continuing to be open to the process. The next stage is to decide on the choice that is mutually beneficial. Once decided, we'll note our choice in writing. We take care to be clear and make sure that we both understand that choice. It is essential that we both under-stand our task as we move on to the next act in which we both partici-pate: we devise a plan for implementing exactly who does what, when.

Finally, we need to set a follow-up time in which we will evaluate the effectiveness of our choice.[4]

This is an elaborate process in which to engage. However, the inten-tionality of proceeding through each step provides us with an opportunity for respectfully and creatively solving those differences that can be resolved.

The wind blew out of the north, bringing flurries of snow that swirled like white misty fog across the gray landscape. Kit resisted a strong temptation to curl up before the blazing fire and lose herself in the Jane Austen novel she'd begun rereading. She could not and would no longer deny that she had a problem—a serious problem. And she must confess to Tom this very evening.

She allowed herself the luxury of thinking about Tom, her husband of just a few months. Solid, responsible, caring, and kind, she thought—a contrast to her own airy spiritedness.

Her intentions had been good, she knew. She'd started her small business in order to have extra money to save for a down payment on their first home.

She left the warmth of the fire and walked into the study, a small second bedroom they'd converted into an office to house the handcrafted baskets she sold through parties. It had seemed like a good idea; the company's district manager had assured her she could make more than $40,000 a year. And Kit had had some success. Her warm, genuine enthusiasm was contagious. Her customers shared her delight in the beauty and diversity, the handcrafted artistry of the baskets she offered. She was successful, she reassured herself. But she shoved the ledger book away in dismay; she had no money to pay the taxes due tomorrow. She felt panic knot her belly as she reminded herself to breathe.

Kit turned at the sound of the key unlocking their apartment door.

I'm home, honey. Tom's full voice comforted her not at all.

We have a problem, she blurted. She'd intended to wait until they'd eaten the curried chicken soup that simmered on the stove. But panic had its way with her.

Tom's eyes filled with alarm while he embraced his wife who seemed more diminutive than usual. She was scared, he knew.

They sat before the fire, green ledger sheets spread about the floor.

I owe more than $1500 in taxes for this quarter and last, plus the sales tax I've collected but not paid.

Tom fought down his own fear and anger. How could she have been so stupid, so irresponsible? Judgments he could make went unspoken as he said, *Yes, there is a real problem here. And I'm scared, too.* He could sense Kit's anxiety easing a bit.

Well, let's look at our options, he paused. *Why don't we have dinner while we talk. I'm starved.*

Kit grabbed his large hand in her own and kissed it soundly, relieved to be sharing the burden she'd carried alone for too long.

Over coffee, Kit laid out the facts: quarterly taxes for September and January, due tomorrow; sales taxes for six months. The total debt was $1485. She had just purchased additional inventory which left a balance of $63.10 in her checking account.

I guess I'll just give up my business, she cried.

That is one option, Tom agreed. *But let's look at some others.*

And so they began creating alternatives, one by one. The most obvious came first: selling the remaining inventory back to the company, having a final party, doing nothing.

But I can't do nothing, Kit wailed.

Tom laid a finger on her lips. *No assessing; not yet. Let's keep thinking of other options,* he reminded her.

They continued. Write IRS and plead for mercy; flee to Brazil; file bankruptcy; pay $50; establish a savings account and bank 50% of all profits; bank all profits until April 15 or until the debt was paid. Emigrate to Switzerland or Mexico or Peru (do they have taxes in Peru?). Wait until they're found out.

They listed the options they'd generated, discovering they had 13!

OK; what do we have so far? They were having fun with the process and they reviewed the alternatives. *I rather like the idea of living in Brazil, don't you?*

Kit laughed. That had been her idea.

Yes, but I'd miss Sara and Mom and Dad too much.

Together they carefully examined each one on the list, deciding to combine a few.

Kit would make a minimum payment, and she would open a savings account tomorrow.

I know I can be more creative with my advertising, and I have several parties already planned. Aunt Ellen called today and wants to have a large group in. I'm sure I'll sell lots of baskets to her friends. And yes, I'll go directly to the bank. No more overstocking. She had a plan and her usual enthusiasm returned.

They agreed to talk weekly for a month to assess the progress, then monthly until the debt was paid. And then they'd celebrate!

Tom took his young wife in his arms, pressed his lips into her dark brown curls, and whispered, *You can do this. And we can do anything.* Kit sighed with gratitude and relief to have someone so wise and caring in her life.

Conflict is the moment of truth in any relationship: how we relate to the differences and the inevitable conflict generated because of those differences has everything to do with the risks we're willing to take with each other and how intimate we're willing to be. What is vital in resolving conflict, creatively, is that we "hang in there" until we have created a solution that is acceptable to both of us. This requires that we both participate in the process: the wisdom of both of us is utilized as we participate in creatively resolving and integrating our differences.

Boundaries of Space and Time

In the New Moon Cycle, we explored in depth the issue of boundaries—physical, emotional, intellectual, and spiritual. In the Waxing Moon Cycle, defining boundaries continues to be important. We remind ourselves of the importance of integrating into a healthy relationship time—intentional time—for togetherness and time for separateness. We may need to begin by setting physical limits. Ultimately, as we're able to trust these boundaries, we can begin to push on them a bit, to explore and experiment with different ways of being together and separate. Some of our most delicious and intimate moments are spent sitting quietly in the same space with our loved one—each involved in an individual activity: sharing a different activity together. There is an especially gentle intimacy in moments such as these.

What is important is to acknowledge that each of us has different needs for space and time. Many of us (especially those of us who have reared children) have learned to take our space internally. We can appear totally immersed in a project when, in fact, we may be miles away, dreaming or meditating or creating a poem. (We mothers become quite creative at taking our space with a little one attached to one leg while the other is demanding to know just what makes clouds white and how birds fly.) Others, however, need to be physically away in order to feel separate and thence renewed.

In the Waxing Moon Cycle, we are probably combining our homes; we may be living together, sharing a home—perhaps for the first time. Designing how we are going to utilize the space provides many opportunities for boundary definition. No matter the size of the space, it is important that we each have a spot that is ours alone. This may be a chair, a corner, or a room. We each need a private space.

Privacy is imperative in any relationship. Privacy is that inner place that is ours and ours alone. What we hold in that private place has nothing to do with our partner; it is not about our relationship. Secrecy, however, does affect the relationship. In secrecy, we withhold information or feelings that, if revealed, could be hurtful to the other and to the relationship. Privacy, however, is an affirmation of our separateness. One's journal, for instance, must absolutely be private, to be read only at the invitation of the writer.

There must be places of sharing in any healthy relationship *and* there must be places for privacy. Each must have *A Room of One's Own*[5]— spiritually and physically, emotionally and intellectually—in order that each of us can return to the relationship with a renewed energy, so necessary for the continual growth of our partnership.

Feelings

Feelings are the foundation of an intimate relationship. Like little seedlings, feelings need lots of room and lots of air, and when those feelings threaten to overwhelm us, we must *BREATHE!*

Feelings must be expressed. We cannot simply ignore what we feel. If we try, the energy will go somewhere underground, and if we aren't expressing those emotions, they will take revenge. They will take control of us. We will get sick or depressed or our feelings will surface when we least expect them to—usually at the most inopportune time—often in the form of an angry outburst or an unexpected flood of tears, a migraine headache, or a pain in the neck.

The relevant issue is not *whether* feelings are expressed; the question is *how* they are communicated. Our feelings are our own feelings: it is *my* responsibility to express *my* feelings. I may scream in my car, punch some pillows, journal what I feel; I may walk, literally, through them; and I will, at some point, want to share them.

To disgorge, regurgitate, or blast our feelings onto someone else is not acceptable; we do this by blaming and shaming another for our own feelings. Let's assume I am very angry with you. Imagine that I'm putting my anger—and it's a lot!—into a huge, 30-gallon, 3-ply trash bag. I tie it up and I lift it—heavy as it is—and I toss it. If I, disrespectfully, throw this at you, you still have three choices! You can stand there and tolerate it, letting the bag split open so that all my anger spills onto you—in which case my anger has now become yours to deal with. Or you can heave the bag back to me, and we can proceed, throwing it back and forth, each reacting to the other's behavior. Or, in response to throwing my bag of anger at you, you can take two steps backward and let the bag fall on the floor between us. You acknowledge it, but you take no responsibility for it. It's my bag, after all! Ultimately, it is I who must make respectful choices as to what I'm going to do with my own feelings.

Basically, we feel sad, mad, glad, scared, lonely, or ashamed.[6] When we say we feel *disappointed,* we're usually mad and sad; *confusion* is often scared and mad; *frustration* is mostly anger; and *upset* or *weird* are some more of the many euphemistic words that help us deny or minimize our feelings—both at which we seem to excel.

Feelings are "words made flesh,"[7] and we are often challenged to find the words to wrap around the funny little twinge in our belly or the set of our jaw or the tightness in our chest. It is in our bodies where we must begin to untangle the labyrinth of knots, pangs, and gurgles that accompany our feelings and serve as cues to our awareness.

Our bodies are a metaphor for our feelings, and this is where we begin to explore those feelings. We catch hold of the thread that is attached to that mild ache in the small of our back, and when we follow that thread, we soon discover we are, in fact, still mad at our brother-in-law for his insulting comments on New Year's Eve. We may be holding in our shoulders the burden of resentment (more anger) from the never-ending demands of our boss. Or we realize that our intrusive neighbor is becoming a *real pain in the neck!* or that our clenched jaw is preventing us from being forthright with our words as we clamp down on our feelings that we want to express to our great aunt Sally! The lump in our throat may be still more, unshed, tears over the loss of a dear friend. So we need to stay with the clues our bodies give us, to honor those until we can name the feeling. In fact, we may not know *why* we feel a certain feeling. Our search for explanations often distracts us from simply feeling our feelings. If we simply honor the feeling, the *why* may follow—and it may not! Either way, the key to emotional health is to feel the feeling!

Feelings, in and of themselves, are not bad or good, right or wrong: they just *are*. It is what we decide to do with those feelings that may be a good or not-so-good choice. But we can't begin to choose our actions—what we do with our feelings—until we become aware of and then name them. (And if we don't name them, they may choose our actions for us, leading us to feel out of control of our own lives.)

It's important, in deciding what to do with those feelings, to have a whole repertoire of behaviors from which to choose. We can begin by imagining what we'd like to do. (We can, after all, think anything!) From our fantasy, we can make some appropriate choices. For instance, if we have the urge to "punch someone out," we can alternatively punch a pile of pillows, hammer nails in a block of wood, or play a game of racquetball. If we see ourselves running away, we may, in reality, need to "walk off" our feeling of anger or fear. There are many ways of creatively and appropriately expressing our feelings. A journal can be a very useful vehicle for not only expressing feelings but for acquiring clarity about what lessons our feelings may have for us.

Not only do our bodies give us the necessary clues, but we need to attend to when a song or a movie particularly touches us in some way. These things often serve as a gentle reminder that we have some old, unresolved feelings that we now are ready to explore.

Feelings are transitory. I once heard feelings compared to clouds. We love watching the clouds, noticing them as they lazily float above us. But we don't get attached to one cloud and watch it from one horizon to the other. Nor do we judge its rightness or wrongness: the cloud simply *is*. We notice it, then let it go, moving our awareness to another—or to the trees or to our lover who smiles appreciatively at our delight.

Just as we are learning to trust the rhythm of the cycles and our ability to flow respectfully through the phases, so we are learning to trust our own rhythm and ability to risk our feelings in this relationship. We are learning to allow ourselves to breathe into those feelings as we become aware of them, to breathe as we name them, and then to choose what/if we need to do anything with them.

Healthy connections begin from the place where our feelings live. The Waxing Moon Cycle is the time to make a commitment to the expression of feelings. Magic will happen when each of us makes an I-feel statement to our partner every day. Try it!

As we learn to trust ourselves, we may need someone to accompany us on the journey into the unfamiliar world of feelings. This may be our partner, a trusted friend, or a therapist. I firmly believe that nothing comes up for us for which we're not ready. But we may sometimes need to ask for support from someone we trust—someone who's willing to walk with us.

Money Issues

Money issues must be confronted in this Waxing Moon Cycle. Certainly this is so if we are combining households. In the illumination, the safe brightness, of the full moon phase, let us tackle what is for many the most challenging of issues.

Women are often at a disadvantage in the world of finances. We are quite capable of being financially responsible—in fact many of us have had to learn to be masters of frugality. However, not having been schooled in the ways of money in our early years, we tend to avoid even talking about money. Furthermore because our styles of negotiating tend to be *different* from men's, we tend to feel uncomfortable with money talk. We women typically go within ourselves—negotiate with ourselves, so to speak—and then come to the discussion with our fairest offer. Men, on the other hand, seem to prefer the *process* of negotiating, so they tend to start high and negotiate down.

Women typically don't much like dealing with money issues, which makes negotiating on our own behalf challenging. This can be especially problematic when there is an economic differential between us and our partner. More important to the health of the relationship, however, is that most unresolved power struggles get played out around money.

That money so often remains an issue is baffling, because it is one of the few areas that is a tangible one. We know how much we have, or don't have; we can touch it, count it, and plan what to do with it. Nevertheless, we can certainly see how money often serves as a metaphor in the relationship. How we create (or avoid) boundaries around money is often an indicator of how we set limits around space, feelings, food, time, and so on.

In negotiating our finances, some of us combine all monies into a single account from which everything is spent. (The two become one!) On the other hand, some choose to keep everything separate. (Disengaged.) Each writes a check, for instance, for half of the mortgage payment, half of the groceries, half of the utilities payment, and so on. A third option (yes, there is nearly always a third option) is to budget—a word that threatens to become extinct—for household expenses and establish one account for these. Each contributes equally into this account, or in the case of unequal incomes, a formula is agreed upon that reflects the relative incomes. All remaining monies are retained by each of the partners to be used at her own discretion.[8]

As we negotiate the economic area of our lives, we see not only the possibilities for playing out the control issues, but we also notice the attitudes and rules around money that we bring to the relationship. As we negotiate our monies, we are challenged to draw on all aspects of our relationship—from how we make decisions to what we value.

Work and Play

The Waxing Moon Cycle presents many tasks, for we are going about the business of building a life together. In this process of framing the structure of our relationship, we are no doubt doing projects together both in work and in play. How we work together and how we play together bring new differences into focus.

Some of us work quite well independently, while others are skilled at teamwork. Some are used to leading, some following; some are quite good at collaborating, while others prefer to be more autonomous. Our individual rhythms come into focus as we attempt a joint activity— whether it's playing tennis, preparing dinner, doing housework and yard work, or building a porch. Some of us prefer working alone, some are self-motivated; some of us pace ourselves with regular breaks, while others "keep on truckin'." Some of us are better initiators; some have difficulty bringing a chore to completion. Some focus on the "big picture"; others are adept with the smaller details.

Once again, we need to notice how we are alike and how we differ as we proceed to develop a blending of our styles into one that serves to utilize all our skills. We simply recognize that how we play and work with one another provides us with yet more information as we go about the business of evolving into the rhythm of the relationship.

Trust and Jealousy

Trust continues to be tested and to grow throughout the cycles. As we face each new challenge in the relationship, we are asked to trust ourselves, the other, and the integrity of the relationship. Most important, we are continually being challenged to trust the natural rhythm of the cycles. Jealousy is a negation of this trust, for it has little to do with the object of our affection; jealousy is more a reflection of our own self-esteem. If we are unsure of ourselves, if we seem unable to trust our own vulnerability, we are more likely to feel unstable in the relationship. Often, to focus on our partner's behavior and to feel jealous is simply another distraction from ourselves, and from what we need to be doing to be respectful of ourselves.

Of course, jealousy may, in fact, be our intuition alerting us of the other's indiscretion and that, in fact, the boundaries of the relationship have been violated. More often than not, however, jealousy is an internal experience—and an indication that we need to turn within to examine our own insecurities and to nurture ourselves.

Sexuality, Sensuality, and Intimacy

We are warmed by each other's presence; we anticipate the pleasuring of each other. We delight in our moments of ecstasy. It has been so easy—this rapturous flowing between us when we allowed ourselves to merge in moments of utter bliss. Now, as we move through the Waxing Moon Cycle, we may find our sexuality becoming a more gentle passion, and we begin to acknowledge that there are, sexually, differences between us.

We pause again to reflect on how we came to be where we are. In the sharing of our sexual stories with one another, we cannot ignore the reality that we all suffer some form of sexual repression imposed upon us by a patriarchal culture whose powers that be teach that sex has only to do with procreation, where the pervasiveness of pornography not only exploits women but misguides men, where women are objectified in a media that reinforces the myth that we are either virgin or whore, where our bodies have been torn from our spirit.

We grow up in this society inevitably being sexually shamed, confused, and probably violated. Both women and men seldom feel comfortable and clear about themselves as sexual or sensual beings. More often than not, our sexuality is an extraneous part of ourselves, separate from the wholeness of our being. We struggle to integrate our sexuality within ourselves—to allow what is normal and natural and beautiful and playful and exciting and creative and connecting and spontaneous—to simply flow rhythmically in celebration of life. We yearn to remember, to reclaim the ancient knowing that sexuality, a metaphor for the precariousness of life, is the energy that is the creation of the life force, shared with *all* living being-ness, and that being sexual is about affirming life, affirming the self and each other.

Our rhythms may vary within and between us, and it is important that we remember that sexuality is yet another means by which we connect and communicate with one another. And it is vital that we find ways in which to talk with one another about sex—about where we connect and where we differ.

As women, as men, as heterosexuals, and as lesbians and gays, our differences are most clearly manifested through our sexual, our sensual, and our intimacy needs. Intertwined with the perception of our own sexuality, for many, is the puritanical dogma that defines morality for both women and men. Particularly for us women to embrace our passion, we must first overcome the rigid dicta of the badness of being sexual. Inevitably, both women and men must navigate through a mine-field of homophobia, sexism, and religiosity in order to reach wholeness as human beings and the freedom to be wholly in relationship. Ultimately, we must cross the chasm that divides us and oppresses us, that defines us by gender, race, age, and affectional orientation. We must heal from the conflicting propaganda that divides our bodies into parts, that diminishes our humanity by separating our spirituality from our physicality, that separates us and prevents us from being in relationship with our own bodies and thus with each other.

Infused as we are by the patriarchal proscriptions regarding sexuality, many of us miss the fullness of our sexual expression by limiting our awarenesses to what we do in the bedroom. As whole human beings, our sexuality is an important facet of the total definition of ourselves and hence of our intimate relationships—if those are to be whole and healthy and life-giving. We join together in that special place of vulnerability, each aware that our individual rhythms may vary, that our needs, our desires may differ. Yet we are committed to naming those places of divergence, to talking with one another about what our preferences are, what feels good and what we need and want, and to exploring and expanding the boundaries of our passion.

Reminding ourselves that each of us has individually varying rhythms as we wax and wane, as our energies flow and ebb, so do the energies of the relationship flow and ebb and flow once more into that moment in time when all that exists is the energy of our loving, when we willingly suspend all awareness of physical reality and surrender to our vulnerability and to each other. We remind ourselves of our own sensuality—to reclaim our sense of wonder as we touch and see and hear and taste and smell—exploring and celebrating in the delights of our loving. We remind ourselves that our sensuality and our sexuality have many forms: a gentle touch in the darkness of a theater, a quick parting embrace on a crowded city street, a midnight massage—delicious scents of oil wafting into the candlelight, a shared bubble bath surrounded by the sweet sounds of Sibelius, a quiet talk before the smoldering embers of a campfire, a candlelit, gourmet dinner for two—in bed.

When we increase the awareness of our sensuality, we nurture our sexuality; we allow ourselves to become more integrated and we move to a place of deeper intimacy. We play and celebrate and weep in ecstasy. We discover that when we slowly and sensuously utter *intimacy*, we hear *into me*, and we know the vulnerability of letting you *into me*—the blending, the merging, the moments of oneness into that sacred private place to which the two of us withdraw to renew the primacy of our love.

Through our sexuality we celebrate with unencumbered childlike wonder what it is to be male, to be female; we see our own beauty and hear our own voice so that we may meet one another in our *lightness of being*, free to reverently and lustily share our vulnerability with another. In this place of wonder—a paradise revisited—this articulation of the life force, we feel our miraculous transformation as we become gods and goddesses.

Spirituality

It is impossible to separate our spirituality from the other areas of our lives. As we move through the Waxing Moon Cycle of our relationship, we recognize that we celebrate our spirituality in different ways. Sharing and celebrating our unique expressions can be an enriching experience. However, once again, if diversity is not an honored value in the relationship, the different ways of expressing ourselves spiritually can become divisive.

To honor the rhythms of ourselves, of our beloved, of all living things is to honor the Spirit, to integrate spirituality into our lives. And so, we have cycled around to where we began—we have come full circle—for just as we cannot not communicate, when we honor the cycles of living, the rhythms, the ebbings and flowings, the waxings and wanings, we cannot not be spiritual. We are one with the Spirit. That we have a spiritual bond that connects us with one another and with the Universe affirms our relationship. It is in the spiritual realm where our differences are integrated into strengths, where those differences are transformed, where all our rhythms are in tune, and where we are truly one with the Universe.

In the full moon phase of the Waxing Moon Cycle, our more clearly defined relationship is elucidated: we are creating a new family system. In this full moon phase, we are strengthening the boundary around ourselves as a *couple*. To some extent, the investment in our relationship necessarily is made at the expense of other relationships. That is not to suggest that all other relationships are eliminated; this would leave us with a *closed system* and all of the problems that accompany it. But the investment of time and energy into our relationship takes priority.

One of the ways we affirm the significance of our relationship is by establishing rituals. We may choose to have a commitment ceremony, although this may not occur until a later revolution of Waxing Moon Cycle. In the meantime and in addition to a commitment ceremony, we have many other rituals: our wishing each other *sweet dreams* as we part for the night, greeting each other with a gesture of affection as we come and go through our daily lives, celebrating special anniversaries (one week, one month, six months, yearly, our first date, first kiss, etc.), committing to scheduled mid-week dates, planning regular *nurturing* days—all are ways of celebrating ourselves, of being purposeful, and of nurturing the relationship. Rituals, often playful as well as ceremonious, go a long way in keeping our relationship alive and full.

We tend to stay longer in each phase as the cycles progress. In the fullness of the Waxing Moon Cycle, we luxuriate in the brightness and the expansiveness of this rich time as we celebrate ourselves and our increasingly defined relationship. We delight in our successes while we honor our commitment to meeting the challenges of the many tasks we are called to do, continuing to invest ourselves in this growing relationship. But inevitably the full moon begins to wane, and once more we surrender, reluctantly still, to the lengthening shadows. We begin the process of separating in order that we may integrate the many lessons of our deepening relationship. We turn inward.

WANING MOON PHASE

Once again, we yield to the decreasing light and, *staying connected with a dotted line,* we become more mindful of our own needs. Having confronted the many issues illuminated in the light of the full moon phase, we must separate for a while, allowing for time and room to integrate the awarenesses and feelings evoked from the recognition of these differentnesses. We have many feelings and we need time to integrate what is true for us.

For some, the waning moon phase of the Waxing Moon Cycle may, in fact, be precipitated by our discussions and plans for a *commitment!* Commitment, for many, creates fear—whether we're contemplating a commitment to complete a project or a commitment to share our remaining years with another. Fear, even phobia, of commitment often creates extreme anxiety which, as with many of our feelings, may be manifested in physical symptoms.

> A roaring fire diminished an early autumn chill. Snuggled together under an afghan, Sara and Emily had begun to talk of plans for a ritual. They'd been living together for several months now, and it seemed time to honor the commitment they were ready to make to each other.
> Sara could not ignore the growing distance between them as their discussion continued. Emily had begun to withdraw; her body tensed. Her soft voice seemed edged with fear. Sara had noticed that when Emily became afraid, she often appeared angry and her voice began to rise and tremble.
> *What's wrong, honey?* Sara inquired gently. *Are you OK?*
> *I'm fine.* Her reply came from that "mother voice" and Sara felt wary.
> When Sara had met Emily's mother, Louise, she was astonished at the similarities between the two women. Not only did each woman resemble the other physically, but their voices, gestures, and behaviors were mirrors of each other's. In the heat of an argument, Emily's voice sounded amazingly like her mother's.

Encouraged by the warm fire, Sara enclosed Emily's hand in her own, deciding this was as good a time as any to share her fears.

I need to say something about what seems to be going on here.

Emily just nodded, but much to Sara's relief, Emily absorbed the information and acknowledged the truth of the observation that Sara made.

Responding, Emily asked, *And are you aware, my love, how much like your father you sound when you get mad?*

Sara agreed that yes, she could sound and even act like her parents—particularly her father, whose anger was masked in harsh and rigid judgments. And both women had to laugh as they realized that neither chose her behaviors.

Surely there are healthier ways of handling our differences.

The room became a stage as Emily took on her mother's persona, and Sara did a hilarious impersonation of her father, improvising a skit starring Emily and Sara as "Louise" and "Ted" bickering and arguing—through uncontrollable giggles. Taking their bows before their imaginery audience, they congratulated each other on their great insight.

Thanks, sweetie, Emily carressed Sara's flushed cheek. *I didn't realize how much I'd been worried about how we'd been struggling lately.*

In fact, they both felt renewed as they began to talk of their definition of commitment and how they wished to celebrate that.

Actually, said Emily, *I feel stronger in my commitment to you now than I have for a while.*

And that's what commitment means to me, Sara rose to refresh their glasses of wine, *Being able to walk to the other side of the hard stuff and to come out feeling stronger.* They settled back into the sofa, tucking the old afghan around each other.

Now where were we? Emily's eyes glistened in the firelight as Sara gently stroked her thick black hair.

Emily smiled. *To us,* she said, raising her glass to Sara. *May we always honor moments like these.*

● ○ ●

To make a commitment is to make a promise, a pledge of ourselves and/or our time, money, energy, presence, and love to a person or a project for a specified period of time. We may disguise our fears of making a commitment in terminology that implies a preference for spontaneity or for our freedom or for lots of space. Regardless of how we attempt to reframe our fears, that fear of commitment will, unfortunately, preclude our experiencing the intimacy and connection that foster our growth. In the delightful movie *City of Hope*, Joan challenges Max, suggesting that we all have three choices: to run, to spectate, or to commit! While fear of commitment may rear its unwanted head at any time throughout the cycles, it is quite likely to do so as the fullness of the Waxing Moon Cycle begins to wane—when we've been together long enough that it really is appropriate to name the relationship more definitively, to formalize our future together.

There are many reasons we may experience fears of committing to another person.[9] We may fear closeness and intimacy; we may have unresolved shame or feelings around past relationships. We may have diffuse boundaries and be unable to trust ourselves not to get forever lost in the other. We may fear being abandoned, rejected, or hurt. And we may, having spent years of overcommitting, be afraid to extend ourselves at all.

Sometimes our fears are legitimate: warnings that the other is desperate and overly dependent, cautions that we ourselves aren't ready or that this simply isn't a relationship that is good for us. We invite another person into our lives to learn lessons from and with each other, but this does not mean that all relationships are meant to be *til death do us part!* We value what we've learned, and as we know from the New Moon Cycle, we create a respectful ending.

Like all feelings, our fear of commitment must be honored: we begin by being *aware*. We simply pay attention; we don't control the feeling, nor let the feeling control us. We make choices about what we do with the feeling.

We are always, throughout each cycle and in each phase of the cycle, being challenged to commit. At the beginning when the cycle is waxing, we commit to taking that leap. In the fullness when our creativity is high and we have many tasks before us, we commit to persevering, to "hanging in there." And in the waning, we must commit to staying with the rhythm, to honoring the entire cycle to its completion. So it is with all our undertakings. Always we remember, particularly in the waning time, our ultimate commitment is to ourselves, to the honoring of our knowings, our own rhythm.

In the waning phase of the Waxing Moon Cycle, we reflect on the differences between us—the issues we confronted in the full moon light of the cycle. Now we must assess our own truth: are we able to live with the differences that have emerged, to integrate them, to grow through them and still maintain our own integrity? Or are these issues so problematic as to be terminal for our relationship? Ultimately, we must decide whether the differences are opportunities for our growth—individually and for the relationship.

We seem able to accept in our friends their imperfections, but when faced with these same flaws in our lovers, we must learn over and over how to let go of all those expectations. In our love relationships, we are faced with one of life's most difficult challenges: "the most emotional as well as the most romantic of all human dreams has to be consolidated into an ordinary working relationship."[10] This is the reality that we confront in the waning phase of the Waxing Moon Cycle: the transition from a romantic relationship to a working relationship!

We continue to be challenged to tolerate the ambiguity of the waning phase. We are tempted to ease the pain of the confusion and of the unknown, to rush into solving all the problems *now!* Yet we've come to know that problem solving must be timely, for it is often a distraction from the real issue: simply honoring our feelings and respecting our own and our partner's rhythm by listening to ourselves and to the other. Only as we listen to each other and to ourselves can we determine how healthy the relationship is and how healthy we are within the relationship. Ultimately, we must honor our personal integrity, for when differences revolve around a conflict of values, we risk surrendering our own integrity for the sake of the relationship, and doing that is disrespectful to ourselves, to the other, and a violation of our spirituality!

There is much reflecting and serious contemplation to be done in this waning phase of the Waxing Moon Cycle. We have been confronted on many levels. Our individual patterns and issues have been brought into focus as we more clearly begin to define our relationship. We see ourselves in the reflection of the other, and we necessarily begin to question our values, our feelings, and our behaviors.

At this juncture, we must be truly and scrupulously honest with ourselves about the health of our relationship. Too often, we mistake complementarity for compatibility. A *complementary union* is one in which two halves equal a whole. One who is a caretaker inevitably is drawn to one who is needy; a passive person attracts an angry, aggressive partner. We choose a partner who will express those traits that we must ourselves deny or those that we yearn to express but can't. Ultimately, we rage at our partner for expressing the very characteristics to which we initially were attracted. Often when we grow into our own wholeness, we no longer need those to which we were attracted: we say, we "outgrow" our partner.

Now, we move into this waning phase continuing to remain connected to the other, *with a dotted line*, as we evaluate for ourselves all the challenges of the fullness of the cycle. As we inevitably loosen the embrace of the relationship, of the other, in order to make more room for our own contemplation, we confront once again the fears of aloneness and we react out of the old, familiar feelings of alienation and abandonment. Can we really face the darkness alone? Can we trust ourselves to honor our own shadow? Can we trust the other to return from the darkness recommitted to us?

The waning moon phase presents opportunities to examine and test those differences that we so courageously confronted in the full moon phase. Once again, we must trust the ambiguity of the separating as we make room for the questions that are sure to emerge out of the decreasing light and the ensuing blackness of the new moon phase.

NEW MOON PHASE

Within the blanket of silence and darkness, we go deep within—gentling, nurturing, tending to ourselves. We sit in the stillness, simply allowing ourselves to *know*. This is a significant time for both of us and for the renewal of the relationship.

Although our rhythm and our styles may differ, we are less fearful now of the darkness and are increasingly more trusting of the silence—of ourselves in the silence. We have some history now; we are more able to honor our own rhythm and to know that, if we choose, if we *dare*, another waxing surely is soon to appear.

Quietly, in the stillness, we celebrate ourselves with a private ritual, for the new moon phase is a private time. This is the time for deep reflection and meditation.

If we are to proceed into the third cycle, the Full Moon Cycle, of the relationship, we are well advised to honor this time of darkness, to move deep within ourselves in search of our own truth. We must be still in order to hear the questions and then to open to the answers that can only come out of the stillness. This is the time of both integration and completion. We honor the darkness, as we alone face our truth, our dreams, our hopes for the ensuing cycle. At the same time, we honor completion of the Waxing Moon Cycle; we recognize all that we've learned, the risks we've taken, the successes we've enjoyed. And as we open ourselves in the silence, we mourn the endings and the losses as we embrace that which awaits us in the cycle that follows.

The waning phase is inevitable when we begin to confront our *necessary losses*—the loss of our independence, our illusions, our expectations, and perhaps our hopes. Now, in the dark of the moon, we rest in the knowing of just what deep implications those losses have for us.

All human relationships will end, and the threat of loss, of abandonment, of death is what we confront during the waning of each cycle. The fear, the threat of the loss of our beloved is greatest when our love is the deepest. So, as our love intensifies in the Waxing Moon Cycle, so does the fear of the loss of that love, and paradoxically, our awareness of loss deepens our love.[11]

It is the new moon. We are still. We rest in our love, knowing that when it is time, we shall venture into the waxing phase of the Full Moon Cycle.

Lessons of the Waxing Moon Cycle

In the second cycle, the Waxing Moon Cycle, of a relationship, we are beginning to be more comfortable with the rhythm of cycling, to trust our ability to honor the ebbing and flowing through the phases. We have successfully moved through an entire revolution, through the New Moon Cycle, and we have increased our awareness of the boundaries between and around us. We have actually survived conflict, and, as a result, our trust has deepened and has continued to grow.

We are ready to get down to the business of doing this relationship, for there is much work to be done. In the Waxing Moon Cycle, we are establishing an identity of this Relationship that now has a capital *R*; our partnership is taking form. So one of our first tasks is to examine just what it is that we bring to the relationship. From our families of origin, from our culture, we have brought certain rules, expectations, hopes, and illusions. Only when we have clarity about those rules and expectations are we prepared for the task of creating a form that is uniquely ours.

Each relationship has its own emotional contract that begins to evolve in the Waxing Moon Cycle. This contract, typically unstated, comprises the rules we choose, the dynamics of our relationship. In traditional marriages, in which roles were clearly defined, the emotional contract was based on gender: the wife provided the emotional support for the relationship, while the husband was responsible for more practical matters. Clearly, as we have seen, this dynamic is limiting and is not relevant to a relationship committed to mutual growth and nurturance.

The challenge for us as we enter into the Waxing Moon Cycle and prepare to establish our own unique dynamic is that we utilize all our skills, tenuous though they may be, to consciously, purposefully devise the framework that is to become our contract. A contract of any kind, we must remember, can always be open for evaluation and renegotiation. So we may choose a specific time in order to be intentional about this process. Often couples choose the occasion of their anniversary, New Year's Eve, Hallowmas (the witches' new year), or another holiday especially meaningful in which to spend time together reviewing (using, perhaps, the criteria discussed earlier) what has worked and what needs special tending in the relationship. The contract may in fact take the form of a vision—articulated to one another, naming our goals, dreams, values, and wishes.

Industry

In our youth, we resolved the "psychosocial crisis" of industry and inferiority, as we began leaving the shelter of our families in order to make a commitment to a group beyond the family. We began broadening our perspective, developing more varied points of view. So it is in the waxing moontime of our relationship. We remind ourselves that the waxing phase is the time for initiating and for connecting, so in this Waxing Moon Cycle, we begin working together to develop a willingness to decide just how our relationship will work for us.

We are establishing our own family. However, we must first be willing to challenge those myths and roles of our families of origin; we must examine the rigidly defined rules of our childhood. We cannot marry another until we sufficiently separate emotionally from our family of origin, in order to make primary the commitment to our partner.

Presumably we have physically left the family; now we must leave emotionally. This does not mean not doing what members of our family of origin do, or doing what they don't. Emotional leaving means evaluating and choosing our own way. This is the task of the cycle of the waxing moon.*

In order to make change, to clearly define for ourselves, to be intentional with life-changing choices, we must begin by making explicit that which is implicit. It behooves us to examine, once again, whence we came. Throughout the Waxing Moon Cycle, we will be purposefully defining the rules that are to guide us in our growing relationship, which makes it important that we become aware of the rules that prevailed in our families of origin.

Whatever the family rules, they reflect just how open the family system was—or how closed, how rigid were the boundaries or how diffuse. Looking at how our family of origin handled diversity is an important place to begin. In addition to fostering the dualism of win/lose, right/wrong, good/bad, we often experience the lack of acceptance of differences in parental attitudes toward other cultures. Racism and homophobia, grounded in fear, are often used to control our intellectual boundaries and to justify a family's credibility in an attempt to create a sense of status. Racism and sexism and homophobia flourish in families that are unwilling to accept diversity.

In many families, three rules prevail: *don't talk, don't trust, don't feel.* All of the rules that follow, and many more, fall into these categories. While rules are vital to the healthy functioning of any relationship, it is imperative that we be clear about what rules prevail, which are currently relevant and which should be discarded. For instance, a mealtime rule in my family of origin was *Don't sing at the table.* In spite of many

---

* There are exceptions, of course: economic or health circumstances may preclude the physical leaving. The family system must then support the emotional/psychological boundaries required for an adult primary relationship to be formed.

inquiries, I have no idea what the rationale for this was. I suspect that some self-defined singer several generations ago was atonal and the matriarch desired a respite at least through mealtime. Nevertheless, this is a rule I've chosen to delete: I'm convinced that singing aids in the digestive process.

Let us begin by imagining our family seated around the dinner table: many rules come clearly into focus here. How was mealtime? Was it fun? tense? Were friends welcomed? Were we expected to wash our hands? dress up for dinner? clean up our plates? try at least three bites of everything? Were we warned not to talk with a mouthful? Was food tasty? imaginative? prepared and presented creatively? Or did we have chicken every Sunday, macaroni and cheese every Monday, meatloaf every Tuesday . . . ? Who talked with whom? Did everyone talk at once? Was conversation interesting? inclusive? stimulating? Or was there strained silence? bickering? fighting? Did mealtime consist of a quick drive-thru at McDonalds? on the run from one activity to the next? an occasional sit-down meal in a restaurant? Or maybe there were no family mealtimes! Where/when did the family meet together? or did it?

Many of the old saws reflect the rules in the family.

- *Idle hands are the devil's workshop* and *Busy hands are happy hands*. Both carry strong messages not only about time but about work as well. With these messages, curling up on a Sunday afternoon before a fire with a "no-brainer" book or an electronic game would not be allowed! There are many rules around how we spend money and time. If an attitude of scarcity or stinginess prevails in one of these areas, that attitude will be reflected throughout the system.

- *A penny saved is a penny earned.* Money has been noted to be the area of greatest discomfort among many couples. Was someone in the family *a spendthrift? Tight as a new boot?* How was money handled in the family? Was there an attitude of having enough or was nothing ever enough? Did clothes come from K-Mart, Goodwill, or the bargain basement? Or was only Ralph Lauren or Perry Ellis acceptable? Was money used to control members of the family? Were we able to earn money? have an allowance? have a job? Did someone trouble to teach us how to handle money? have a checking account? savings account? Our relationship with money may serve as a telling metaphor for the relationship with each other.

- *Children are to be seen and not heard. Don't air your dirty laundry in public.* (And just what is dirty laundry, anyway?) As children, were we talked at? interrupted? yelled at? listened to? criticized? Were our imaginations nurtured? or were we laughed at?
- *Save yourself for your husband* and *Boys only want one thing! Wives must always be available for their husbands.* There are many rules for sexuality—many that are quite different for boys than for girls. Was sex openly discussed? questions encouraged? answered? How comfortable were our parents? Was privacy allowed? Was nudity prevalent? modesty? Was our body respected and valued or shamed and violated?
- *Keep a stiff upper lip. Don't be a cry baby. Nice girls don't get angry. You're overreacting! Don't be so dramatic.* Many rules exist about feelings. What happened when we cried? or got mad? or excited? Was affection and love saved only for special occasions? Were we allowed only to have happy feelings?
- *What will the neighbors think?* Families are often very concerned about how we look to others; maintaining a good public image takes precedence over being real and responsive to family members.
- *Spare the rod and spoil the child*—a license for physical abuse, indeed. Was discipline used to teach about limits and boundaries or rather was discipline used to shame, to control, to punish? to vent our parents' anger?

Rules and rules and rules! Along with these injunctions, there are rules about family and friends, rules about church and school and hygiene and language—and we haven't even begun to explore the rules in relationships.

Just as it is imperative that we identify and evaluate the current relevance of the rules that regulated our family life, so it is important to examine what relational rules prevailed.

Family rules not only determine our actions but influence the expectations we have of others' behaviors. Similarly, the rules we came to believe were *normal* with respect to relationships, as gleaned primarily from our parents' relationship, influence what we expect to have happen in our own relationships.

We realize again that the *no trust, no talk, no feel* rules may, in fact, be the dominating dynamic. In preparation for choosing the rules we want to incorporate into our relationship, let us explore more carefully those with which we have become—consciously or not—most familiar.

- Decision making: How did our parents make decisions? Did each consult the other? Was there consensus, or were decisions made *because I said so?* Did Dad make all the decisions, or did Mom just make Dad believe he made all the decisions? Were decisions made after much research and in a timely manner, or were they impulsively made?
- Communication: How did Mom and Dad talk *with* one another? Or did they? Was their language filled with sarcasm? Ridicule? Did one consistently put down, discount, and negate the other? Did they tell shaming tales about each other? Did they talk about each other in the third person even though s/he was present, as though s/he were invisible? Was Mom protective of Dad, making excuses for his behavior? Were they disrespectful? Did they indulge in name calling? Was there collusion against Mom? Dad? *We won't tell your father.* Secrets? Were opinions solicited?
- Conflict: Was there fighting? arguing? screaming? violence? Was there cold, silent anger? passive aggressive, indirect expressions of anger? Did the 50/50 rule prevail: each one having—appropriately or not—to own 50 percent of the problem? Were differences resolved? Did fights get fought and re-fought? Did someone have to be right and someone wrong? Was there a scapegoat?
- Feelings: Was there emotional honesty between Mom and Dad? Were warmth and affection expressed? Did Dad do all the anger and Mom all the sadness? Were parents allowed to be vulnerable? Both parents?
- Parenting: Were both Mom and Dad partners in their parenting? Collaborative? Cooperative? Or were they competitive? Was one absent, or were both active and involved?
- Trust: Was there jealousy between Mom and Dad? Was Dad faithful? Mom? How can we know that they trusted one another?
- Sexuality: Were there clear sexual boundaries around parents' sexual relationship? Did they talk of their sexual relationship with us? of things we didn't want to know?

- Roles: Was Dad always right? Was he the breadwinner? Were roles rigidly defined? Did Mom take care of the interior and Dad the outside?
- Celebrations: How were life's passages honored? Were there birthday parties? Did each person have special days? Was there acknowledgment of achievements, successes, life transitions?

From our parents as models, we learn how to give and, equally important, how to receive—how to risk ourselves and to support the other. We learn about stinginess and generosity—on many levels: how stingy (or sharing) we are with feelings, money, time, words. It is important to examine what we observed in the marriage that was modeled for us and decide what we want to take and what we wish to leave behind. That particular rules prevailed for our parents—and may, in fact, have worked quite well for them—does not mean those same rules will necessarily work for us. We must decide what is relevant for us as we find our own way.

The too-familiar pattern had been set in motion once again. Their lovemaking had been delicious, yet Kit and Tom found themselves arguing, bickering about what neither could be sure.

What's going on? Kit wondered aloud, tears gathering in her soft brown eyes.

Tom, anticipating yet another sleepless night, said wearily, *Oh Kit, please can't this wait until tomorrow?*

But Kit insisted on finishing their "discussion" before they went to sleep. After all, her mother's rule was to *Never go to bed angry!*

I don't want to go to bed mad. Her mother's rule had become her own.

But Kit, Tom's voice was heavy with frustration. *We'll both be exhausted and irritable, and I have an early appointment in the morning.*

It was true, Kit had to acknowledge, their exhaustion inevitably led to more arguing, and while their disagreements eventually dissipated, Kit was increasingly left with gnawing feelings of a growing distance between her and the man she loved.

Let's break the rule. Just for tonight; let's agree to disagree and kiss goodnight, Tom suggested. *Meet me for lunch tomorrow and we'll talk then.*

Feeling fresh and clear and excited for their date, they met at Charley's Cafe. Over lunch, they delighted in simply listening to the other, opening to each other's perspective.

I think I can give up that old rule, Kit laughed. *This is fun, having a midday date.*

It's almost illicit, isn't it? Tom said.

Relieved of the pressure to win, assured that there would be time for reconnecting, they were more willing to let go and trust whatever was to emerge. Having had some time and distance, the issue of the previous night seemed more manageable and less threatening in the light of day.

You know, said Kit thoughtfully, *I wonder if our fighting after we've made love serves the purpose of diluting all that intensity and the intimacy that sometimes seems to overwhelm us.*

Tom had to agree. He'd wondered the same thing. *Obviously,* he added, *there are healthier ways of taking care of ourselves.*

They smiled into each other's eyes, savoring the intensity beginning to flow once again.

Having examined the rules of our family and of that parental relationship—our primary guide for relationships—we mindfully declare what rules we wish to incorporate in our relationship. Assuming we wish for a life-giving, mutually-supportive relationship in which we reciprocally approach our dreams and desires, we begin the process of deciding how to decide! We are deliberate and respectful as we talk with each other, communicating clearly and honestly. Conflict—and we will have conflict—can be creative when each of us is willing to take responsibility (ability to respond) for what is ours. We are not limited to a 50/50 rule. Although we are not blaming, we know that often one of us may take 80 percent of the responsibility, or 30 percent!

We express our feelings openly; we are committed to honesty and to remaining as current as possible. Along with the open sharing of feelings, we are committed to honoring our individual needs for privacy. We want to be intentional in separate time and time together.

Our commitment to one another is to trust ourselves and each other. We each choose to honor our own body and the other's, knowing that as we integrate our sexuality, our sensuality, and our trust, our differences will serve to nurture the deepening intimacy between us. And always we honor the Spirit that guides us, that nurtures the connection between us and with the Universe, even though these expressions may differ.

As a couple, we begin to take our place in our community. We take our unique loving and expand beyond our relationship into the world. We do our work, not simply our jobs, but believing that *we* are greater than the sum of the two parts, we begin—working together, affirming our own competence and supporting our partner's—we move into the world. Together, from our vision, we develop a goal; together we cultivate a mission.

Identity

We are forming our identity as a couple. Our relationship is evolving into an entity that is unique and well-defined. We are creating a new system, and as we do so, we are strengthening the boundary around ourselves as a partnership. We remember this is not a rigid boundary, but one that is flexible, allowing for the inclusion of family and friends. We are negotiating a relationship with each of our families of origin who concurrently are adjusting to the inclusion of our partner while adapting to the separation from us. This may be an especially difficult transition for those couples who confront lack of affirmation from families in whom diversity is not accepted. Same-sex couples, mixed-raced couples, and cross-class couples tend to suffer alienation and disappointment during this time of identity. Homophobia—the fear and hatred of homosexuality—prevails to an astonishing degree and has a profound impact on everyone. And tensions about racial and class identity may run high in families for whom accepting the new relationship is a stretch.

Individually, we nurture ourselves by reconnecting with friends. As a couple, we begin developing friendships that sustain us. We choose friends who affirm our relationship, who encourage our growth and celebrate our joys, and who walk with us through the times of pain.

We are mindful of our commitment to each other, affirming ourselves and each other and our relationship. We are vigilant, not only of the values of our relationship, but of ourselves, for in the face of violating our own integrity, we shatter all meaning of the relationship. We remind ourselves that to define our relationship—to marry, to commit—does not negate the definition of ourselves: *we* are comprised of *you* and *me!* All three entities must be honored.

As we affirm the identity of the relationship, so we continue to affirm our own: there is couple identity that coexists with our individual identity. The relationship, in order to be a life-giving one, must have room for those places of our differences and of our mergings as well. We are two individuals who, because of our unique abilities and desires, have invited one another to share a life, so that the two of us may grow together, moving into a greater good.

Necessarily, there will be some blending of values. We've each invited the other to join us on this journey, and that is an expansive venture. We gift each other with unique, perhaps brand-new, perspectives and visions, and each of us may choose to integrate these into her own value system. This process must not be an automatic fusing; rather, we must examine and choose what fits for us, for our own belief system.

No doubt, we will utilize the waning phase for affirming our separateness, for introspection, and for integration—to question, to evaluate, to *re-e/value/ate* the values presented to us. We may proceed through a process of experimentation that is essential to any new value orientation and then reevaluate our choice. All of this is a necessary process through which each of us must go as we formulate the identity of our relationship and of ourselves as part of a newly formed partnership.

Finally, the process of identity is formalized in ritual. We establish special times to celebrate ourselves; we become betrothed, engaged, married—committed to each other. Whatever form we choose, whatever language we prefer, it is time for that naming to be intentionally defined.

Resolution of the Waxing Moon Cycle

We have reconnected with one another in the Waxing Moon Cycle, waxing with greater awareness into a gentler passion as we nevertheless deepened our loving and our commitment to one another. In the illumination of the full moon phase, we worked oh-so-hard defining the expectations and hopes for this evolving relationship. Not knowing how, exactly, we knew we had invited each other to share this wonderful journey, and we committed to each other to travel together in loving honesty and with integrity as we set about the task of defining our rules and our relationship. And in the waning phase of the Waxing Moon Cycle, we reflected on what we had done. Quietly and with less of the fear we felt in our first waning, we assessed our own values, determined to maintain our own integrity in the face of the delicious blending.

A busy cycle, indeed, is this second cycle: we have been hard at work creating the structure of our relationship. We want the frame to be strong, the boundaries well-defined, for it is our hope that this will withstand the stresses of time and the pressures of the tasks that await us. We may experience many waxings and wanings through this cycle, for the tasks are many, the lessons profound.

If we have been diligent in our work, we move with grace into the dark of the moon phase to rest, to reflect on our job well done, to marvel at our own growth. We rest in the silent hush of the darkness of the new moon phase, and we surrender to the questions that emerge out of the stillness, courageously and willingly exploring the resulting answers.

If, on the other hand, we have misstepped, hurried through our tasks, or ignored the challenges presented to us, and if we have subverted our own personal integrity in order simply to have this relationship, then we have failed: we have failed ourselves and ultimately our desire for a healthy, life-giving relationship. If we have isolated ourselves from family and friends, if we've not honored our place in our community, we have succumbed to the dis/ease of fusion; we are vulnerable to becoming enmeshed. Ultimately, in that case, our relationship will become static, recycling the same issues, void of any life-giving energy. Certainly, we have more invested here, for some remain in this cycle for many years. Finally, in a new moon phase, we may recognize that, indeed, we've reevaluated and we know, from within, that we must, after all, honor ourselves. We must let go; we choose to leave.

In enmeshed relationships, there seem to be only two options: we're either *all the way in* or we're *OUT!* For that reason, many relationships end this cycle harshly. Knowing we no longer wish to be *in*, we simply get *out*—angrily and disrespectfully of both people. Most relationships end as they have been throughout. If the coupling has been enmeshed, the leaving will be difficult and ill-defined. If the relating has been tumultuous, so will the parting be. If the couple has been distant and disengaged, so will the final separation be relatively without passion.

But there are other options. We can use our leave-taking as a learning. Indeed, the separating provides us rich opportunities to let go with honor, honesty, and respect. However, if we choose to avoid these lessons, any unfinished business will inevitably be dragged into our next relationship.

There is no timetable for any of the cycles, but many move through this cycle several times before knowing their readiness to proceed into the Full Moon Cycle. We must honor our unique rhythms, allowing ourselves all the time we need for achieving the tasks so important to creating a life-giving, life-changing relationship. The Waxing Moon Cycle is where many relationships remain: unwilling to invest in the tasks inherent in the Waxing Moon Cycle, most stay here, never growing into the fullness that follows.

The many issues we confronted through the examination of our differences are not all neatly resolved. Resolution may take a very long time; we are travelers on the journey, after all, and learning our way. We have named our differences; we have acknowledged the areas of concern. Most significantly, we are now committed to tackling these challenges; together we are willing to grow through them. We have made a commitment to ourselves and to each other to meet honestly the challenges that await us and thereby to honor our own integrity along with the integrity of our relationship.

The second cycle presents us with many opportunities to celebrate ourselves in ritual: betrothal, engagement, the joining of households. I share with you, dear reader, a marriage ceremony—a very special celebration, indeed. This is the marriage of my niece to her husband. And while I was truly blessed and honored to preside over their union, they created their vows, not I.

A Commitment to Marriage

We gather in a small, open chapel by the sea. It is late afternoon at Summer Solstice and while the setting sun will soon yield to the waxing moon, it continues to warm us, its rays casting gems of glistening lights upon the azure blue of the Gulf waters.

The old, plain, clapboard chapel, weathered through many cycles of seasons, has been transformed into a summer garden, fresh and radiant with youth and promise. Flowers of the season create splashes of brilliant color brightening every corner and adorning all available space of the small chapel: flowers of every description bedeck the worn pews, fill the sconces on the walls, and lay strewn on the altar. Impertinent fuscia cosmos, delicate white daisies, golden black-eyed susans mingle with the softly thistled periwinkle bachelor buttons, the rainbow of silly snap dragons and the fragile baby's breath all creating an enormous spray of color upon the altar.

Anticipating the arrival of the bride, we greet one another excitedly. The groom stands with his father before the simple altar, casting nervous glances at the arch emblazoned with the summer posies through which his bride will momentarily emerge.

Along with the brilliant bouquet, a gift from the Earth, the altar is bedecked with three white candles, symbolizing Fire; the candles are white, representing the Spirit that is present. A bowl of water borrowed earlier from the sea glistens beside the rose incense, its gentle fragrance purifying the Air, as it wafts amidst the gentle ocean breeze that mischievously teases the candle flames. All is in readiness for the celebration of the young couple who have invited us to join in their union ceremony.

Gentle sounds of a harp swell into fullness as all heads turn and we smile upon the elegant bride whose beauty and joy emanate from the very center of her heartspace. Dressed in a simple gown of creamy white silk, its deep luster only enhanced by the folds of delicate lace that cascade from her tiny waist and sweep the ground, her lovely face is modestly covered with the delicate lace-trimmed veil that flows from a simple garland of flowers. She carries a small nosegay of daisies and baby's breath, and she pauses in the archway to smile upon the man she is about to wed. The bride, escorted by her brother, gracefully walks down an aisle strewn with petals of wildflowers. Her groom mirrors her happiness and he extends his hand, tucking her arm into his own as she kisses her brother reassuringly in a gesture of farewell. They turn toward me and I catch my breath, for I am awed by the sacredness and beauty of the moment. And then I read their words—so carefully and lovingly chosen.

> We come together to share, to celebrate, to witness this new beginning—the essence of which is the taking of another person in his and her entirety—as lover, as companion, as life mate and friend. In reverence of this celebration, we honor the Spirit that embraces and unites us . . .

> We honor the Spirit that guides us, for we are blessed to be here in Your presence in a spirit of love, remembering that love has no other desire but to fulfill itself, and when we love, we let these be our desires:

- To melt and be like a running brook that sings its melody to the night
- To know the pain of too much tenderness
- To wake at dawn with a winged heart and give thanks for another day of loving
- To rest at the noon hour and meditate love's ecstasy
- To return home at eventide with gratitude

And then to sleep with a prayer for the beloved in our heart and a song of praise upon our lips. Blessed be.[12]

The groom, unabashedly joyful, smiles at his bride.

We honor the parents of the bride who gave the world a sensitive, gifted, and beautiful woman, one who has learned resilience, forbearance, and compassion; and we honor the parents of the groom who have given us a quiet, intelligent, and determined man, whose dedication and vision enriches our world. The bride and groom thank you and honor you, their parents, for the gifts of your creation, your love and nurturance.

My sister glows in joy and pride as she gazes upon her lovely daughter and the man who now joins our family.

A childhood friend, sitting before her dulcimer, gifts the bride and groom with a lovely song she has written, an adaptation from First Corinthians, Thirteenth Chapter, known as the love poem. Her full lilting voice blends with the sweet sounds of her instrument and melds with the songs of the gulls and pipers who gather with us in celebration.

Kathleen and Thomas, you both know that neither a minister, a priest, a rabbi, nor any public official can marry you; they can only witness and certify your marriage. Only you can marry yourselves. Marriage is your mutual commitment, your willingness to continuously nurture your relationship in order to create an atmosphere of caring, consideration, and respect; it is your willingness to face the conflicts and fears inherent in and woven through the human experience and your realization that love does not consist of two people looking at each other, but two people looking together in the same direction.

I am touched once more by the wisdom and love these two young people have articulated so poetically and I look upon them now, their faces filled with promise and hope. Surely anything is possible through their love. And I continue putting my voice to their words.

> Marriage is the form that allows for and nourishes the growth and deepening of the two people within. It is the outward manifestation of the intimate sharing of two lives, for this sharing must not diminish, but rather enhance the individuality of each partner. In love, all of life's contradictions dissolve and disappear; and only in love are unity and duality not in conflict; rather, differences are affirmed, integrated and celebrated.

> Marriage is a single soul dwelling in two bodies. And love, like fire, can only exist in eternal movement. Love ceases to live as soon as it ceases hoping.

> A healthy and balanced relationship is one in which neither person is overpowered or absorbed by the other. It is out of the tension of separateness and union that love exists.

> Kathleen and Thomas have come here this evening to express to each other, to the Spirit that embraces us all, as well as to each of us as their witnesses, their commitment to each other. The spirit of their commitment is diversity, and the celebration of being different and equal.

The bride's heart-sister, her cousin, comes forward to share a reading that speaks of the two women's dreams as they journeyed together through girlhood. Her eyes glistening with unshed tears of joy, her voice firm and filled with love, she offers this as a gift of her love and a blessing for the couple.

> All I really need to know about how to live and what to do and how to be I learned in kindergarten. Wisdom was not at the top of the graduate-school mountain, but there in the sandpile at Sunday School. These are the things I learned:
>
> Share everything.
> Play fair.
> Don't hit people.
> Put things back where you found them.
> Clean up your own mess.
> Don't take things that aren't yours.
> Say you're sorry when you hurt somebody.

Wash your hands before you eat.

Flush.

Warm cookies and cold milk are good for you.

Live a balanced life—learn some and think some and draw and paint and sing and dance and play and work every day some.

Take a nap every afternoon.

When you go out into the world, watch out for traffic, hold hands, and stick together.

Be aware of wonder. Remember the little seed in the Styrofoam cup: The roots go down and the plant goes up and nobody really knows how or why, but we are all like that.

Goldfish and hamsters and white mice and even the little seed in the Styrofoam cup—they all die. So do we.

And then remember the Dick-and-Jane books and the first word you learned—the biggest word of all—LOOK.[13]

Spontaneously, the bride winks and grins at her cousin. Surely, these two—my niece and my daughter—are 5- and 7-year olds, still. And now the diminutive bride looks up at her husband-to-be and a silent peal of laughter falls from her lips. Her groom squeezes her hand, knowing they are about to exchange the vows that together they have created.

In the acknowledgment of their unique truths and the diversity of their spiritual traditions, the bride and groom have chosen to exchange three rings—symbols of the trinity—while acknowledging they are separate and they are one.

As a symbol of marriage promises, a ring of gold has special significance. Being circular, it represents nature's most perfect and enduring form, created by uniting opposite poles: it has no beginning and no end. The use of precious metal signifies its resistance to the tarnish of an imperfect world; it is a symbol that continues to shine with beauty despite the stress and abuse of everyday living. Just as the Maiden, Mother, and Crone guide you on your journey together, let these three rings now, and for all time, become a sacred symbol of your love, commitment, and unity.

Turning toward one another, the bride and groom smile into the eyes of the other and exchange their vows of love and commitment, saying,

"I give you these rings as a symbol of my respect, loyalty, friendship and love. I promise to celebrate our differences, to nurture our changing love and to share life's challenges and joys."

Once again I am lost in the moment—in this moment of grace—and I utter a silent prayer that they may always be able to touch the love, the commitment, the hope and joy that is so clearly visible in the sacred time. And I continue with their words.

> Inasmuch as each of you have made promises and expressed your intentions to this gathering of your family and friends, and to the Spirit Within and Without, that you are and shall hereafter be husband and wife to each other—it becomes my privilege on behalf of those assembled here, and on behalf of those present in spirit, to affirm that you are now and henceforth shall ever be husband and wife.

Their faces glowing with love and happiness, the young couple shares the symbolic kiss uniting one to the other.

> And now, please join your family and friends who will forever cherish the gift you have just given by sharing this very special time with all of us.

The sun has set into the sea leaving behind a lovely lavender sky that soon gives way to the rising crescent waxing moon and thence to the stars that dance in celebration as they illuminate the summer sky. All who have gathered now light candles, all of which reflect the many colors of the wildflowers, while we wish the bride and groom a multitude of blessings of prosperity, passion, love, hope, fertility, peace, fidelity, creativity, and spirituality.

Blessed be!

Chapter 6

Full Moon Cycle

Midlife   Autumn Equinox   Differences Affirmed

Come ride with me, my dears,
In my magical chariot so fine.
For I am Selene, Goddess of the Full Moon,
Mother of the Night Sky.
Travel with me through the cosmos and
let us embrace the stars—
their sparkling dust made
more luminous by your love,
more brilliant by your acts of beauty
and more radiant by your passion.
Come, dare to journey with me into all your fullness.

Like an exquisite wine, we ripen into full-bodied pleasure and satisfaction. We are most certainly in the fullness of our lives, and our relationship reflects the full moon quality of our being and our being together. This, the third cycle, presents different kinds of challenges. While we have tasks to perform, in the Full Moon Cycle the tasks are about nurturing what we know, deepening what we have, and enriching what has become comfortable and familiar. We are now flowing into the mature fullness of our relationship. Everything that has occurred until now has been preparation for this cycle, and all that follows is actualization of what preceded.

We are faced with being purposeful. In cycle one, we have laid the foundation; in cycle two, we created the structure; and in this, the third

177

cycle—the Full Moon Cycle—we are about the business of *being* in the relationship.

● ○ ●

Typically, the Full Moon Cycle is the cycle of the most longevity. We enter into the Full Moon Cycle filled with hope—our visions clear, our hopes more refined. We have plans and dreams—the moon is full: we are luminous with abundance; we enact our possibilities. Feeling safe and comfortable in our relationship, we broaden our horizon and begin to consider many options. Shall we buy a home? have children? make advances in our careers? We define and clarify our life's work.

What was the central focus of our lives—our relationship—becomes the touchstone from which we develop other interests and priorities. We are more worldly now, and our relationship is the haven of safety to which we return for renewal, for strength, for encouragement. Our relationship is *home.*

Our differences no longer seem to be problematic; we have learned to enjoy and even to affirm those ways in which we differ. Through our early years together, we are smitten in the blush of romance, and the extraordinary energy of our impassioned loving facilitates our facing the differences and conflicts that inevitably exist between us. As we begin to turn our focus beyond the two of us, we are fueled by our commitment to our life's work, our careers, our childrearing. We have little enough time for each other, and we celebrate those rare times when at last we are able to steal a few moments from the many tasks in our daily lives to enjoy being together. There is an illicit quality to those precious times when we are at last able to push aside the many demands that seem always to be present. Our differences are woven into the fabric of our busy lives.

Just when we feel overflowing with the utter abundance of the Full Moon Cycle, we career into a terrible and frightening slump: we confront the proverbial midlife crisis. Without question, the greatest challenges of our middle years revolve around issues that have to do with our love relationships. The Full Moon Cycle is characterized by change: change of lifestyle, change of values—*change of life.* This cycle is a vigorous one, filled with growth, abundance, and vitality. Particularly in these waning years of the twentieth century, we are faced with great confusion and conflict around relationships. Those of us who are currently moving through midlife and beyond grew up with the promise of "'til death us do part." We were told that with the appropriate dedication, commitment, sensitivity, and perseverance, we would have a happy and exclusive relationship; we would—with some challenges along the way, of course—endure through the years. No one told us of the major revolution that would transform the complex institution of marriage throughout the last third of the twentieth century. No one reminded us that "'til death us do part" had a very different meaning a few generations ago when marriages often ended in the early death of one of the spouses. One has to wonder if divorce serves the contemporary function that death provided in earlier times—that of changing partners.[1] Marriage for love is, after all, a relatively recent phenomenon.

I have deliberately avoided attaching any limits of time to each of the cycles, and I continue to do so. To attach a time to a phase—how long do we remain in cycle one? how many times must we go through cycle two before we progress to cycle three?—negates the intention of this book, and further, is a submission to the linear way of thinking. The patriarchy has taught us to be forever projecting into the future—always asking, how long before we get there? Our true purpose is to be attentive to our own rhythm, our unique pace. The natural *process* of relationship is one in which we wax, reach fullness, then wane. We initiate connections in the waxing phase, we reach our optimum of creativity in the full of the moon phase whereupon we wane into a separateness that allows for the integration of what we have learned, and then we rest in the stillness of the new moon phase. We are transformed and, with renewed vision, we prepare for the returning energy of the waxing phase.

Waxing and waning, our energy ebbs and flows. To honor our own individual rhythms and thence to honor the rhythm of the relationship is our task. We are challenged to honor the different rhythms of our partner and the varying rhythm within ourselves as these blend to create the tempo of the relationship. To attach a timetable to this natural phenomenon would be ludicrous, for just as each of us has her own expression of her rhythm, so does each relationship move uniquely to its own beat. We simply allow for that which is inherent in the entity that we call *relationship*. After all, as Deepak Chopra reminds us, time is a concept that has no basis in reality and the flow of linear time is completely a psychological event.

We move through the first waxing phase of the New Moon Cycle only once; falling-in-love—limerence—is a singular event in any relationship. However, we may make several revolutions through cycle one before we flow into the Waxing Moon Cycle. The second cycle presents many significant tasks for our consideration, and many relationships remain there for many years. There are no rights or wrongs here. However, in each cycle there seem to be particular opportunities for learning; each cycle has distinct characteristics. To remain in one cycle does not imply that we are slow or bad or wrong; we simply *are* where we are and our task is to honor our own particular rhythm which will move us along perfectly. Dis/ease occurs when we abort what is natural, when we fail to first honor our own rhythm and our partner's; dysfunction occurs when we fail to trust that each is capable of feeling our own feelings, when we forget to make, respectfully, the choice that is best for us at the time.

As we flow through our individual cycles, each of the cycles becomes increasingly more expanded. So it is in the relationship cycles. We flow into the Full Moon Cycle as our relationship is leaving its youth, and we, typically, move into the Dark of the Moon Cycle as our relationship prepares for its waning years.*

Simultaneously, we must remember that along with the prevailing cycle of the relationship, we are experiencing our own individual cycles that may be daily, monthly, and seasonal. Necessarily, the relationship will be affected and, in fact, may be waning in the midst of the individual's waxing phase. Confusing and contradictory as this may seem, it is not unlike a snap of cold weather in the midst of June or a record-breaking warm day in the middle of February. These seeming incongruities simply need to be honored.

Furthermore, with each major life transition, we return to the earlier cycles—at least briefly—in order to re-learn the lessons necessary for the changing of life's circumstances. For instance, as we shall see, when we add children to our lives, a new system is formed, and we must therefore

---

* While a second marriage will have a different rhythm, it will, nonetheless, flow through the cycles.

develop trust in each other and in the rhythm of the new family. We have additional boundaries to define, rules to evaluate. However, having successfully moved through those cycles, we have a proficiency that will enable us to more gracefully and respectfully flow through the subsequent process. We are able to trust the rhythmic flow.

● ○ ●

Creating a healthy, life-giving relationship is challenging. However, continuing to nurture the relationship into a mature, mutually satisfying partnership is an even greater challenge. We yearn for those earlier days of romance when life was an enchanting adventure filled with anticipation and desire, yet there is something powerful and empowering about a relationship in the fullness of life.

A couple I knew in our youth—when we were all entering the Waxing Moon Cycle—was recently featured in the Sunday newspaper. With great interest, I read of their many accomplishments through the past 30 years. They've reared their children; both have highly successful and creative careers, serve on many local boards, and are currently corecipients of an award for excellence from their alma mater, Howard University. When asked what their prized possessions are, she responded "a stack of photo albums" and he, "my father's watch." Her number-one anxiety is that there is "so much to do, so little time," and his goal for the coming year is to build a house for his wife. In their mid-50s, this couple is obviously in the fullness of life, still eager to take in all life has to offer while reciprocating as well.[2] No doubt their 30 years together have brought many challenges and changes, for that's what living life fully promises. Yet, a healthy relationship is a "friendship with possibilities."[3] And indeed, what more could we want in our middle years—or ever—but a *friendship with possibilities.*

WAXING MOON PHASE

We flow out of the darkness of the new moon phase into the waxing phase of the Full Moon Cycle exuberantly eager to live our lives fully and completely. We are committed to sharing this grand adventure with our beloved. Having celebrated our love and our commitment to one another in an affirming ritual that we've shared with our friends and family, we feel settled into our relationship, prepared for the challenges that await us.

Having experienced the rhythm of two complete cycles, we are no longer attached to hanging on to the waxing; we no longer fear the darkness of the waning. We are trusting the rhythm, and we recognize that as delicious as the waxing time may be, there is value—and learning—in all the phases; we need not dread the darkness, for we trust the light that soon follows the dark.

Less fearful of the differences between us, we see these as questions to be answered, paths to be explored. Feeling comfortable to name, then acknowledge, the ways in which we may differ or conflict, we now see these as an exciting source of renewed energy. We recognize how stimulating challenges can be as we wax into yet another beginning.

We have created quite workable skills for problem solving; we are committed to talking with and hearing from one another. While we are regularly confronted with new differentnesses as each continues her own growth, we are comfortable in the knowledge that we trust ourselves and each other with the *hows* of dealing with those differences. We have utter confidence in our potentialities; together we can do anything! We believe in all the possibilities; we set about exploring what choices we wish to make.

We know that the waxing is the time of new beginnings, of initiating new projects, developing goals. We are excited to be alive and open to all of life, to all our feelings; and with this sense of confidence we begin to push on more of our boundaries, perhaps trying on new behaviors. We explore the edges of our lives.

All intimate relationships develop a rhythm. Relationships between mothers and daughters, between sisters, between friends wax and wane, ebb and flow. At times we feel a deep closeness; at others we feel distant. The lessons available to us in these relationships are as vital to our own self-awareness and growth as is our relationship with our life partner. Honoring these rhythms is not only important, it can be even more challenging. We are more likely to remain in old, well-established—albeit unhealthy—patterns, content to accept the status quo. In fact, changing rules, creating new patterns is apt to be one of our greatest challenges; it often seems easier to start anew. Yet these relationships are fertile ground for renewal.

Sari? The familiar voice was soft, pleading, drifting slowly through the telephone.

Hello, Kit. Her words escaped through a closing gate, securing, protecting the place only her sister could touch, could hurt. Yet she'd acquiesced to Kit's request. Kit had wanted to talk. Since their meeting at Winter Solstice, the chasm had neither widened nor healed; it lay like an open wound needing tender care.

Now Kit was at her door, waiting, wanting. Awkward courtesy masked fear, but there was no embrace in their greeting, meeting each other politely as though strangers, not sisters, not friends—not yet.

The room into which Kit entered was ablaze with white candles—tall, slender tapers touching the ceiling with flickering light; stout, squat cylinders casting soft vanilla-scented circles; and votives, twinkling like stars, nudged away all darkness and set the room aglow with irresistibly reassuring warmth.

I'm celebrating Candlemas, Sara offered an explanation although none was required. Their mother had always honored the eight holy days of her own mother's earth-based Celtic religious tradition. Of course, Kit remembered, this cold first day of February was the celebration of returning light.

I'm nervous, Kit's body was stiff and small as she huddled in the over-stuffed chair by the fire.

Me, too. Sara was not inclined to rescue as she'd always been wont to do. Then, *Let's sit closer to the fire.*

Two women, sisters, curled up on a sofa, a blazing fire warming their bodies, warming hearts grown cold with distance. Little girls, still, snuggling under Grandmother's afghan of many colors. Sara, the wild one, curly untamed hair falling beyond her shoulders in careless abandon, her brown eyes were deep pools of warmth sparkling with fiery intensity. And Kit, small-bodied, round and soft, selflessly nurturing; her black hair, smooth, stylishly cut, framed her delicate features, full-mouth, blue eyes, cues to her Welsh heritage. How could anyone have ever thought them twins, even in the sister-sister dresses Mother insisted on. *You're so fortunate to have each other,* she'd say. Dresses of yellow and pink flowers splashed on crisp, shiny cotton, lace trimming the neck and puffy sleeves and wide velvet ribbon of moss green sashes encircling their waists. One plump, one slender, one dark, one fair, yet each a mirror of the other somehow, reflecting a reality they shared but hadn't an inkling how to wrap words around the fears, the questions that always hung in the air. *Why is Mommy so sad? Where did Daddy go?* Instead, they filled the hollow

nights with whispering games of *Riddleee Riddleee Riddleee
Reee, I see something you don't see and the color of it is purple.*
Now Kit looks shyly at this person who's shadowed her
since she was three. She can't remember when Sara was not a
part of her life. Indeed, their lives were inextricably woven one
into another—threads sometimes frayed thin only to be
rewoven with firmer cord. Once more, it was time to do just
that, Kit knew.

I'm very sorry I've been so far away, Sari. The old name fell
softly into Sara's heart. *When you told me about you and Emily,
I was sent reeling. I've needed time to get used to it, I guess.*

Sara remained silent, though her body began to relax into
the cushions, the gate to her heart slowly wrenched open.

*I've been so afraid this would get between us, and I've
managed to get between us, instead. I just didn't know what to
say. I've been so afraid.* The words she'd so carefully rehearsed
evaporated. These words just fell from her heart.

Sara said simply, *I'm so sad. I've been missing you.* No need
to reassure; no need to explain. This was Kit's own truth she'd
have to wrestle with, not hers.

*I've struggled through some really crazy places with some
really crazy thoughts. I've felt jealous and envious and scared
and angry. But I want you to know, I am happy for you.*

Words became balm healing wounds of separation. Shared
feeling became the strands strengthening the tapestry of their
love, for they knew that only in the land of feelings could they
truly meet and heal into the closeness they both valued.

A healthy relationship is like a safe home base from which we can
venture into uncharted waters, returning for encouragement, renewal,
and affirmation. Most likely we begin, in the safety of our relationship,
to nudge some of our own boundaries—testing ourselves physically by
developing new skills in our play and in our work, both on our own and
with our partner. We may push some emotional boundaries, taking new
risks with a friend, a sister, sharing feelings at an even deeper level.
Intellectually, we may be ready to delve deeper into the philosophy and
meaning of life—our own and others. In our state of high energy, we are
grabbing onto life, celebrating being grown-up in our relationship—being present in our own life with our partner! We are free now to venture
forth—into new career opportunities, friendships, community involve-
ment—coming home once again to the delicious security of the relationship that supports us.

Our relationship is greater than the sum of the parts: we are high on life! We seem to be carried along on an ever-renewing energy. We hardly stop to catch our breath. The issues and explorations of our second cycle seem a part of us now, and we are free to enjoy the ride through this waxing phase of the third cycle. We begin to explore deepening our commitment to one another even further: we talk of having children, buying a home, creating a project together, initiating a business venture.

As our children are born—whether those be babies or projects we've created—we begin to see shifts in the level of energy. We notice the tempo seems to change. On one level, we are waxing into fullness, but as our family members increase in number and our productivity grows, the system changes as it adjusts to a new balance. As we expand to include each child and each undertaking, the sands beneath our feet begin to shift. Through the transition we may indeed feel out of sync, out of balance with ourselves and with each other. During these times of change, we, on a deeper level, return to the earlier cycles as we adjust to trusting ourselves, each other, and the rhythm of the system—our relationship—in its new configuration. With each change in lifestyle—birth of each child, each career change, relocation, and each necessary loss, we not only need to renew our trust, but we need to adjust our physical boundaries, particularly those of time and space. We shift our emotional boundaries as well, as we make room in our lives—and our hearts—for more family. Furthermore, we must once more redefine ourselves as parents and to whatever other roles we assume. And always we're open to reevaluating our rules, our skills, our styles.

The challenge of the waxing phase of the Full Moon Cycle often becomes one of finding time and room in our lives for nurturing our relationship, for those necessary rituals—those intentional ways in which we nourish ourselves and our relationship as we get swept along in the rushing flow.

FULL MOON PHASE

The full moon phase of the Full Moon Cycle seems to be a culmination of all our efforts, of our many learnings. All the investment of energy comes to fruition as we move into the full moon phase. We are, in a sense, at the pinnacle of our life together. We are at the peak of energy, of our creativity. What is true in the full moon phase of all the cycles is especially poignant in the Full Moon Cycle: this is a time of expansiveness. The brilliant light of the full moon illuminates our creative efforts; we are filled to overflowing with our indefatigable pursuits.

At the same time, as we continue to take risks with one another, to push those personal boundaries by being ever truthful and open—as we remain committed to celebrating ourselves and our life together—we are continuing to deepen the intimacy between us. A sense of excitement prevails as we each remain committed to our own creative endeavors and growth. When each of us is dedicated to creating her own adventure and sharing that with her partner, we are always enjoying the renewed exhilaration and intrigue of meeting and falling in love once again with the person we married.

Life is an adventure. We are solidly establishing our *home*. We may have fulfilled the great American dream by buying a house. We may be busy parenting the children we've invited into our lives and who are teaching us endless lessons about loving and feeling while challenging us on every front and essentially confronting all our boundaries.

We begin to notice subtle shifts in our relationship. While we are no longer troubled by the differences between us—in fact, we can actually affirm them and enjoy the excitement that comes from the ways in which we are dissimilar—we cannot deny the *changes* that inevitably occur. What happens when the woman we fell in love with—the one totally committed to being a homemaker and rearing our children—suddenly decides to run for the United States Congress? What happens when the gentle man we married who wished for nothing more than to be the very best high school English teacher suddenly decides, at age 35, to go to medical school? What happens when the woman with whom we've made a life commitment finds her successful marketing career in trouble, loses her job to a younger man, and now simply wants to stay at home and garden?

What do we do with the inevitable disappointments, the losses, those visions of successes? After all, we are absolutely committed to our own choices and dreams. We cannot jeopardize our own integrity in order to please another. Yet each of our choices necessarily affects the relationship. How do we make room in our lives, particularly in this full moon phase of the third cycle, for those changes?

With each change and shift in the relationship, we feel afraid. Few of us really welcome change—and even those who do welcome it experience some accompanying fear as the sands shift beneath our feet. Change is unsettling!

We re/member those earlier lessons. We talk with one another; we listen, really *hear* one another; we express our feelings; and then we make decisions and problem solve together. In the utter busyness of our lives, we cannot ignore the basic values—the foundation, the very structure—of this venerable partnership that together we've created.

We take time to nourish ourselves, to evaluate, and to be proactive in the face of the many external pressures and demands that threaten to impinge upon us. This is the ultimate challenge in the Full Moon Cycle: to find healthy ways, in spite of the patriarchal culture, to remain respectful of our own rhythm. The temptations to do otherwise are great. We are invited time and time again to forsake our own knowings and to forget all that we know to be true for us. We are human, after all, and it is normal during times of stress to retreat to the familiar ways. An enormous amount of energy flows in the full moon phase—some stressful and disruptive, some exhilarating and renewing. We are cautioned again to be purposeful and mindful of our actions and our words, and always to be respectful of the rhythms, intense as they now seem in the midst of all the vigorous activity of our lives.

To regularly and purposefully check in with ourselves and with one another is certainly one way of remaining proactive in our relationship. Let us, then, return briefly to the criteria we outlined in cycle two in order to assess just how we're doing:

- Are we being honest and open in the discussion of our feelings—all our feelings—and what of our differences?
- How direct and honest is our communication with each other?
- Are our expectations realistic enough to allow for each other's humanness and vulnerabilities and imperfections?
- Do we have trust in ourselves and in each other?
- Are we playing and having fun together?
- Are we willing to confront issues, so that we may move ahead toward growth and the inevitable change of cycle three?
- Are we truly honoring of our individual rhythms and the rhythm of the relationship?

An unmistakable reality in the middle years of our relationship is the realization that our time is running out; we experience (as we do on an individual level in midlife) a sense of urgency. This confrontation with our finitude may disturb some of our neat and heretofore workable (albeit unhealthy) collusions. To risk a serious look at our relationship offers us the opportunity to renegotiate the terms of our commitment.

This sense of urgency, in tandem with our feelings of anxiety, may serve as a catalyst for our descent into the waning phase. We are seldom able to remain unscathed by the fear of divorce, of aging, of changing roles as our children leave and our careers wane. We are likely to be affected by our friends' fears as well as our own. How we manage the stress of the changes in our lives becomes the primary challenge of the third cycle.

WANING MOON PHASE

As we attempt to affirm the differences between us in the Full Moon Cycle, as we move through the many changes of our lives, as we adjust to disappointments and reevaluate our expectations, we may feel as though somewhere along the way we've lost the connection we once enjoyed. The sense of mutuality we so valued has waned. Our busy paths may have separated us into parallel journeys.

Those who remain together through the Full Moon Cycle may experience a decline of satisfaction in our relationships. Our focus on work and on family responsibilities often contributes to having less time together and hence less play time—our social life is lacking. Our lives may be weighted with *shoulds*. We may feel restricted, in turmoil and crisis. We yearn to explore new frontiers. This waning phase offers us the opportunity to seriously review and evaluate our relationship. In the waning time, once again, we detach and move within ourselves to attend to our own rhythm.

We may, in the waning phase, experience a sense of deadening, a numbness to life. The light has been dimmed; our relationship seems lifeless: life-taking instead of life-giving. We may feel bored—one of those euphemisms often used for anger. While we may feel comfortable, we recognize that, probably through benign neglect, we feel no passion. There may be little, if any, play, sex, or excitement; we lack creativity. There are many cues to alert us to possible dissatisfaction, and the sooner we attend to these—becoming aware of and naming them—the more opportunity we have to resolve the ensuing conflict in a respectful manner. Addictive behaviors, such as workaholism, abuse of alcohol, drugs (including prescription drugs), or food are always indicators that we are looking for a *fix*, a distraction from our feelings.

Midlife crisis is commonplace terminology used for the waning phase of the third cycle. The accompanying dissatisfaction is often indirectly expressed through extramarital affairs. Affairs during the waning phase are often indirect expressions of our feelings of dissatisfaction. They are another distraction from what we are feeling within ourselves. I do not mean to imply that affairs only happen at this time; of course, they can and do occur throughout the cycles, but they always occur during the waning phase of a cycle. What becomes problematic is that when one engages in an affair, that relationship is in a time of waxing: energy is high, romance blooms, lust abounds. Simultaneously, however, the primary relationship is waning! When we attempt to make decisions about the relationships at this time, we are hindered with conflicting information: we are trying to compare apples with oranges—a lesson in futility, indeed.

A multitude of stressors assert themselves in the middle years of any relationship. We may be caught between our adolescent children and our ailing parents—and be expected to parent our parents at the same time we are parenting our children! We may be confronted with the illness of friends and our parents. We are affected by changes in relationships of our friends, our children, and our families. Indeed, we are caught in the middle!

Even if we as a couple have continued to grow and have been together for many years, we may suddenly feel as though we're involved with a stranger. In the face of the many changes we experience as individuals, we have remained committed to someone we chose when we hardly knew ourselves, much less what each of us might become. It is less a wonder that so many couples divorce and more a marvel that so many stay together!

Yet many do stay together. And if we have been respectful of our rhythms, we may not only willingly acknowledge the waning phase of the Full Moon Cycle, we may welcome the decreasing of the light—the time for integrating, for reevaluating. We may de-light (excuse the pun!) in the waning, accepting this as a time of renewal of ourselves; we take a personal inventory in the context of the relationship. We have been in relationship with our partner for many years by this time, and it becomes increasingly imperative that we maintain our own individual integrity. Moving through our fears, we can reaffirm our differences, and we can recognize anew the incredible richness and value that comes when we have room in our relationship for our contrasting styles and interests and energies and rhythms.

We stay connected through this waning phase, as in all the others, *with a dotted line:* we are detached, yes, but we continue to be inclusive, to have times of sharing, of "checking in" with one another, although we may—perhaps for the first time—dare to vacation alone or with a friend, to have intentional time apart. We take the time not to *get away* from our partner but to *be with* ourselves. In the face of our busy lives, a separate vacation, a retreat—even overnight at a nearby lodge—can be not only a courageous act but an affirming one.

> I am having a wonderful adventure: my spiritual celebrate-me-I'm-turning-50 journey!
>
> I have written an affirmation for this trip: I am a loved and loving child of the Mother and I am being led in right ways. My journey is safe, fun, and creative, and I am spiritually deepening in profound ways. I am grateful.
>
> Although my intention was to leave by 6 a.m. on Saturday, I managed to have all my goodbyes said—to all four cats, to both dogs, and to my sleepy Jennifer, warmly snuggled down in her quilt and to Tom who, while admitting to missing me was encouraging me, still.
>
> So, off I went, at 6:50 a.m.—into the sun, brilliantly, steadily emerging on the horizon. And what a vividly colorful landscape I drove into—all the tones and hues and shades and textures of the Midwestern countryside. The dew still glistening like a carpet of minute gems, the freshly combined fields of soybeans, the harvested fields of brown juxtaposed to the half-shelled cornfields; cows, sheep (will their coats really be thick enough by winter?), and horses languidly greeting a new day. And, sadly, the many animals—particularly those little bandits, the raccoons, and the skunks whose pungent odors live long beyond them—lying dead in the road, victims of a world that has passed them by.
>
> As I've traveled cross-country—alone, I've taken in exquisite beauty everywhere—from the golden plains of the Midwest into the rolling hills amassed with grapevines and thence to the awesomely gorgeous Green Mountains of Vermont, with all the trees colorfully adorned in celebration of autumn, I've been keenly aware of the Mother's presence, Her gifts of beauty embrace me at every turn. And now I am here at the beach, abundantly filled with sounds—of the pounding surf, of tempestuous seagulls, of whispering barnacles on Beetle Rock, emerging from the waters, and of heavenly silence! Her gifts

abound: the full harvest moon majestically rising over Massachusetts Bay, the early autumn sun that warms the sand and my body, the distant whale regally making her way southward!

My first morning to awake—alone! I do feel very safe here in the beach "Coddage," quite content with my own company. Sleep was undisturbed except for the lullaby of the waves immediately carrying me back to gentle dreams.

As I travel more deeply into myself, I want this time alone to be intentional yet not rigid; I want to be aware of the choices I make with my time and energy. I want to write and read and weave and just be with myself and with my father, whose presence is especially close to me here. I think of him often, of those last days with him here at the "Coddage." I miss him and yet I feel his presence, sitting quietly in his old frayed chair before the paned window, the backdrop of a rolling ocean turbulently pushing against his backside. The raging sea thrusts its angst into him and he, helplessly flailing in its power, knows not at all how to channel the force of passion he knew and could not know. Please, Daddy, won't you, can't you guide me through my own raging storm I've come here to ease?

Kit's journal entries: 9/24—10/4

The waning phase may be a time to engage in a singular venture, taking us into a labyrinth of surprising revelation and desire. Often, in the waning time, the most thoughtful poem or reflective essay will surface. But the waning phase of the Full Moon Cycle, characterized as it is by change, indeed can be fear-filled as well. What impact will all the shifts have on our life together—our life that seemed so serene just a short time ago? How will we relate when the children finally leave? As each of us changes and grows, can we, will we be able to stay and grow together?

My partner and I periodically claim a day or more of silence together. We spend the day journaling, writing, and meditating; and while we share our meals, we do this in silence. We often are in adjoining rooms and while we see one another throughout the day, we remain silent. We have found this to be an exquisitely intimate experience—sharing silence together. And when we reconnect, we are always amazed at how renewing and exciting it is to share with the other the richness of our experiences throughout our time of retreat.

The waning phase of the Full Moon Cycle offers another opportunity for deepening of the self. We can support one another's efforts to be reflective as we struggle with the weighty questions that inevitably challenge each of us. And then, we emerge with a renewed feeling of closeness—to ourselves and to our beloved.

NEW MOON PHASE

We move from the time of decreasing light of the waning moon phase and into the dark of the moon. We have left our fears behind and we honor the dark stillness, quietly waiting—waiting with ourselves for our inner wisdom to be revealed.

Her marriage, like an old copper pot carelessly abandoned beside an ocean cottage, was eroding, corroded by salty sea air into gray-green decay that no longer bore any resemblance to the lustrous shiny vessel that once held rich and hopeful dreams.

She snuggled her trim body deep into her woolly sweater, pulled the collar high, a shelter against the cold misty wind blowing in across the bay. A real Nor'easter is brewing, she thought. She'd come to the cottage alone. The week's retreat had been a bittersweet time, yet she'd filled her solitary days, balancing her time with journaling and weaving, cooking and reading. Never before had she spent time alone. She'd left the safety of her family for the safety of a forever-and-ever marriage. She'd never lived alone, had never left home. Not really. And now it was time.

What had happened along the way? Where had they misstepped? Tom had lost the ability to feign interest. Somewhere, sometime, he'd receded into a fiery, volcanic pit of anger, erupting more and more often into wounding, lacerating sarcasm. She was beyond blaming, beyond hurt—melancholy had become an inner density. She simply felt utterly sad. Her deep sorrow washed over her like the mounting waves of the incoming storm, howling into her body and filling the hollows of her heart with tears.

Still she held onto a vague promise of hope. Tom arrived tomorrow and they would talk. Finally, they must speak the words they'd never said, embrace the despair, the frustration of unmet needs, of unrealized dreams.

Many of us must acknowledge that we have grown and changed in ways that are no longer compatible with the person to whom we committed ourselves long ago. This is the sad truth—our truth. This is not what we have planned or hoped, yet we have finally accepted the inevitability of change in our relationship. We were young, immature, and unprepared when we started the journey. We have learned much from each other along the way: we have given and we have received through the exchange of the gifts of ourselves. We have shared pleasure and we have experienced pain, and now some of us must finally know that in order to honor our own integrity, we must leave. We must unravel this tangled fabric we've woven together. We must let go of the security, of that which is familiar, if we are to grow into our own fullness. As we face the waning years of our life, we know we must fly away—alone.

With courage and honesty, we examine the many waxings and wanings, and we discover that we have learned much of ourselves: we are wiser and more compassionate, having moved through the cycles in love and hope. And now, oh so sadly, we let go. We grieve the unfulfilled dreams, the illusions of what might have been—and, if we dare, we grieve the love that we shared, the laughter, the tears, the times of anger along with the times of play. We mourn the loss of it all!

Others of us come to stillness acknowledging with deep gratitude the love and the hope that continue to grow within ourselves and in our relationship that we hold so dear. Through the differences have come change: we have grown—separately *and* together. We are continuing to encounter in the other a familiar stranger who intrigues and excites us!

Courageously, we have looked within ourselves, and now, resting in the quiet, we are secure in the knowing that we are where we need to be—growing, caring, changing together. In the spirit of honoring our rhythm, we've transcended the disappointments and hurts; we've renewed the trust which may have been threatened; we've re-established boundaries and redefined values and we've recommitted ourselves one to the other. Now out of the darkness of the new moon, the light begins to glimmer again. Our energy stirs as we anticipate waxing into the coming cycle. We feel transformed and renewed; our relationship experiences rebirth.

Lessons of the Full Moon Cycle

It is paradoxical that in midlife our greatest lessons, those of intimacy and generativity, are learned in the context of our relationships while, at the same time, these middle years present us with the greatest challenges to those relationships.

We come to the Full Moon Cycle with a great deal of experience; we have honored the waxing and waning rhythm of two cycles. We have established trust, defined boundaries, determined values and rules, and, in ritual, have formally celebrated our relationship. We are now ready to *be* together: to work and play, to build a home and create our life's work through our childrearing and careers. The Full Moon Cycle is a full one, indeed!

We will be challenged on many fronts as our differences become changes—in lifestyle, values, priorities, interests, and energy. We may be threatened by our fears—of change, of divorce, of infidelity, and of aging. We are vulnerable to losing our focus in the busyness of life, being swept up in the tasks of managing family and career and community commitments. One in two marriages is likely to end in divorce, and the wonder is that as many couples as do are able to successfully maneuver the minefield of the middle years! It is easy to lose a relationship in the shuffle of meeting report deadlines, wiping runny noses, driving carpools, getting to teachers' conferences, preparing gourmet meals for corporate bosses, volunteering in the hospice support program, paying bills, planting the herb garden, tending to the four-leggeds, and keeping the dustballs at bay.

Our tasks are those of deepening and enriching our life's experience. We have the opportunity to grow more fully intimate with each other, or we may succumb to the struggle and become bored with and isolated from each other. We can find ways of developing common goals and generating, together, creative projects for the greater good of all—or we can become stagnant with each other and in our participation in the world. The autumn of our lives, the cycle of the full moon, has to do with bearing others, responding in community with others. We are expansive, embracing others and taking our place—as a couple—in our world. This is the time of harvest, when the seeds we planted at the new moon, nourished in the waxing moon come to fruition. We are full, ripe with abundant creative energy. Our challenge is to honor this creativity in ways that are respectful of our rhythm, of our integrity and of one another.

Intimacy

Some people believe that only after we've been together for many years can we truly experience intimacy. I believe intimacy, like trust, to be more of a *process*. We are, in healthy relationships, always moving to a deeper place of intimacy, as we allow ourselves to be more vulnerable and more trusting of ourselves to risk our thoughts, our feelings, our visions, and our fears.

We struggle with what it means *to us* to be intimate, for intimacy can be about playfulness, closeness, sharing, connecting, taking risks, and feeling special. Intimacy is about companionship, friendship, sexuality, and familiarity. Is intimacy also about exclusivity and monogamy? For most of us, being intimate has to do with empathy, vulnerability, mutuality, and tenderness.

Throughout these active Full Moon Cycle years, we are deepening our friendship with each other—for what greater happiness than to be married to our best friend! In spite of the extraordinary pressures the midlife of the relationship imposes upon us, we are, in healthy relationships, deepening the delicious intimacy between us. When we know that love is not a finite quantity but is expansive and inclusive—and when we know that we are able to be generous with ourselves, accepting that there will always be enough—then we are free to develop and deepen our relationships with ourselves, our partner, our children, and our work.

Mutuality is implied in our primary intimate relationship. We have, through practice, struggle, and experience, developed a win/win dynamic between us. In heterosexual relationships, by midlife, women typically have become more assertive in their relationships, while men have become more vulnerable, a combined growth that allows for greater mutuality and therefore deeper intimacy.

Assuming that each of us has been doing her own work throughout her individual cycles, we have by these middle years developed a confidence in ourselves that enables us to freely and wholly be available to the other in the relationship. We have developed a strong sense of self, and we are able to maintain that sense of the self in the context of our relationship. Clearly, as we become more intimate—vulnerable, playful, tender—with ourselves, we are free to be more deeply intimate— vulnerable, playful, and tender—with our beloved. We are, therefore, certainly more willing and capable of honoring the needs of our partner.

While we are not responsible for meeting all those needs, we *honor* them by listening and supporting one another. What seems to be most significant in the process of deepening intimacy is being open to the knowing that our personal gratification is subordinated to the needs for *mutual* satisfaction in the relationship. That is not to imply that either of us subordinate our needs to the needs of the other, but that we are each willing to participate in the process of exploring a third option: what is best for both of us. This is *mutuality*.

We have reached a place, potentially, in which we are truly able to integrate our differences—to affirm that we are different people with different rhythms and needs and feelings and thoughts and interests and priorities *and* that there is room in the relationship not only to name and acknowledge those things but to say *oh yes! this is interesting; let me hear more about that.* We are no longer threatened; instead, we are interested in, even intrigued by, the ways in which we differ. We have, in the nourishing environment of this relationship, moved to a place of sexual maturity. We are secure in our personal identity, and our values are clearly defined. We know ourselves, and we share this knowing with our partner.

But be warned! In the middle years of our relationship, we tend to confuse complacency and security, comfort and familiarity, with intimacy. We mistake material success—the *Better Homes and Gardens* image—for a healthy, life-giving relationship, in which case, we have the form with little content. Attachment to the image of *looking good* increases our vulnerability to escape into an affair where, at least temporarily, we feel alive and passionate and real.

If our efforts to grow in intimacy are unrequited, if one or both of us seem unwilling—or unable, perhaps—to meet the other in that risky place of vulnerability, certainly we will experience isolation—from each other and from ourselves. In that case, we have a prevailing sense of alienation. Our relationship, our life together, has little or no meaning. We flounder in our efforts to connect with the other; we find ourselves leading parallel lives. We have become strangers to one another; we become visitors to our own home. We distract ourselves with thoughts of divorce; we contemplate fantasies of affairs that often, then, "just happen."

The issue of monogamy/exclusivity in relationships is a volatile one. Due to my socialization and life's experience, I am (like most, I suspect) unable to look at this issue as objectively as I'd like: I admit to my bias, which is that nonmonogamy and intimacy are mutually exclusive. Conceptually, I know this not to be true. We are capable of loving more than one person. I have adamantly argued the point of inclusiveness, and I know love is an entity which is infinite. However, I believe we can have only one primary, affectional, intimate relationship at one time. To be involved with more than one person at the same time—in a primary way—seems to be a distraction from our own feelings and a violation of the intimacy that exists between the two. Logistically, the thought boggles the mind! Exciting? Yes. Stimulating? Certainly. Freeing? Perhaps.

In my experience, seldom are both parties in the primary relationship equally invested in the kind of sexual freedom that allows for multiple sexual partners. The sexual revolution of the 1960s, 1970s, and 1980s took an unexpected turn in the 1990s as the AIDS epidemic began to invade all levels of society. With the high level of risk having multiple sexual partners entails, particularly careful intention must be given to developing outside intimacies that exclude or impinge on the primary relationship.

We know that relationships wane; couples in long-term relationships *do* have affairs. This is a fact of life. No doubt many are distractions; others are vehicles out of a relationship that has lost its luster, perhaps its life; some are alarms that provide opportunities for renewal of the relationship. Some relationships grow through infidelities; others do not.

Deciding to have an affair often hinges on whether we believe our partner is willing—or capable—of changing and meeting our needs. Some of us find ourselves in situations in which we love our primary partner deeply, yet we absolutely don't want to end the new relationship, the one in which our needs currently are being met. These needs may have nothing to do with sex: we simply have found someone who listens, who is open with expressions of caring! Inevitably, there is wrenching pain upon discovery and/or revelation, yet this is true throughout any process of growth. Once again, we must acknowledge that the quest for wholeness is more desirable and healthy than the despair and emptiness for which many seem to settle.

There is as much controversy around the question of whether to reveal the existence of an extramarital affair as there is around whether to have one. Whether this information is private to the individual or just a secret is a call only those involved can honestly make. Some whose partners are having affairs prefer not knowing; others believe the pain of deception far outweighs the pain of infidelity. But the decision to have an affair calls for looking at these issues carefully.

When the commitment is strong and when we as a couple are courageous enough to face the implications of infidelity, we are almost invariably rewarded by a deepening in the relationship. Conversely, if the ramifications of the affair are not dealt with, the relationship will tend to return to the status quo and eventually deteriorate.

It is a challenge—and some believe unreasonable to expect—to live with one other person for 30 years or more in a state of monogamy; for some, this expectation conflicts with our value of individual freedom. But there is grave danger in choosing nonmonogamy, for ultimately we are faced with the fact that in most relationships it is not the case that both partners are equally enthusiastic about the choice to *open* their relationship. Further, we have difficulty honestly evaluating the degree to which the choice to have an affair is a distraction from feelings for which we must take responsibility or an attempt to sustain a troubled marriage. Whatever our choice, we must clarify for ourselves what we value. We must separate childhood illusions and rules from those that are relevant for us now.

In long-term relationships, we need to continue feeling special to each other, so it seems to me that it is important to honor the boundary of primacy. We can and do love more than one person at a time; in fact, I would hope for each of us to have the experience of loving and being loved by many in our lives. Yet we have choices to make. As we experience attraction for and attraction from others, we must navigate those attractions—perhaps into friendships. We need not sexualize friendships. To have loving friendships outside our primary relationship is completely possible without having to sexually and emotionally violate the boundary of primacy.

Just as we need to examine the issue of infidelity, so is it essential that we attempt a realistic perspective on divorce. Divorce (or infidelity, for that matter) is not always a symptom of awful failure. It may indicate that we are trying to live our lives meaningfully. To terminate a marriage is no disgrace. The challenges for relationships can be overwhelming. And divorce in the middle years may be an affirmation of our ideals—that we have been growing and must continue to grow—not simply a disavowal of a commitment often made quite early in our lives.

Furthermore, second marriages in the midlife are often quite successful, especially when those involved have courageously and honestly examined the lessons learned in the earlier relationship. In a second marriage, we tend to have a greater self-awareness and bring to the marriage a different, more honest understanding of what it means to be in relationship. The movement through the cycles—and yes, in subsequent relationships we do return to the cycle of the new moon—is often done more rhythmically and with greater mutual respect.

Meanwhile, we are middle-aged people who are becoming increasingly aware of our aging; we are middle-aged people who are in relationship—typically—with another who is also in midlife, making even more undeniable the realities of aging! We are challenged to honestly and courageously meet our own shadow—both singularly and with our partner—and in the sharing, our fears may be alleviated. We are all too aware that we are aging and that our lives have an edge of finitude to them, but the coming of old age and the threat of disease and ultimately death makes more poignant our loving, more acute our intimacy.

Relationships in the Full Moon Cycle have the potential for an intimacy that is precious indeed. We have every right to expect that in a spirit of adventure and imagination, our long-term relationships can thrive. We are reminded of the importance of those intentional acts, those rituals that allow us to celebrate ourselves and all our endeavors as we honor the waxing phase when we connect and reconnect with one another, and the times of waning while we honor our own and our lover's need for separateness. We honor the fullness when intimacy is easy and the dark of the moon when we connect with ourselves. For intimacy evolves out of the wholeness of the cycle. Intimacy is about closeness and separateness when, we are reminded, *there are spaces in our togetherness and the winds of the heavens dance between us.*[4]

Generativity

Just as intimacy is a significant challenge for us in the Full Moon Cycle, so is the resolution of generativity and stagnation. Indeed, in the midlife of the relationship—as in our own middle years—we are stirred by intense urges toward creativity, and these nudges often spur us into the most prolific time of our lives. We may be supporting one another in a demanding project or commencing one as an individual; we as a couple may be undertaking a commitment in the community.

We may be using our creative energy in one of the most challenging and honorable endeavors of all—childrearing. Yet, as many of us are working outside the home, often as an economic necessity, we leave our children to face many difficult situations alone. Our roles are changing so drastically that often we are unable even to support one another. Balancing all our activities seems to require an administrative assistant— or at least a lot of patience and mutual support and encouragement and affirmation and love and sometimes just rolling up our sleeves and cleaning the stove together! The job of parenting is too big for one person; we must participate with one another.

We are fine tuning our mutual decision making. Our rhythm, as we work and play and make love and talk and plan, flows more easily now. While we are very present-centered in our busy lives, we are also investing in our future. We are becoming more and more responsive—developing *response/ability* for sharing our skills with one another. We are developing a commitment to creating and deepening our collective resources for an improved quality of life.

Increasingly, we are focused and purposeful as we search for a creative expression of our collective meaningfulness. We collaborate to formulate a philosophy of our life together that reflects our creative productivity. We are developing an altruistic vision of life and exploring various means of manifesting our redefined values.

We discover that to be generative is to be life-giving and that the expression of life may take many forms: we claim our *passion*. We as a couple are becoming role models for younger couples; we find ourselves supporting others as they develop their own creative endeavors, for we are becoming not only mothers and fathers to our own children but to our community as well.

We can no longer afford to remain isolated and confined to our own secure space. Now, in the Full Moon Cycle, we must be more expansive; we must reach beyond our own homes and into our neighborhoods, our towns, our country—our planet. In the autumn of our lives, in the cycle of the full moon, we open wide our arms and we embrace life—all of life. We search for—and hopefully we begin to feel—a greater connectedness to the universe.

In celebration of these connections, in the autumn of my life, my family and I left the city of my birth and relocated to a sacred piece of land resplendent with hickory and beech, maple and sycamore trees, a meadow wild with flowers and grasses that defy description, where we have created a sanctuary for the many birds and deer, beaver, possum, coyote, and fox that roam the land.

We've learned to honor the sounds of the seasons. Our relationship with the moon has deepened as we celebrate the reappearance of the waxing moon in the sky and we pause, awestruck, to witness Venus as she so exquisitely and perfectly rests in the cradle of the crescent moon in the clear, cold winter sky. We feel utterly seduced by the brilliance of the full moon haunting us with her dazzling beauty, and when we become quiet and introspective as the moon wanes, we affirm the cycles, the rhythm of all nature, of all life, of all there is; we acknowledge how intimately connected we are with our universe.

How, then, can we not feel utter rage when we hear of yet another spill of oil in the beautiful waters of the Atlantic? And what do we do with the anguish that threatens to overwhelm as images of oil-drenched mallards and seals, laden with ugly black slime, foist themselves upon us from the television screen? And what do we do with the tears that crowd our throats, threatening to become screams, as we stand by helplessly watching DNR* workers fill barrels and barrels with dead fish pulled from the creek now contaminated by careless and illegal disposal of asphalt—the creek that runs through our woods—the creek that is home to the beaver and the great blue heron, to the deer and the raccoon?

---

*   Indiana Department of Natural Resources

Tragically, and perhaps irrevocably, our lovely, sacred Mother—Mother Earth, is being raped and tormented, abused and exploited, every day. And what has become quite clear to many of us, is that what happens to our Mother, happens to each of us! When the elegant whales are hunted down and slaughtered in Norway; when the magnificent elephants in Africa continue to be desecrated; when lush, life-giving rain forests in South America are systematically raped and destroyed, so am I—so is each of us! Likewise, when the people of Somalia starve, when the women of Bosnia are raped, when the child in a downtown apartment lives in squalor, so do I—so does each of us!

So just as the moon in all her fullness evokes passion within many of us, so the cycle of the full moon is the time when our passion for life deepens: we become political; we become activists! We write our representatives in Congress; we march for equal rights for lesbians and gays; we recycle; we consume less water and gasoline; we speak out at town meetings; we campaign for the school board; we send letters to publications expressing our outrage at their continued use of chlorine-processed paper. We find our voice—and we use it! We become accountable! We become passionate! For ultimately, each of us must confront the egocentricity of living only for ourselves.

Think not forever of yourselves, O Chiefs,
nor of your own generation.
Think of continuing generations of our families,
think of our grandchildren
and of those yet unborn,
whose faces are coming from
beneath the ground.[5]

We are reminded that we all come from mothers; we all mother in some way; we all need mothering and we all return to The Mother. Whether or not we have children of our own, we are responsible for and to each other. We are all part of the universal cycle and we have no time to lose in working toward a society that reflects ecofeminist values: one in which no one exercises power *over* anyone or anything, a society in which we are all mindfully integral to the interconnected web of life. The universe is that web and each of us a significant part of the weaving of the web. The world is not something outside, external to ourselves, to be conquered and exploited. An ecofeminist society is one in which the fate of the whales in Norway is my fate; in which the exploitation of the South American rain forests is the exploitation of me! The Palestinian woman's struggle for home is my struggle; as the old one walks a mile in the frigid cold of Bosnia for a cup of water to drink, so do I.

We must redefine for ourselves our personal ethics as we move into this radical shift in consciousness. It is clear that if our planet is to survive, the traditionally female values are the only ones that will make this happen, and we remember: "We are the mothers. We must *be* The Mother!"[6]

Achieving, then sustaining, a healthy, healing perspective is our challenge: this is generativity. We must commit ourselves to remembering the knowings of the ancient ones, of our foremothers, of those who honored the earth, honoring those who related intimately *with* the cycles of all living things. In the cycle of the full moon, we are invited to surrender to the magic, to honor the rhythm of the cycles that surround us, for by honoring our own cycles, those of each other and of our planet, we may heal—ourselves and our Mother Earth.[7]

Resolution of the Full Moon Cycle

The Full Moon Cycle is one of expansiveness and extends over a number of years, encompassing many life-changing events. As we wax into the cycle, our relationship is challenged to make the transition from a romantic into a working, functioning partnership while retaining all the elements that attracted us to each other in the beginning. We face, in the autumn of our relationship, a time of activity, as we go about the business of solidifying our partnership. We have formalized our love through a commitment ceremony and now we bring into fruition the promises, the hopes, the visions, that have emanated from our loving one another.

If, through the years of the Full Moon Cycle, we are able to navigate through all the busyness and the many changes—both of which are inherent in this cycle—and if we continue to nourish ourselves, each other, and the relationship, then we will have successfully deepened the intimacy between us, and we will have collaborated to become a responsive couple: two people who have found expression for whatever empassions us. Through our children, our politics, and our values, we are expanding our world view beyond ourselves, becoming compassionate and altruistic. We are a team—a powerful and empowering team, and we are claiming our place in the world as we, feeling more secure with one another, are free to take risks beyond the limits of our home base. Realizing that change is inevitable in life-giving relationships, we as individuals still feel affirmed by each other, and from the safety and nurturance of the relationship, we are—individually and collectively— free to explore an ever-deepening relationship with ourselves, with each other, and with our world.

We must face a number of cold realities, however: couples do get bored, couples experience infidelity, some fear the vulnerability of intimacy, and many are unable to balance all the tasks of the middle years. We may lose our way, lose touch with each other—and probably with ourselves.

Out of our fears—of intimacy, of aging, of change—we often become isolated and lonely within the relationship. Others seem to neglect themselves. Boundaries become blurred and the two indeed become one; the relationship becomes one of fusion. The relationship becomes static and dead . . . and deadening. The cycle stagnates; there is no generativity. Both people in the relationship become self-absorbed; we are two isolated individuals leading parallel lives. People choose to remain in relationships like this for a variety of reasons. Some rationalize that continuing to stay married is best for the children. Others are unwilling to lose the material investment made through years of being together. Most, however, fear what may lie ahead—loneliness and a reduced standard of living.

The middle years of the relationship offer us the opportunity to amend, to redefine, and to make peace with previous conflicts. We can explore new ways of *being* together. As women become more assertive— and more political, perhaps—and as men become gentler and less aggressive, each freeing the heretofore concealed aspects of themselves, we can begin once more to collaborate and to find a new meaning for our lives.

For some, the reward is great when through the middle years we choose to rekindle the flame, to remember those earlier cycles, and to renew our investment. Through the middle years of our relationships, we can abandon the old defenses that continue to lurk and we can renew our commitment to each other. We can redefine our relationship based on empathic acceptance of one another as partner—an acceptance of the other based not on a role as protector, mother, father, or judge. We affirm the differences, loving the other for her humanness, her passions and strengths, along with her foibles and idiosyncrasies. We are simply about the business of negotiating together how to have a meaningful life in the context of a companionship with our best friend. The form will be different for various couples: some may choose to have separate lives, coming together as our own unique rhythm indicates; others share our lives more totally, working and playing together. Whatever the variation of these themes, what is significant is that the choice be respectful and honorable of each couple's unique rhythm.[8]

In some relationships, the affection and understanding is such that we are willing to accept the limitations of the relationship, and one or both of us may seek the fulfillment of our needs and growth outside the relationship. Similarly, when change seems not to be possible, when the differences seem not to be negotiable, when the relationship is no longer life-giving—when we can no longer *live* together—then we must honestly and respectfully consider the options that are best for us.

Divorce is a viable choice, albeit both economically and emotionally expensive, and one that may be chosen after all other options have been explored. For all its negative connotations, divorce can be the result of having worked through our many issues and concluding that, in fact, there is little basis for a thriving relationship: we are no longer able to *be alive* together. Given this recognition, we may both be able to perceive divorce as another opportunity for growth. We accept divorce without bitterness or guilt, realizing that we have grown apart. We acknowledge that we share only our past; we have little on which to pursue a future. We respectfully release each other from our commitment.

There are a number of possible resolutions to the Full Moon Cycle. If we know we continue to feel passion and aliveness in the context of our relationship, we prepare for what follows, remembering that the waning leads to the waxing and to a further deepening of the relationship. We are ready to grow into the cycle of the waning moon. However, if we find we are no longer alive and growing, if we are unwilling or unable to face the changes that are required in order that we may grow into a healthy companionship, then we must consider alternatives. Some of us will remain in the cycle, continuing to recycle old resentments and hurts, in a static relationship of isolation and stagnation. Others will accept our lot: we live without bitterness, yes; we coexist peacefully, yes—but for security we sacrifice our passion! Or we divorce—often freeing ourselves and the other to pursue a new life.

If ritual is an opportunity to celebrate the transitions and changes in our lives, then certainly the Full Moon Cycle—a time of many changes—provides us numerous opportunities for ritual. We may have rituals for blessing the arrival of each of our children into our lives and for blessing our new home. We may have celebrations of special anniversaries, the birth of projects we share. In the Full Moon Cycle, a ritual of recommitment may be renewing. We may have rituals for the losses in our lives as well—of jobs, loved ones, youth.

   One event that occurs often among us, yet is rarely ritualized, is that of divorce. I offer the following ritual with the suggestion that while it is most often performed alone, the ritual of separation can, most appropriately, be shared with the person who is soon to be leaving our lives. Particularly for those of us who have reared children together, we will always be—to a greater or lesser extent—in each other's lives: we will always be our children's parents. So, particularly in instances such as these, a ritual for ending can make the process of separation more respectful.

A Ritual for Divorce

The night is black; clouds cloak the full moon, which has begun to wane toward darkness. Two mourners, we meet at the gate to the park, the park in which we've spent so many hours—exercising the dogs, laughing and playing with our children, stealing away from the busyness of our lives for our cherished walks together. The air is cool in this late autumn night; a windy rainstorm has stripped the remaining leaves from the trees leaving them bare and bleak. And as we walk—slowly and heavily—toward the clearing we've chosen for our goodbye, the leaves rustle and break beneath our feet. A silent lament hangs in the air.

   We have each spent time alone—reflecting, in our own way, on our years together. I looked through 30-plus years of photographs, love letters, and memorabilia, weeping as the many memories of our two lives—so entwined for those many years—flooded over me. In my journal, I have written a letter to the relationship, honoring the love we've shared, the growth I've experienced in this relationship. I've written of the hurt, the disappointments, the unfulfilled dreams, and the illusions I now release. I have attached this to the packet of love letters that I have placed along with the album of wedding pictures in a special box that will sit on a shelf in a closet until such time as I may choose to retrieve it, possibly to transform the contents in ways that at this point remain unclear.

In my journal, I have also written a poem—a copy of which I bring to this ritual—an affirmation of my goodbye as I embrace a new life of love and peace.

We approach our chosen place near the jungle gym that now stands starkly silhouetted in darkness. If we listen carefully, I'm sure we'll hear the childish squeals of our youngsters—now nearly grown—as they beg to swing "higher, Daddy, pleeeeeze!" What happened along the way? I stumble as the tears flood my eyes and he, out of years of habit and concern, takes my elbow. I falter, once more, yet each of us knows: we've talked and cried with ourselves and each other until we finally—sadly and angrily—have accepted that what is healthiest for both of us is this parting.

Quietly, we approach the familiar bench and sit together—the once so comfortable space between us now grown wide.

In the hush of the night, we prepare our altar. We light a stick of incense, its pungent aroma of amber dancing in the night breeze, and we invoke the Spirit of the East, of Air. We light a candle—black for endings—as we invoke the Spirit of the South, of Fire. He takes from his backpack a lovely moonshell from the beach we've walked and combed so many times, and as he lays it among the other symbolic tokens, we invoke the Spirit of the West, of Water; my voice catches in my throat—my feelings threaten to overwhelm me. But I set upon our altar a small white pine tree, while we invoke the Spirit of the North, the Earth.

Each of us names our intention for the ritual: I, to let go of our relationship in a spirit of respect and to honor myself as I journey forward. I place the poetry I have written upon the altar. Acknowledging mine, he adds his own intention to honor our relationship without dishonoring himself or me. He takes from his old backpack—so familiar to me—a drawing he has created—a collage of our years together—and places this upon the altar. And finally, along with our marriage license, I place a piece of rope among the other symbols; the rope, weathered and frayed, represents the tie that has bound us together for these many years.

Having created the altar, a heavy silence sets upon us. And then we do what we've done countless times before, we begin to talk of our children, sharing information about who was doing what, and we find ourselves laughing together about the antics of our youngest child and gloating about the recent success of our eldest. And we acknowledge that while our marriage is ending, indeed we will always be parents of the three children we have born and reared.

I acknowledge shyly how my eyes are changing as I put on my glasses in order to read, in the dim glow of the candlelight, the poem I have written. And even though I have rehearsed it many times, I feel the tears crowding my throat, making my voice husky with sadness.

And then he, his eyes glistening, brings forth his drawing—a lovely pastel collection of memories of our children, our houses, our vacations and travels together.

Just as no priest could truly marry us, no judge could really divorce us. Only we are responsible for those acts—and for all that has happened between the beginning and the end—all those waxings and wanings. We are silent once more, for we both know the time has come. Taking the piece of paper symbolizing our marriage to one another, he touches it to the flame and together we watch it curl and burn in the night. And I take the scissors and together we cut the tie.

We take the small white pine from the altar and, proceeding to a spot near the swings, we plant the tree—a symbol of the family, of our children who will continue to grow in our love.

Honoring the Spirit of the North, we express our gratitude for the gift of wisdom through the years; honoring the West, we are grateful for the depths to which we traveled—in all our feelings. The South gave us passion and energy, and the East inspired us with thoughts and clarity.

And our marriage has ended.

Together we extinguish the candle, now burned low, transformed into heat and smoke and melting wax. A symbol of our relationship that has become reborn into another form.

Blessed be.

Chapter 7

Waning Moon Cycle

Elderhood   Winter Solstice   Differences Celebrated

Ah! My Old Ones
It is time.
We must surrender to the gathering darkness.
Yield to me; rest in me.
For I am Hecate, Queen of the Underworld.
To the slowing rhythm of a poignant lament,
I invite you to give yourselves unto the depths
of blackness, of death,
that you may know once more
the healing light of rebirth.

There is something sacred about a relationship that has endured into the Waning Moon Cycle. As with our individual cycle of waning, this cycle has a sense of poignancy about it. We have reached a place in our life together where we can fully savor the fruits of our labors and yet, at the same time, together, we grow old. The inevitability of loss and grief hangs about us like the dusky twilight of evening. In the waning, there is bittersweetness in living, for dying and death loom. If we are courageous, we recognize that death simply deepens the wonder of life.[1]

The Waning Moon Cycle presents an opportunity for the celebration of life, for all that has gone before is ours to revel in, to savor, to cherish. Long ago, we laid the foundation, we built the structure, and then we created the interior of the haven that is our relationship. Now in the

209

Waning Moon Cycle, our home is a sanctuary, a place of celebration and of deepening. No longer do we need tend to the rhythms of others; more than ever before, we have the room, the time, and the wisdom to honor truly our own unique pace.

We remember, once more, that the waxing flows into the waning, which flows into the waxing; we remind ourselves, yet again, that the waning is no less sacred than the waxing, that the winter is as blessed as is the summer; only by honoring all the phases of our lives can we reach integration and wholeness. Indeed, we continue, in the Waning Moon Cycle, to *grow* into the wholeness of our relationship. Many cycles ago, we fell in love, we struggled through our learnings and our tasks into maturity, and now we've grown old. Yet we know the new merges with the old, the waxing flows into the waning. Surely, we are those young lovers still—growing, aging into wise elders.

There is little cultural support for the growing numbers of us who are living longer and being together through the Waning Moon Cycle, as we struggle with slowing energies, depleting funds, failing health, and isolating loneliness, and oh . . . so many losses! Undeniably, we face many challenges.

This, the final cycle, is one of stillness: we are coming to quiet—in ourselves and in each other. Our relationship, if it continues to be a growing one, has become the realm for our continued spiritual growth; we identify less with the physical and more with the spiritual plane. And, if we are to continue to grow—both individually and together—we honor the Spirit that guides us toward our collective wholeness. Whatever form that which we know as our *Source* may take, we honor that which is divine in ourselves and in each other. In the gathering darkness of the Waning Moon Cycle, we recognize that our relationship nourishes the Spirit within and without, and that the Spirit nurtures us as we confront, with courage and honor and integrity, the decreasing light of the waning.

We have invested years of ourselves into this relationship. We have shared much of who we are and, in kind, have received gifts of our beloved. Truly, we are ever more willing to move to that place of oneness with each other. Our trust in ourselves and in one another is strong. We feel comforted in the definition of our selves and secure in the lines that define us. We have negotiated the difficult and numerous challenges that our middle years presented, and we have emerged strengthened in our love. We feel confirmed in our mutual respect and our achievements.

Through our years together, we have named differences between us. At first, we were tentative and shy with one another, confusing—as we were wont to do—love with sameness. Then, daring to risk more and more, we actually began to affirm those differences—those changes— that so often catapulted us into a disequilibrium and threatened our cherished familiarity. Now, in the elderhood of our relationship, we find ourselves becoming more retrospective and, looking through those years, we actually are able to *celebrate* the variety, the spicy diversity that continues to enliven us.

We often know, after all these years, just what the other is thinking; more often than not, we can complete the other's sentences. We've each shared our struggles, our growth, our pain, our learnings, our disillu- sionments, our hopes, and our shame with the other. Yet we continue to be surprised and delighted by an unexpected treasure of a silly joke, an acute observation, a funny grin, a tender caress, a gentle tease, an affectionate noticing! And we still thrill each time we hear Frank Sinatra crooning "I've Got A Crush On You!"

We look back through the many years—past the disappointments of forgotten anniversaries and misheard wishes, of bruised feelings and careless accusations. We lay aside those shattered dreams, the lost illu- sions, and the broken hopes. Instead, we re/member precious images— of her lovely head bowed over our first born, her silken hair, aglow in the early morning sunlight, sweeping the breast from which she nursed; of the two *boys*—one father, one son—identically dressed in Cubs' shirts and hats, warming up for the Little League Game of the Year; of singing lullabies to the children, *one more time, Mama, please?*; of searching the woods for those elusive Morel mushrooms—the dank fragrance of early spring clinging to our bodies; of the curious questions of death evoked by the unexpected loss of our dear Charlie-Cat; of quiet evenings before the fire—reading to one another the poetry of Emily Dickinson and Adrienne Rich—even daring to read a love poem of our own; of creating silly songs in bed when we're too tired to sleep; of morning coffee on the screened porch to the accompaniment of the little wrens' *tea-kettle,* *tea-kettle* and the *cheery, cheerily* of the robins; of dancing together in the kitchen every time the romantic melody of *our song* emerges from the radio. Oh, the memories, so bittersweet, wash over us as we retrieve

the threads of an intricate web we've woven together; and we acknowledge our life is waning.

Given that we often have little familial—and certainly even less societal—support, the Waning Moon Cycle can be a despairing one, indeed.
We elders are the throwaway segment of a patriarchal society based not
in sagacious wisdom but in shortsighted trends, established on an economy grounded not in integrity but in greed—a society unmindful of the
seven generations. This political amorality is juxtaposed with a cultural
ignorance regarding relationships, so we who struggle in our elder years
to grow and sustain our relationship through the cycle of the waning
moon are confronted with enormous obstacles. It is little wonder that
many relationships are fraught with despair, unable to achieve the desired integrity that is vital to a respectful flow through the passage of this
final cycle. Surely, the relationship that has nurtured us, our life-work,
our children, our community through the earlier cycles, deserves to be
honored in the waning years, for we now have plenty to offer in wisdom
and experience and perspective. We have learned much and we have
much to teach.

We may be in this final cycle for many years or for too few moments:
there is no predicting. No matter the length of time, we are especially
challenged with the one we love so deeply to honor the principle of both
eternal becoming and eternal letting go: we live and we die in each
moment, and as our earthly time grows short, we honor the inevitability
of the finiteness of our time together. We struggle to achieve integrity: to
accept our lives, to honor our scars as we integrate the past with the
present. Our tasks in this final cycle of our life together are to accept our
life's journey utilizing the multitude of experiences to clarify and to
deepen our awareness as we adapt to the challenges that still lie ahead.

The Waning Moon Cycle should be one of gentleness, introspection,
and reflection. We are preparing to enter the *underworld*—a place of
deep connection with our approaching death; we walk with Lady Death
who takes our souls into those dark spaces of non-being. We are learning
to die while we are challenged to live each moment fully; we are living
in those edgeless spaces *between*. May our relationship through these
years of waning remain supportive and nourishing for each of us as we
journey into a deeper meaning of our lives, of our world—our connection with the universe.

WAXING MOON PHASE

Filled with anticipation, relieved of many of our responsibilities, we enter into the waxing phase of the Waning Moon Cycle still excited about what life promises. For many of us, the Waning Moon Cycle will be the best years of our lives—the most fully satisfying years of our relationship. Truly, we are friendly companions.

We experience a dramatic climb in satisfaction with one another, having successfully maneuvered through the Full Moon Cycle—the midlife of our relationship. With the release of many of our professional and familial responsibilities, our life together reaches a level of greater simplicity. We are free to be spontaneous with each other, and with increased room to play and re-create, we feel more tolerant and relaxed with one another than we may have in previous cycles. The differences that were so problematic during our earlier years seem now simply idiosyncratic. We even begin to celebrate and play with those eccentricities. Our successes far outweigh the trouble spots, which now fade into insignificance. We are less concerned with projecting our own unhappiness onto the other and more willing to be responsive—to take *response/ability* for our own emotional needs. We have expanded our perspective and realize that, in the scheme of the universe, it is of little significance that she still leaves too many lights on or that he forgets to put his dishes into the sink. We may be ready to maintain our perspective, as a friend of mine does, by making choices based on what the impact will be ten years hence. In the Waning Moon Cycle, ten years have quite different implications than they did in earlier cycles! We are inclined toward living in the moment.

> The death of her dearest friend lay like a blanket of sadness upon her. She'd pull it around her, comforted in memories of their many years. Had it not been for Elaine's constancy, her encouragement, Grace doubted she could have sustained through the challenges of a marriage troubled by disappointments and indiscretions. Without Elaine, she'd have been lost in a sea of confusion and hopelessness. It seemed ironic that now, after all those years, Ted was finally becoming the husband she'd yearned for. The energy he'd previously extended to other women and invested in his business, now, since his retirement, was being focused in their marriage. If she could only trust that. So many solitary nights of wondering, so many lonely years of waiting.

She was tired, tired of waiting, tired of wanting; she was weary, so very weary. She could no longer deny her waning energies. It must be her 75 years.

Ted sensed her weariness and her sadness, and he had become both solicitous and caring of her. Since the sale of his company, he was relieved of the responsibilities of owning a business. He felt liberated of a cumbersome burden he'd carried too long. He'd come home, and he'd come home to Grace.

She laid to rest her nagging fears, and together they embarked on an adventure they'd dreamed of so many years ago. They took a 6-month lease on an apartment in San Francisco's Noe Valley, luxuriated in the make-believe life of native residents of the beautiful city by the Bay, and they fell in love anew. Ted knew that with Grace, this woman whose quirky humor and intense curiosity sparkled like effervescent bubbles, he'd seen the brightest moments of his life. They ambled among the giant redwoods of Muir Woods and explored the most obscure wineries in Sonoma Valley. They sipped cappuccino on Cannery Row while reading aloud to each other Steinbeck's lyrical stories. Together they indulged in mud baths and sulfur baths in the springs of Saratoga. Each day was a gift in the golden sun of California. An Esalen retreat took them into their inner child, and a tarot reader in Santa Cruz returned them to past lives. Through luxurious candlelit dinners at The Imperial Palace and LeCyrano, they recovered lost dreams, reminisced over old friends, restored broken hearts.

Sitting high above the deep, dark blue of Monterey Bay, they picnicked on sourdough bread and soft brie and a fine cabernet. Time had come to make plans for their waning future. The early winter sun cast long shadows through the stately pines. Each looked upon the other: an old man, still virile, still vibrant; an old woman, gracious and lovely, both softly wrinkled into wisdom and grayed by time. Together they'd penetrated bottomless depths and soared to the brightest spots and highest places. Still, they must design a plan for what lay ahead of them. They spoke quietly, gently with one another about their living wills; neither wished to have unnecessary steps taken to keep alive a body ready to die. And they talked of how they wished to be remembered and honored when it was time to leave. Sorrow and strength and hope wove between them as they, together, faced the inevitable. In the early winter sun, dancing off the blue Pacific waters, death waited.

As the rhythm of our lives slows, as our roles shift, as we move into a new balance, we struggle with feeling useless and purposeless. We are relieved of the awesome responsibilities of the Full Moon Cycle, yet we miss the sense of being significant in our children's lives, in our community. Once again, we are challenged to adapt to a new form. We are asked to clarify what has meaning for us.

As the numerically fastest growing segment of society, we elders have enormous political clout—and we can use it! Many advocacy organizations are fighting the battle against the economic and political disenfranchisement of one of our ageist society's most valuable and underused resources. Of course we're needed: we're needed to advocate for a planet that grows hotter and dirtier, one whose resources continuously become seriously depleted; we are needed to conserve, to recycle, to speak out! As we honor our own rhythms, we honor the rhythms of our ailing Mother Earth. In spite of the culture's attempts to abort our power, we must take our places as the elders. We are needed; our wisdom, our expertise, our perspective is vital. We must remain participants—for our children and our grandchildren—for the seven generations that follow!

In the waxing of the final cycle, we are less disconcerted with those daily distractions and more focused on philosophical and spiritual concerns. We, feeling more at home with ourselves, are far less likely to compare ourselves to others as we become more introspective and insightful. As each of us claims our own elderhood, we are free to be more truly ourselves, to honor our own rhythm, our own integrity. True companionship is now available to us, for we realize, finally, that separateness and intimacy are not mutually exclusive—that, in fact, both are intertwined in the process of deepening and enriching our relationship.[2]

Typically, as we wax into the cycle, our health remains good, we have abundant energy and many of us feel impassioned with a *postmenopausal zest* that supports the challenges of change and renewal through this transition. Who we are and how we adapt to the challenges of the Waning Moon Cycle has everything to do with how we've lived our lives thus far. In many respects we "create our own reality": if we've challenged ourselves to change and remain adaptable throughout our earlier years, we will continue to do so in our later years. If we enter into the waxing phase with a sense of hopefulness, our experience will reflect that attitude. However, if we look toward our waning years with dread and disgust, with fear and regret, the years will reflect our negativity.

While our personalities tend to remain more or less constant throughout our lives, we nevertheless have the opportunity to refine, reorganize, and renew ourselves within our relationship. The energy available to us in the waxing phase allows us to do just that—to cultivate and enhance those capabilities and strengths that will nurture our continuing growth. It is imperative through the cycle of the waning moon that we continue to nurture connections with our family and our community, reinforcing the interdependence that is inherent in healthy relationships.

Retiring from a career or job of many years is often the catalyst for the waxing phase of the Waning Moon Cycle. The process of retirement presents us with many challenges. For those who have made few preparations, these post-career years may stretch before us like a vast barren desert: we may feel utterly overwhelmed with the boredom and emptiness of it all. By contrast, those for whom life is an ongoing adventure see the retirement years as a blank canvas waiting to be filled with bright splashes of color, brought alive with rich textures in the form of new projects, second careers—innumerable creative endeavors for which there's never before been enough time nor room in our lives.

Reevaluation of our roles is a significant task as we move through the waxing phase of the Waning Moon Cycle. As our rhythm slows and our priorities shift, necessarily our roles change. Our success in dealing with those and the numerous other adaptations we're being challenged to make in this time has less to do with any socioeconomic factors and more to do with our characteristic style of handling change in our lives.

We begin, psychologically, to disengage in our 50s. Now, at retirement, we are more clearly making significant shifts in our social behavior and our levels of activity. Typically, we are confronted with conflict in our relationship as we explore our options. One of us may be wanting to remain active while the other is wishing to slow her pace. In the face of these choices, we may also be confronted with societal and/or physical limitations or pressures. We must keep talking and exploring together!

Perhaps for the first time since we were children, we have spaces in our lives to be filled with the realization of our dreams: we can play, paint, write, build, tinker, plant, read, dream, walk, travel, rest. We have time—time for doing and being, time for thinking and creating, time for exploring and discovering—and remembering.

Through the waxing phase, we may begin to notice a shifting in our roles. In heterosexual relationships, women may have become more assertive, men more nurturing. The balance in the familiar dynamic changes. At the same time, all of us tend to become more outrageous; we give ourselves permission at last to claim our eccentricity!

When I'm An Old Woman, I Shall Wear Purple has become a vital symbol for women reclaiming our outrageousness. Long before I had the joy of being introduced to this delightful poem, I envisioned myself at age 60: adorned in a long, flowing, loose-fitting, purple peasant dress, a large floppy-brimmed hat with an enormous plume—purple, of course!—jauntily completing my ensemble. I've not waited to 60 to wear purple, but I'm becoming impatient for that hat!

In the Waning Moon Cycle, we can play together; we are free to thumb our proverbial nose at society, becoming eccentric, whimsical, and even bizarre. No longer encumbered by the need to be conventional, we can march in the streets for the cause of our choice; we can become outspoken and politically active. We have less of our life ahead of us than we've lived. Our time is running out, and we're well-advised to live every moment exuberantly—and outrageously!

We are challenged to honor our own rhythm along with our partner's, for this is yet another time of transition to which each of us may respond differently. And as with all times of change, we refer back to those earlier cycles—renewing our trust, redefining boundaries and values, and refining the rules. We renew our contract—remembering that we must trust and we must feel and we must talk with one another if we are going to continue to have a relationship of vitality. As we wax into this final cycle, it is imperative that we draw upon all those skills in which we've invested so much of ourselves, being clear with one another just what this time in our lives—this time which, each moment, grows more precious—means to each of us.

While economic realities may preclude our retiring at age 65 with a tidy income on which we can modestly live out our remaining years, and because many of us may live well into our 80s and 90s, retirement presents unknown challenges for which we are ill-prepared. Preparations for the Waning Moon Cycle must begin many years prior to our entering its waxing phase, if we are to thrive through the final cycle together.

Moving into the Waning Moon Cycle requires that we be intentional with one another as we assess the decisions we must make, talk with one another of our expectations and needs, reevaluate our time and spatial boundaries, and explore our financial challenges. We will need to be open to our own and each other's sexual and intimacy needs as well.

Freed from attending to others' rhythms, we may explore possibilities of all kinds and pursue many of our dreams, we may embark on a second (or third) career, or we may devote ourselves to grandparenting. For many of us, grandparenting is an opportunity to parent in ways that were not available to us as parents. We *can* make a difference in a child's life—whether they be our biological or "surrogate" grandchildren. Grandparenting is the most usual manifestation of our maintaining continuity with the generations that follow. Whatever form grandparenting may take, it is vital that connections be nurtured among our family and friends and us. To remain linked with the young is renewing for us and certainly can be enriching for those with whom we share our stories and to whom we listen (without giving unsolicited advice!). Of the hundreds of stories clients have shared with me through the years, there is nearly always a grandmother or grandfather, a great aunt, or an elder family friend who made a significant difference in the life of the young person. Often the elder was the only safe person, and indeed—no doubt, unbeknownst to that elder—by doing little but listening and being available, had a crucial influence on the developing child.

It is vital during this Waning Moon Cycle that we remain intentional with our loving. The dominant culture is quick to judge us dirty old men and women or to patronize us as *cute* if we express our passion for one another. Nursing facilities seldom accommodate couples' needs for privacy, and too often we are quick to abdicate to the dicta that make us asexual beings. Many of us have accepted the *myth* of the sexless old person; the relinquishing of our sexual selves is simply the result of a self-fulfilling prophecy. Most of us continue to celebrate our sexuality throughout our lives. The majority of us in our elderhood desire sexual intercourse nearly as often as we ever have, and we have no reason not to continue our sexual activity for many years.

Some physical changes do occur, but these changes result in a *different* sexual experience, not in impotence or absence of desire. While our sexual rhythm slows, our capacity for sexual activity remains well into our elderhood. We are invited to challenge the cultural mythology that threatens to limit us as elders. In the waxing phase of the Waning Moon Cycle, as we reconnect and recommit with one another, we do well to be intentional in our rites of passion.

We are faced with another identity crisis in the waxing phase of the Waning Moon Cycle. Particularly for those of us who have continued to identify ourselves through our work, retirement will be especially challenging. To those of a high socioeconomic status, more opportunities to travel and to maintain social activity may be available. Yet all of us are members of our planet, and we can continue to be *participants* in ways that support our Mother Earth. This is the time in our lives when we deepen the connection with that which is divine—within each of us and without. Religious—or spiritual—in the waxing phase, we discover new ways, perhaps, of renewing, of deepening, of celebrating—both together and within ourselves—that bondedness with all there is, our kinship with all creation.

The waxing into this cycle challenges our most primal assumptions, for life has become exquisitely precious in its finiteness—a rare treasure to be cherished.

Many of us, much to our surprise, find ourselves affiliated politically and even philosophically with young people who refuse to accept any societally imposed status. Being an old person, because of the implied negativity of the aged in our culture, is repugnant to us. To some extent, self-deception through these years may serve a useful purpose. We think young; we remain young.

Gradually, the expansiveness of the Full Moon Cycle begins to contract; our life becomes condensed. We become selective about just how and with whom we choose to use our time, our energy. Purposefulness becomes even more significant in our lives and in our partnership. The light is decreasing; our time together is diminishing.

We recall that the waxing phase of any cycle has to do with renewing the connectedness between us. Certainly waxing into the Waning Moon Cycle holds potential for strengthening the familiar bond between us. We are growing into a comfort and a depth that heretofore may have remained elusive. Undistracted by more worldly tasks, we move into a quiet passion woven out of our many years of struggle, success, understanding, and acceptance of each other. Our love for each other deepens in our gentle familiarity with one another. We are keenly aware, as we wax into our final cycle, of feeling a deeply genuine appreciation for our beloved. Our passion runs deep; our passion remains ardent. Our passion quiets.

> Come to me looking   Come to me smiling again
> as you did 50 years ago   with your mortar and pestle
> arms outstretched   and vitamin pills
> and I will be waiting   because I am given to colds
> virgin again   and coughs that wrack us both
> in white that changes   Oh come to me again
> to splashes of roses   and I will be there
> as we lie together   waiting with withered hands
>   gnarled fingers
>   that will leave their marks
>   of passion on your back.[3]

In this waxing phase, we move into another cycle of our lives—perhaps the most profoundly challenging cycle of all. We feel a sense of renewal that promises new life, renascent dreams, renewed endeavors; we are entering our final renaissance of this life together. We celebrate our rebirth by recommitting ourselves to each other as we venture into the darkness—the waning of our lives. It is the winter of our relationship, of our life together. We've been together since the onset of spring; we've circled the wheel of the seasons many, many times as we've journeyed through the cycles of our relationship. And now we renew our covenant to continue to walk our chosen path together; we vow to grow on this journey to the end of our earthly lives, searching together through the gathering darkness all that life promises, still.

FULL MOON PHASE

The full moon phase of earlier cycles signifies a sense of expansiveness in the relationship, a growing into wholeness; there is room for unfolding. Productivity peaks. Metaphorically, the full moon is the time of ovulation: creativity climaxes. The full moon also suggests manifestation: the fulfillment of all that has gone before. So it is in this the final cycle.

In the Waning Moon Cycle, the full moon phase has even further implications. Fullness equates to expanding the depths of the relationship with our beloved. The renewal of the connection between us deepens in the full moon phase into yet another dimension: we are more fully integrating the spiritual realm into our relationship. This is the theme of the Waning Moon Cycle. Our spiritual journey reaches its peak in this full moon phase which, we pray, may extend for many years.

In the full moon phase of the Waning Moon Cycle, our lives feel complete. We are able to make the most of what life has to offer us. At last, we experience a sense of integrity; all the pieces of our lives seem to be in place. We are satisfied with ourselves and with one another. We feel quite confident in our own wisdom; we have no need to rely on others' opinions. Still perceiving ourselves in terms of our earlier roles, sometimes, we feel quite *middle-aged,* actually. In spite of our bodies' cues to the contrary, we have a psychic sense of well being, a sense of continuity that weaves between us and within us—throughout our lives.

We still have many decisions to make together, and the full moon phase is the time for these. How do we wish to spend these years? Do we relinquish our home for an apartment, a retirement village? When do we consider a nursing facility? And what of our deaths? How do we wish these to be honored? Shall we plan services together? Do we wish to be buried together? cremated? Talking clearly and honestly with one another about the inevitable changes ahead is vital to the continuing connection between us. Facing our endings, we remember that we can have no beginning without ending, no birth without death. Death is part of life; waning and waxing and waning into yet another rebirth.

We can resist death without resisting the awareness of the inevitability of death, and in this Waning Moon Cycle, we have the opportunity to truly honor our cyclic nature by identifying less with our physical selves and more with our spiritual aspects. We know that planning and enacting rituals together is an intentional way of doing this. These rituals may be acts of celebrating the return of the sandhill crane, the lushness of summer, our granddaughter's first tooth, the 47th anniversary of our first kiss, our silvering hair, our status as wisdomkeepers, or creating our own memorial services.

In contrast to earlier cycles, we are clearly experiencing a gentling of the pace of our lives: our rhythm slows. We take time—all . . . the time . . . we need. . . . We celebrate ourselves; we celebrate each other—our accomplishments, our joys, our learnings. We affirm the worth of our relationship. We have achieved much in our collective efforts, and we celebrate the manifestation of our endeavors through our work, our children, our connections with and into the world. We celebrate the wisdom into which we've mutually grown.

In our wisdom, we are able, together, to reflect on the journey we've shared. We search as we move more deeply toward integration. Objectively, we can now examine our disappointments; we can see there were no failures, simply lessons to be learned, boundaries to be nudged, edges to be explored. Still we grieve all those many losses—though they be necessary ones: lost hopes, visions, illusions, friendships, years, youth, health, loved ones. We go about the business of completing what must be done to finish that which is unfinished, to say the unsaid. Secrets thrive in the darkness, and I wonder at all the secrets taken to the grave. We know that the keeping of secrets hinders our journey to the healing of the soul. We must say our secrets. We grieve them, yes; but the telling allows us to "leave the death cult of secrets behind. We can grieve and grieve hard."[4] We are warned as we search for the spirit within, and then we come out of our grieving "tear-stained rather than shame-stained." We emerge into a deeper relationship with ourselves and with each other; we feel fully acknowledged and renewed in this full moon phase, when all our feelings are felt fully—profoundly and passionately.

Life and death,
a twisted vine sharing a single root.

A water bright green
stretching to top a twisted yellow
only to wither itself
as another green unfolds overhead.

One leaf atop another
yet under the next;
a vibrant tapestry of arcs and falls
all in the act of becoming.

Death is the passing of life.
And life
is the stringing together of so many little passings.[5]

In the process of our ever-becoming, we exorcise all that precludes our living fully—those fears, secrets, resentments. We let it all go, for we are healing our own psyche, our own spirit. And through our love, we are walking with our partner who, likewise, struggles to prepare for what lies beyond, in the gathering darkness.

In this experience of fullness, we are able to forgive ourselves and our beloved—for our humanness. We remind ourselves in this time that to be open to healing is to prepare for death; to be open to death is to be open to life. As we prepare for our dying, as we ready ourselves for the inevitable loss of our beloved, we are challenged to do all that must be done in order that we may live our life together fully and honestly and with an acceptance of our humanity, of the limitations that continue to challenge us.

By the time we reach the full moon phase, it is especially important that we have a friend, a confidante with whom we can share our feelings about the changes in our lives. Community is vital to us elders, and each of us needs a friend. While our very best friend may be our partner, we need other friends as well. The support and nurturance of a group of peers can indeed be life-giving. For women, this may be an easier task than for men, for through the years, we have most likely nurtured friendships.

Many elders find support in their church groups. The Sunday School Class of which my mother is a charter member celebrated its 57th anniversary this year! And the group continues to grow. It is with these women and men that my parents have exchanged abundant support and energy and continuity as, through the years, they birthed and launched their children, playfully celebrated their joys and painfully shared their sorrows. Now, as one by one they lose their spouses, together they endure their grief.

Recently I had the truly heartwarming experience of having dinner with my mother and her dear friend Alice, who has known me since my birth. Oh, the stories the two of them wove—one melding into another producing a lovely tapestry of woman/spirit. How delightful to see the two old friends giggling together like girls as they reminisced! We need continuity in our search for integrity, and that comes only when we nurture those precious connections, when we continue to weave the web.

In the face of death, we reflect on all we've been; we celebrate the delicious journey we've chosen to travel together as we've waxed and waned through all the cycles. We celebrate ourselves and each other—our wisdom, our spirit!

We continue on the path—ever searching, ever deepening as we challenge our values, our beliefs about life and death. In this full moon phase, we become more subtle, more internal, and we recognize, through our exploration, that as we've moved through the cycles, our cloaks of protection become less dense and more sheer, allowing our very souls to shine through.[6] As we grow older and older, we are able to know the spirit within the body. Truly we are becoming body/mind/spirit—wholly integrated.

How utterly wonder/filled to feel met by our beloved in this most sacred of places! Living in each moment, honoring the hallowedness of each moment, we are free to let go of ourselves and of the other—free to be in that place of *nonbeing,* to live in the spaces between.

> If you would indeed behold the spirit of death, open your
>   heart wide unto the body of life
> For life and death are one, even as the river and the sea are
>   one.[7]

WANING MOON PHASE

The end grows near: the waning phase of the Waning Moon Cycle.

The waning phase of each cycle is characterized by our learning to tolerate the ambiguity of the darkness of separation. In the Waning Moon Cycle, we are being asked to honor the ultimate darkness, as we move ever more deeply within. We are challenged to trust ourselves, to surrender to the inscrutable blackness that forms on the edges of our lives. We are, as we move into the waning phase of this final cycle, entering the darkness of death. We must have courage; we must trust.

As elders, we are challenged to honor our own sense of integrity or to submit to the despair that, tragically, we see consuming so many of our peers. We live with a perpetual reminiscence of death. Our friends become ill and die; our own body weakens, we face death in our illness or our partner's. We plunge into the darkness of waning.

The longer we are together
the larger death grows around
   us.
How many we know by now
who are dead! We, who were
   young,
now count the cost of having
   been.
And yet as we know the dead
we grow familiar with the
   world.
We, who were young and loved
   each other
ignorantly, now come to know
each other in love, married
by what we have done, as
   much
as by what we intend. Our hair
turns white with our ripening

as though to fly away in some
coming wind, bearing the seed
of what we know. It was bitter
   to learn
that we come to death as we
   come
to love, bitter to face
the just and solving welcome
that death prepares. But that is
   bitter
only to the ignorant, who pray
it will not happen. Having
   come
the bitter way to better prayer,
   we have
the sweetness of ripening.
   How sweet
to know you by the signs of the
   world![8]

In the waning phase, we come to accept the unacceptable: we must be dependent on others; we must rely on others for help. We must face another of the *necessary losses*—the loss of our independence.

As we age, we grow increasingly susceptible to disease. We are reminded of the correlation of stress and disease as the many changes in our later years impinge upon us. As a matter of fact, 6 of the 13 most stressful life changes are characteristic of the Waning Moon Cycle: death of a partner, death of a close family member, injury or disease of the self, a partner's serious injury or illness, retirement, and sexual dysfunction. Our stress level may be such that our ability to deal with the changes may push us to the limit, resulting in serious or terminal illness. How long our bodies will maintain themselves has much to do with our environment, our level of activity, the food we eat, our social system, our expectations and attitude toward aging, our ethnicity and heredity. Those of us who tend to live longer are less anxious, have always been independent, and have a zest for living; we tend to be highly adaptable, preferring to live in the present moment (not in the past) and enjoying the companionship of our partners. And couples can expect to live five years longer than singles![9]

The waning phase is, we recall, the time of separating; the waning phase of the Waning Moon Cycle is the time of the final separation from our beloved. And how reluctant we are to let go, to release the one with whom, indeed, we have become one. Yet let go we must, for we must each journey through this final passage alone. Witness each other's passing, yes, we can do that, but the tie that binds stretches and grows taut as each of us moves more deeply within. We each need time alone to reflect, to accept, to integrate what this life—our life together—means . . . has meant. We have a torrent of memories to nurture us. Yet in the waning phase, faced with illness, we stave off those fears that haunted us in the earlier wanings—our fear of aloneness, of pain, of death. While we know the Source of our strength sustains us, we ebb and flow into our fears. *We don't want to let go!*

It is not death, now, so much as the dying that we fear.

To take control of our own dying is what most of us prefer. Indeed, four out of five of us prefer dying in the familiar comfort of our own home. In reality, however, four out of five of us will die in institutions.[10]

Terminal illness for some presents another journey to be taken. Many of us choose to use the time to die in our own way, to reckon with our life and to focus on the authentic connections that exist in our lives.[11]

There is probably no experience more intimate than to walk with another during the process of her dying. To move through the dying surrounded by those with whom we feel safe and by whom we feel loved offers all of us the opportunity to participate fully and deeply in the waning into the next waxing—into the cycle that follows. We share in the profound sense of fulfillment and completion that allows for less resistance to the unknown; we are embraced in that which is familiar. To die at home is to die in the midst of life and love.[12] To share moments of passing through the fear, to be open to the utter powerlessness of moving into the darkness is to touch something profoundly sacred. We are humbled in the true joining with another as we encourage and support her passage.

> Stillness lay upon the land like an old quilt of colors once vibrant now muted and faded, edges worn and frayed by years of tender use. A waning moon fell wearily into a bank of dark clouds gathering in the morning sky. As the rhythm of the wheel of the year slows toward Winter Solstice, so has the rhythm of her days, of her life. Darkness envelops, holds her in

warm embrace, she submits more and more to the seductive comfort of the shortening days, approaching the longest night with characteristic wonder and curiosity.

She gently lowers her tired, frail body into the familiar old rocker beside the bedroom window, allowing the *creak, creaking* rhythm to soothe the disease that ravages her body. Something had drastically shifted inside her, something that no amount of blood transfusions, no experimental medical treatments could change. No longer could anything stave off the irrevocable ebbing of life energy draining from her body. Grace is dying; her final tasks are simply to prepare for the journey into darkness, into the light that lies on the other side of the underworld into which she now descends. She grieves the passing of her own life, not with remorse—she has no use for regrets—but with compassion gleaned from memories woven with sweet reminiscences of a life blessed with wonder and curious meanderings. For Grace, life has always been a wave to ride, a path to explore, a song to sing. Why should dying be different? In fact, she has never been so keenly present, each discrete moment dissolving with full awareness into the next and each breath, each sound, each movement exquisitely, poignantly sharp, bright. She knows that each one may be the last of this dance and the first into the next. She feels a curious blend of desire to hold onto every moment yet wonder about the next.

Her journals, leather-bound and bulging with a lifetime of conflicting wisdom, of privacies unspoken, secrets revealed, dreams lived and buried, rest on the top shelf of a nearby closet. Wisps of last night's dream tug at the dark edges of her mind, waiting to be gathered onto the final volume of the journal lying in her lap. Since Hallowmas when, some say, the veil between the worlds is very thin, visions of those who've gone before have filled her dreams. She removes the cap from the familiar fountain pen and begins in a heavy, firm scrawl to recapture the elusive dream. Her grandmother, young, graceful, lovely in a gown of glistening, filmy white and encircled in an aura of golden light, beckons to her, urging her to join in a game—or is it a spiral dance? She'd felt shy, reluctant, yet curiously drawn into Grandmother's gentle, persuasive invitation to the dance.

The pen drops from her hand as weariness once more consumes, and her eyes roam the winterscape, the woods, the meadow which had nourished her soul and given sanctuary to many. So tired . . . so weary. . . . Too weary to don the old parka and boots, to pull on hat and gloves to walk once more

the paths worn clear by critters large and small making their
way to the creek, to tune her ears for the raw-edged laughter
of the pileated woodpecker, to catch one more glimpse of the
white-tailed deer slipping among bare trees, to nurse yet
another abandoned baby squirrel or rabbit or hawk. Sweet
memories flow as her life energy ebbs, woven into stories
shared with family and friends who have gathered to walk the
narrowing path.

Sounds of Kitty and Sara bickering in the room down the
hall; Sara running—she never walked—through the hall
downstairs, the back door carelessly slamming behind her on
her way to the woods. Kit's sweet voice, *I'll be home by 11,
Mom*—and of course she would; Grace could count on that.
Sari impatiently running her fingers over the piano keys,
Hanon exercises becoming improvisational jazz—so she
insisted. Kitty absently humming as she curled up to read *The
Secret Garden* for the umpteenth time. Memories like an aged
quilt, piecing the years together with laughter and tears and
pleas and endless tasks.

The texture of her life has been rich, the threads strong.
She's been neither famous nor infamous, yet she rests in
knowing she's tended her corner of the world with kindness
and respect. Somewhere along the way, she released the
burden of self-loathing and hindering, plaguing doubts that had
lain so heavily upon her youth. She feels deep compassion for
the young woman who negotiated the treacherous path into
womanhood. Birthing her daughters had freed her to rebirth
herself into a fullness of womanness, thence, sagaciously into
cronehood. Had her mothering become too much? Had she
sacrificed her marriage to become the mother she'd never
had? Ah, her truth is, she's met the challenges of her life and
her marriage with integrity. She and her husband have finally
healed those gaping wounds. Both have found places to put
the loss of youthful dreams, to reconcile regrets of unmet
needs of those middle years. She rests in the knowing that this
has been a very good life. The threads may be worn, some
bare, many faded, yet the aged fabric remains soft and warm
and deeply comfortable.

The chiming grandmother clock tolls the late afternoon
hour, and she yields to the shortening day yearning for the
comfort of the darkest night, the release to the sacred void
where there no longer exists the awful weariness, the pain that
has come to consume her. She knows that in the darkness
Lady Death beckons, waits like a comfortable old friend urging
her home.

She rouses to find herself under the canopy of their four-poster bed. Ted's eyes, so sad, and Sara, why, she's weeping. It 's Kit's hand stroking her own, skin spotted and thin as fine parchment. She can no longer will her old body to move. She feels drained, her energy spent. Light fades while tiny particles dance in the sun's rays across the soft, worn quilt that swaddles her frail, tender body. She sleeps.

Gentled by the lilting sounds of "Claire de Lune" floating, embracing her, she stirs and smiles into those kind eyes of the man she'd always loved and who she must now leave. And to her daughters, so very dear, silently she bids them farewell.

Please, my dears, she whispers, *don't let your sadness burden you for too long. I shall be with you always.*

She knew when Death came. The solid earthiness of her body melted into a heavy quiescence. And as the earth element dissolved into water, she seemed to melt like fluid beyond all the edges of her self. Water dissolved into fire as she became warm like a mist rolling off the summer lake at dawn, vanishing into a lightness of being. As fire flows into air, so all feeling of warmth and cold dissipated. She felt neither comfort nor discomfort. She paled as she floated into an ethereal emptiness and air element dissolved into consciousness itself as her outbreath lengthened and her inbreath shortened and her outbreath dissolved into the place of nonbeing, of purity.

Grace, their mother, his wife, friend to many, caring steward of the earth, slipped away on the waves of "Claire de Lune," in gracious, graceful beauty, a spirit of gentle kindness and love her legacy.

Although few of us may have the courage to journey with another, given the support of some of the realities we might expect, perhaps more of us will dare to open our hearts to the experience. As we make the commitment to walk with our beloved as she faces Lady Death, it is vital that we follow our partner's lead: we must not impose our fears, our needs, nor our values. We are, after all, being invited to walk on the path of our loved one, not our own.

A supportive network is imperative to nurture both of us; we will need rest and renewal through the process as well. We are being invited to simply *be* with our beloved as she prepares to pass into the cycle that follows.

As each of us faces our own dying, we find ourselves measuring events more by our distance from death than by our age. As we celebrated the *firsts* in our lives in the New Moon Cycle, now we begin to notice the *lasts:* the last time we walked on the beach, our last birthday party, our last vacation. And when our beloved dies, oh! we grieve—fully and painfully and often for years, we grieve. We bargain with our god. We rail and we weep, and for moments in time we may even deny the truth of our awful reality: we are alone. Never are we, can we, be prepared for the utter blackness of grief. But in our grieving we feel all the pain and eventually we live beyond it. For we still have choices: when our beloved life partner dies, we can choose to die as well; we can choose to live only half a life. Or we can begin to create a new way of being through the pain and with our memories. We let our loved one go *and* we take her into our being. We accept the awful and difficult changes our loss creates for us and then our grieving wanes.[13]

I don't know that grieving ever *ends.* My sense is that our grief grows into scar tissue, and we have many scars, which are stronger than our skin. We must remember to honor these scars. Our pain, our grief is unique to each of us, and we must gentle ourselves through our healing—being open to the Spirit who will hold us while we grieve . . . the Spirit who hears our wailing, our "wishing to die without dying . . . [who will] put the best medicine in the worst places," and who will feel our pain, bear our pain, and never leave us as we move into and through all our pain.[14]

We are reminded once again that the ancient ones saw all existence not in a static state of *being* but rather a dynamic state of *becoming.* Life is in perpetual change, transforming its shapes and colors, its sunrises and sunsets—all that is is in constant and fluid transition—flowing and ebbing, turning and growing, waxing and waning. That which appears lifeless is in process of renewal and that which is alive is becoming dead.

We always remember that it is in the Spirit where we are joined with our beloved, and while the form of our relationship is changed, we remain connected in our love.

NEW MOON PHASE

We are alone, truly, utterly alone—perhaps for the first time in our lives. We are alone. Our beloved has died: we hold close the memories, the gifts of our loved one; we take them into ourselves.

We are still. We honor the darkness of the New Moon. And in the quiet we listen once more for the voice to guide us through the deep shadows as we begin to recreate our own life. In the hush, we know there are still many lessons. We have yet another role to assume: we are widowed. The implications are solemn indeed. *Widow* . . . we taste the word—yet another identity is this? We feel different with ourselves and with others. We feel alienated. People seem awkward around us, not knowing what to say, how to behave. Do they fear their own pain of loss? of aging?

We've known few other widows to remarry, although our widower friends seldom are single for more than a year—often marrying a younger woman. And many of our widowed friends marry one another—having known each other for years. Second marriages that occur in these later years seem highly successful.

How confusing life seems now: in the midst of our sadness, we feel some anticipation—a sense of freedom, perhaps. We peer ahead as we look behind: into the black darkness a tiny beam of light begins to glimmer. The past melds into the future, and this present moment is recreated. There is much to contemplate in this new moon phase.

We remember that the dark of the moon is the time of integration, and we sit in the stillness taking in, sorting through all that has transpired. Truly, this is our reckoning, and as we recreate our own life, we are challenged to honor our unique rhythm, our own cycle.

> One leaf left on a branch
> and not a sound of sadness
> or despair. One leaf left
> on a branch and no unhappiness.
> One leaf left all by itself
> in the air and it does not speak
> of loneliness or death.
> One leaf and it spends itself
> in swaying mildly in the breeze.[15]

Out of our passing grief, our aloneness, we see a glimmer of light that flickers among the deep shadows, holding within the promise of a gleaming crescent moon. In our aloneness, we feel stirrings of renewal; we are reclaiming ourselves, we begin to re/member that in death there is rebirth.

Lessons of the Waning Moon Cycle

The Waning Moon Cycle offers us the opportunity to learn the most profound of life's lessons—the meaning of our lives—as we struggle with the dilemma of achieving integrity or plunging into despair. Sadly, as we have observed in the individual life cycle, there is a grave probability that we will end our lives more in despair than not. Integrity for us as elders requires the support of personal integration and interdependence with our community. Given the bleak fact of ageism, and all that that implies in our youth-centric culture, we are likely to fall into despair. Poverty, isolation, disrespect, and alienation of us as elders leaves an astonishing portion of our aging society to live our waning years in a state of wretched hopelessness.

In spite of the disheartening facts, we who have navigated through the *I-should* of our young adulthood, the *I-can* and *I-must* of our middle years, now, in our elderhood affirm the *I-am* of ourselves. Released from the constraints of others' expectations, we are, through the winter of our lives, free to truly become all that we were meant to be in this lifetime. Accepting ourselves and each other—our gifts *and* our limitations—together we face death without great fear. We celebrate our collective competencies, acknowledging that both as individuals and as partners, we have been empowered—achieving many creative endeavors.

At the same time, we are in the process of reducing and rechannelling our energies; our world becomes simpler as we make careful choices for ourselves about how we expend our time and energy. Together we confront the future, still in search of a deeper meaning of the lives we long ago committed to one another. Together, we reflect not only on our collective successes but on our disappointments as well, in order that we may integrate these into the definition of our partnership. We continue to grow toward an integrity—integrating those many losses, along with the achievements—of our lives.

We more clearly affirm our interconnectedness with all there is. We've been the Mother's guest here on Her Earth for many, many turns of the moon, and we know of the interdependence of all existence. We humbly honor the unique expression that we are in relation to all things. We cannot not accept our own mortality as we, in the winter of our lives, take our place among all that lives and dies and is reborn.

We have observed numerous waxings and wanings, births and deaths. We honor all on the cycle of life. No matter the path we choose, if we are to achieve integrity, we must recognize that we are not actors; we are, throughout all the cycles, *participants* in our lives, on our planet. All of life is sacred, and ultimately our integrity reflects our relationship with our beloved and with the Spirit that is within and without: to be fully integrated is to be spiritually, emotionally, physically, and mentally whole. How blessed we are to have someone in our life with whom we can explore and deepen these knowings! Our relationship is the vehicle by which we manifest the expression of that which is sacred. When we honor the Spirit, we honor all that is—the Spirit in our daily lives, for indeed, She is everywhere. We are able to see as we move into a spiritual deepening that honoring the sacred is a continuous act of *becoming*: we are consciousness in a continual state of creation that is manifested in our relationships.

Often, we despair as our body changes; we feel betrayed by the increasing limitations age imposes upon us. We struggle with wrinkles, narrowing chests and shoulders, broadening pelvises, atrophying muscles, stiff joints, and fragile bones. Our digestive process is more sensitive, our senses work less well, our reactions slow, and we have insomnia. In frustration, some of us get just plain mad; we become sometimes irritable and often fearful when we are no longer able to perceive and interpret our surroundings as quickly and accurately as we'd like. Too often, our partners, who, no doubt, share our frustration and similar limitations, become the target for our frustration with these discomforts.

Integrity

Whether our relationships last 10 years or 75, we are, in the Waning Moon Cycle, challenged to deepen and to continue to grow in our love, in our spirituality. We persist in sowing seeds, honoring the cycles of birth and death and renewal. We mentor; we grandparent; we learn; we teach; we share the gifts of our experience and wisdom.

Hope, an essential ingredient for achieving integrity, aids in mobilizing our energies, increasing our ability to weather the many changes the Waning Moon Cycle presents. Hope is manifested through the telling of our stories—hope for us and for the young ones. Ahhh, our stories, our memories: we reminisce about who we are, where we've been. Such treasures these—such gems we have to share with those who will hear. Moreover, having our stories heard is vital; this is how we integrate our lives while sustaining a feeling of continuity. We have a personal sense of all our cycles, and looking back and wrapping words around our memories allows us to come to terms with our lives.

Some of us seem to be natural storytellers, always ready with a tale that, although oft-told, comes alive over and over again. A friend's father wove wonderful tales of his 96 years—years that spanned the developing frontiers of the Wild West to the conquering of outer space. A god-fearing, teetotalling man, a twinkle in his lively blue eyes, he'd tell of adventures in Paris where he was stationed during World War I. Much to his dismay, he learned many years after his frequent visits to the sensational Parisian cabarets, that these famous saloons were actually infamous *brothels!* With each telling, his old, wrinkled face would be transformed into a blushing, naive, young American soldier grown up much too fast amidst a culture of war. He'd describe in exquisite detail his family's move from Illinois to Oklahoma in a covered wagon, of riding the flume in the logging camps of the Northwest at the turn of the century, of teaching school at age 16 to kids older and larger than he! He'd protest, *Aw, you don't want to hear those again,* and his grandchildren would plead until once more he'd regale us all with his fascinating tales of a wondrous time gone by.

Others of us, reluctant, shy—or ashamed—keep our stories private. Such a sad loss this is—for all of us! For we need to speak our stories; we need to be heard as we move toward the wholeness of integrity. Without the telling, without the hearing of our elders' stories, we are left with ugly, frayed holes in the fabric of our lives—valued pieces torn from the web that connects us one to the other. Those released secrets are the precious threads of burnished copper that strengthen and become the warp in the weaving of our lives.

When we achieve integrity, we are able to *integrate* the spirit—our connection with that which is greater than ourselves. We acknowledge that we simply *are*—one with all. Thus there is the constancy of change: ebbing and flowing, waxing and waning—always transforming.

Ah, but what of the hopelessness that befalls us? What of the darkness of despair that threatens us in this final cycle? Often our children live great distances away. We fear widowhood and dwindling resources. We live in terror for our own safety. We have no community. We become frail and too old to care for ourselves. Is our only option to end our lives the pawns of bureaucratic institutions?

Most appalling of all, we fear death! To the degree we identify solely with our body, that is the degree to which we fear death. This struggle is our final task. When we are attached only to our body and our mind, we must acknowledge our impermanence, and this is the source of our fear. We despair. So many of us fear the process of dying. Having walked with our friends and loved ones to the valley of death, we fear the pain of the journey that lies ahead. Whether we grow ill and die in an institution or in the familiar surroundings of our own home, death to the despairing one is likely to be an experience of utter aloneness and abandonment. As we approach death, we often behave differently, becoming more withdrawn; we are in the process of leaving. We generally move through at least five stages of dying: we may *deny* the possibility of our death; we may *rage* at our god and *bargain* for our life. We become *sad and depressed* before we finally *reach a place of acceptance* of our life.

As elders, we are neglected, discounted, and often discarded. Through the very time of our lives when we need to be in community, we are alienated. Through the very years when we need to be respected and acknowledged, we are neglected and invisible. Through the very season of our lives when we most need to simply *be* in our homes—to rest, to be secure, we are removed to unfamiliar surroundings and we are isolated. We are subjected to a society void of compassion and respect for its most valuable resource—the elders. We are victims of a culture afraid to honor us because of its own societal phobia of aging and death.

When we forget, when we *dis/member*, to honor the cyclic nature of all there is, we see death as separate from, outside of life. We see life, and death, as something to be controlled. Thus we perceive aging and death as an outrage to our existence, for in fact, we have only the illusion of control over our lives and our environment. We are unable to integrate our death into our life: inevitably we plunge into despair. Unwilling to yield to the natural rhythm of the cycles of life and death and rebirth, we feel powerless and hopeless.

Inevitably, the despondency with which we as individuals struggle has grave implications for our relationship. We miss our children. We feel bored and boring. We are isolated from a community that has nourished our relationship in the past. We feel unable to care adequately for each other, and when we look at our partner we see an *old person*—our own oldness mirrored back to us. And the loneliness and isolation grow large between us.

Each day, we grieve the missed opportunities; each day we miss another possibility. We have no passion for life: we await death. Introspection becomes self-centeredness; internal exploring becomes self-absorption. Old arguments and resentments surface; we are unwilling to let go of the past. The self-centeredness of those who remain invested in the illusion of *power-over* precludes the requisite surrendering to the natural rhythms of the cycles. Desperately, fearfully, tragically, we hang on—mistaking the past for life.

The developmental tasks of integrity and despair seem more personal, somehow, than those of earlier cycles through which we gathered strength and experience for our middle years; now we are clarifying and deepening—accepting our own life, and our many experiences of living, as we maneuver the changes and loss that constantly challenge us.

And yet, each moment presents another chance to risk our feelings, to confront death, to forgive—ourselves and our partner—and to remember our courage, our achievements, our connectedness.

Each moment presents itself to us—giving us yet another opportunity to die. We know we are dying; the self we have created is physically finite. And yet, surely, in the winter of our lives, we can know that spring is soon to follow, in death there is life. So in each moment as we die, we can be reborn—if we dare! We must, no matter the worldly realities, surrender to the process which is innate—available from within. When we free ourselves from the fear that paralyzes us, that aborts the rhythm that is inherent in all there is, we know that death is as sacred—as essential—as is life. We connect; we separate; we reconnect. There can be no life without death; there can be no waxing without the waning which holds the promise of rebirth. Each phase of each cycle is sacred and commands our reverence.

To negate the waning, to succumb to patriarchal precepts that drown us in despair is blasphemous, but the journey into integrity begins not in the waxing of the Waning Moon Cycle. No; that journey begins at the waxing of the New Moon Cycle, for it is then that we set out upon the path that leads us into a life-giving, Spirit-filled relationship.

Resolution of the Waning Moon Cycle

There is a tragically high probability that many of us elders—particularly those who are widowed—will reach the end of our lives in a state of despair. However, those of us who have honored our cycles, the many waxings and wanings of our lives, and have continued to nourish our relationship, are more likely to resolve this final challenge in the Waning Moon Cycle with a sense of integrity.

The divorce rate in the Waning Moon Cycle is extremely low; any dissatisfaction no doubt led us to divorce prior to this. We now prefer marriage to being alone. However, those who are unable to adapt to the many changes of our final season together, may project onto the other the unhappiness, the frustrations, the fears that are our own. We remain attached to the illusions of what might have been as we regret the choices we've made, the path we've walked. We feel hopeless and lonely, despairing of the connection with one another and with the Source from which hope emanates. The separateness inherent in the waning phase becomes not an opportunity for deepening the connection with ourselves and the Universe; instead we become withdrawn, alienated from life. Often the effects of an ageist society and the inherent discrimination that supports poverty, isolation, and disrespect of its elders impinges too heavily upon our relationship, and we are tragically estranged from our loved one. Adrift in our struggle for survival, we lose our way and plunge into despair.

For many of us, however, the Waning Moon Cycle, with all its changes and challenges, is one of deepening and enriching the relationship that has now moved to profound intimacy as we celebrate the integrity of our union and of each other!

Truly, *the longer we are together, the larger death grows;*[16] yet this is a poignant time of our lives as together we face death. How precious the time has been; we savor all that we've been together. The Waning Moon Cycle is a reflection and a deepening of the totality of our years together.

And yet, inevitably, the Waning Moon Cycle must end in death: *'til death us do part.* Once more, we affirm that in the waning there is the promise of waxing—of rebirth; and, as through our earlier wanings, we are challenged to trust ourselves in the dark ambiguity of the unknown. So we say goodbye to each other . . . for now. We celebrate our dear one and the life we've shared. We let go of one another, passing on now into the next cycle with grace and dignity and integrity.

We celebrate our love as we release our beloved into death with the celebration, the ritual we've created together. We've walked to the door of death with our beloved, and now with tears of sorrow and gratitude, we release the one with whom we've shared our laughter, our pain, our joy, our visions—our very lives. Symbolically and in ritual, we release our beloved—ashes into the sea, balloons into the air, seeds into the earth.

Farewell, dearest love.

An art form, ritualmaking is a significant way of supporting ourselves through the inevitable changes—the beginnings and the endings—of life. We honor the subtle space and time between transitions. Ritual marks the place—a bridge between—where the inner and outer worlds meet, resulting in a balance of strength and energy and conflict. Ritual provides a context within which renewal occurs. To create ritual is to invite renewal—*re/creativity*.

In the Waning Moon Cycle, the creation of a letting-go ritual can be as transforming as the enactment itself. Play, imagination, symbols, art, music, myth, and actions are significant aspects of both the creation and enactment of ritual—all part of the transformative process. In ritual, we transform the abstract into the language of the unconscious by mindfully clarifying the intention, choosing symbols, blessing the senses; we make explicit what is inevitable in our life together in these waning years.

A Ritual for Letting Go

The night is still. The waning moon has long since disappeared into the horizon. This is the longest night of the year: Winter Solstice. On this sacred night, my beloved and I must bid farewell. My life partner approaches the door of death and I may go no further.

Together we have created this ritual, yet my heart is heavy with the weight of my love and my mourning. Amongst candles, incense, and an offering bowl of water on the altar, I've placed the Goddess-made stone, a gift of Her womb and a souvenir of our honeymoon those many years ago. The figure of Hecate, Goddess of the Underworld, sits in the center of our altar; She watches over us, Her arms outstretched, inviting us into the depths. Her craggy face reassures us of Her wisdom and guidance. To the poignant sounds of "Claire de Lune," *I light three candles: black for death, white for rebirth, and red for our everlasting love that is now in transformation.*

Tenderly, I anoint her brow with the cool spring water; the rose incense embraces us in sweet fragrance. My heart aches; tears fill my eyes and I struggle to say the words that together we've written for our letting go. . . .

Rest into your body, my dearest love, feel the heaviness, the weight of it, and give your body room—room to breathe—in and out . . . breathe into your body and release that breath—in and out; gently, quietly breathing all through your body. Surrender to your breathing; let your breath breathe you. . . . All else fades into the mist of being and you simply take in a breath and release that breath.

Simply be in this moment . . . breathing in easily and gently; there is only this one breath. Breathe out and breathe in . . . ebbing and flowing.

There is nothing more. There is no pain. There is no yearning. There is simply the ebb and the flow.

Release the body into the mist that surrounds. All there is is an awareness of being in this moment. Breathe gently and easily. See your breath—each breath as it moves into and out of your body. Feel each breath—in and out, easily and gently.

And now let go. Surrender your breathing to the mist that embraces you . . . holding on to nothing. Surrender to this moment. You are free . . . there is nothing. Let go of all there is and surrender to the edgelessness. Float into the spaces between. You are safe and free. Move through the mist and into the light that simply is. The mind melts into the heart as the wind dissolves into the light. Go now. Move through the wind and melt into the light. You are free and safe. You simply are. You are floating into the light that embraces your being.

Go now. . . . Let go. . . . You are free in the emptiness of nonbeing. You are in the spaciousness of the light. Go now; free the breath from its restlessness. . . . The Mother awaits.

You are released from this incarnation, and now you dance in the light of the Mother. Let yourself die into the spaciousness of the heart.

And now you breathe in—a first breath . . . breathing anew. Rebirth. You are the light. You are one with the Mother. She welcomes you home.[18]

Blessed be.

Chapter 8

Dark of the Moon

Hush now.
Listen to the sounds
of your tears flowing
into the silence.
Let me hold you close
as you surrender to the darkness.
While the silence embraces you,
know that together we await the return of light,
the birth of a new moon.

We await the celebration of Spring Equinox: the days and nights are nearly equal in length. Frogs in the creek ambitiously serenade us; a courageous robin appears in the melting snow, optimistically singing her cheery song of welcome to spring. Green shoots of daffodils and hyacinths push their way up through the wet, muddy ground, making a cautious appearance; the bright sun valiantly encourages their return. Audaciously, a lone crocus displays herself in all her purpleness. At last! We are waxing into spring.

I complete this book as a new cycle begins. Indeed, endings flow into beginnings; waxing and waning!

Coming Full Circle is about honoring: honoring the rhythms that are inherent within us and around us. Cycles are everywhere, in everything—in each of us as individuals, in our relationships, in nature—in all there is. *Coming Full Circle* is an invitation to participate in life, to dare to surrender to those rhythms inherent in all there is. The moon has been our teacher; she is our guide. Just as she cycles in relation to the sun and the earth every 28 days, so do we cycle—rhythmically—daily, monthly, seasonally.

Coming Full Circle is about relationships. Relationships in all expressions of life are cyclical. We wax and we wane; our energies ebb and flow. We wax into connectedness, reach a fullness of creativity, wane into separateness, and flow into the dark of the moon: we integrate our learnings.

Our individual and relational cycles go on; the cycles of our inner life unfold as the cycles of our relationship evolve while the cycles of nature flow and ebb. We are a microcosm of our Universe; we are a part of the web that is our universe. *We are the flow; we are the ebb. We are the weavers; we are the web.*[1] All is intricately woven; all is in perfect rhythm: we have only to honor the rhythm that is within all of nature. But as we have seen, we need courage to yield, to surrender and to honor those rhythms. This is our challenge!

To some degree, the cycles—none of which are meant to be resolutely tied to chronological age—are progressive. However, let us not be seduced into the patriarchal perception that we start at the beginning and move forward to the end: this is linear thought. We flow through the cycles, we wax and we wane, and as we grow, encounter challenges, and experience transitions, we may necessarily re/cycle the tasks characteristic of a particular passage. Some of us get stuck, both individually and in our relationships, in specific cycles. If, for instance, when we enter the world, we encounter a place that is unsafe and abusive, we quickly learn that, for us, the world is untrustworthy. Thence, throughout our lives, we most likely will be challenged by the task of learning to trust—ourselves and others.

The issue of trust, reflected in our relationships, may remain unresolved for a very long time—until such time that we do the work required to heal the wounds of childhood. So it is in relationships. Our lessons progress; our experience grows. Yet along the path, we stumble. We may need more time to learn to trust another, or we may need more help in setting boundaries, honoring our feelings and listening. Our lessons are many, after all. Some, for instance, become attached to *falling* in love and are unwilling to risk what is necessary to flow and grow into the cycles that follow. Unresolved issues, both in our relationships and within ourselves, will be problematic in ensuing cycles. We notice these and we honor our own rhythms as we do the necessary healing of those old wounds. No need to judge our cycles; no need to punish ourselves.

We simply notice; surrender to the rhythm and embrace ourselves in both the ebb and flow.

Characteristic of each cycle are particular lessons and tasks; we are asked to reevaluate, to examine our values and our relationship to life. Major transitions and losses often are catalysts for returning to earlier cycles. Formal commitment to a relationship creates a reevaluation of what rules are now relevant as we move to a new level of trust. Likewise, the birth of a child evokes a return to earlier cycles as we adjust to the balance with this new configuration, this redefinition of family.

Alternative lifestyles may have different challenges. Homophobia—both internalized and externalized—has unique implications for lesbian and gay relationships. However, while the issues may vary, the *process* is the same. We wax; we wane. We honor the rhythm of the cycles.

Being respectful of diversity is vital. We are two individuals who are attracted to one another not because we are alike, but because each of us has qualities of interest to the other. So we invite one another into our lives to explore those differentnesses. Of course, the very differences that at first intrigue us inevitably become the source of our conflicts and therefore the catalysts for our growth. Furthermore, each of us will have different rhythms, needs, feelings, wants, interests, priorities, perspectives, and values. Our primary challenge throughout the cycles is to honor our partner's rhythm *while honoring our own*.

Coming Full Circle invites participation. We are currently faced with challenges that will seriously impact the future of humankind, the seven generations. We can no longer afford to ignore the cycles of our precious Mother Earth. We must renew our commitment to honor the rhythm inherent in all there is. No longer can we act upon this ailing planet—scarring the land, desecrating the forests, toxifying the air, polluting the waters, and annihilating Her creatures. We simply must *participate* with our Mother Earth; for what happens in the West African plains, the Norwegian waters, the Oregon forests, happens to each of us. Each cell in our bodies is a microcosm of the Universe; we are, indeed, one with all there is.

Yet we have become out of sync; we have systematically alienated ourselves from the natural rhythms of life. In the patriarchal culture in which we live, we have come to believe that there is no room for diversity: either/or dualism prevails. We must re/commit ourselves—each of us—to restoring the balance; we must surrender to the rhythm that is within ourselves and among one another—within all that exists. To *participate* requires courage. To participate means letting go of the need for *control-over* one another and our planet. When we *participate with*, we are in *relationship with* one another and our planet.

What we know, as we honor our cycles, is that all coexists; we can *both* honor our own *and* be respectful of our partner's rhythm, of our planet's rhythm. When we start from a place of trusting, then naming our differences, we come to acknowledge the richness of diversity; we are then able to celebrate ourselves in the context of the blending of us as healthy individuals. For indeed, any relationship is only as strong, life-giving and healthy as the individuals who have chosen to be together in relationship.

We cannot truly *honor* our cycles without acknowledging the Source of all there is. Whether we call that spirit Goddess, God, Mother Nature, the Wind, or our support group, it is our spirituality that sustains us and allows us to surrender to the rhythm of life. Celebration of life, of our spirituality, is often done through ritual. In ritual we are reminded of the sacredness of all life. And what could possibly be more sacred than to share our vulnerability, our vision, our very *being* with another, as we walk the path together on this blessed earth?

This is a book about *healthy* relationships, for I fervently believe that, in spite of pressure to the contrary, we can have healthy, life-giving, respectful, and loving relationships. We simply need to re/member how.

> To be of the Earth is to know
>   the restlessness of being a seed
>   the darkness of being planted
>   the struggle toward the light
>   the pain of growth into the light
>   the joy of bursting and bearing fruit
>   the love of being food for someone
>   the scattering of your seeds
>   the decay of the seasons
>   the mystery of death
>   and the miracle of birth.[2]

Now, in the dark of the moon, the new moon, we can rediscover the magic that is everywhere. But we must surrender—surrender to the rhythm. Hush now and listen! Can you hear it? Can you feel it? Can you know it? Do you dare to participate in the magic of the rhythm of the cycles?

Spirit of the North
Powers of Earth
I thank you for blessing this work with wisdom.
May I know the ground of the creation
As you part.
Blessed be!

Spirit of the West
Powers of Water
I thank you for blessing this work with feeling.
May I know the depths of all emotions
As you part.
Blessed be!

Spirit of the South
Powers of Fire
I thank you for blessing this work with energy.
May the flame of passion continue to burn
As you part.
Blessed be!

Spirit of the East
Powers of Air
I thank you for blessing this work with inspiration.
May I remember to know and to speak Her truth
As you part.
Blessed be!

Notes

Introduction

1. Gilligan, p. 8.
2. Teresa A. Peck, p. 282.
3. Starhawk, *Dreaming the Dark*, p. 3.
4. Harding, p. 11.
5. Wagner, pp. 202–203.

Chapter 1: Moon as Metaphor

1. Mountainwater, p. 117.
2. Harding, p. 64.
3. Starhawk, *Spiral Dance*, pp. 202-203.
4. Stein, p. 70.
5. Rush, p. 54.
6. Downing, p. 9.
7. Stein, p. 71.
8. Stone, p. 92.
9. Stone, p. 292.
10. Stone, p. 292.
11. Stone, pp. 81–82.
12. Bolen, p. 27.
13. Monaghan, p. 265.
14. Spretnak, pp. 77–83.
15. Stone, p. 208.
16. Spretnak, p. 83.
17. Downing, p. 13.
18. Rush, p. 26.

Chapter 2: Cycles of the Individual

1. Starhawk, *Spiral Dance*, p. 143.
2. Starhawk, *Spiral Dance*, p. 209.

3. Starhawk, *Spiral Dance*, p. 203.
4. Starhawk, *Spiral Dance*, p. 41.
5. Hazvat Inyat Khan, *Music of Life*, 1967, cited in Gardner, p. 102.
6. Schaef, p. 100.
7. Rush, pp. 261-262.
8. Rush, p. 293.
9. Gardner, p. 76.
10. Stein, pp. 72–73.
11. Lacey, p. 115.
12. Harding, p. 77.
13. Harding, p. 73.
14. Harding, p. 74.
15. Harding, p. 74.
16. Harding, p. 74.
17. Viorst, p. 3.
18. Erikson, p. 247.
19. Gilligan, p. 156.
20. Gilligan, p. 6.
21. Gilligan, p. 7.
22. Gilligan, p. 18.
23. Viorst, p. 9.
24. Viorst, p. 10.
25. Newman and Newman, p. 111.
26. Erikson, p. 255.
27. Viorst, p. 140.
28. Gilligan, p. 33.
29. Viorst, p. 161.
30. Viorst, p. 166.
31. Gilligan, p. 62.
32. Gilligan, p. 127.
33. Miller, p. 83.
34. Gilligan, p. 156.

35. Gilligan, p. 159.
36. Gilligan, p. 164.
37. Gilligan, p. 166.
38. Erikson, p. 267.
39. Gilligan, p. 23.
40. The term was coined by Betty Friedan in her book *The Feminine Mystique,* which helped catapult us into the women's movement more than two decades ago.
41. Miller, p. 87.
42. Bateson, p. 5.
43. See Morris Berman's *The Reenchantment of the World* for a comprehensive and provacative exploration of the science that has impacted society, causing us to act upon rather than participate with our planet.
44. Jean Baker Miller's *A New Psychology of Women* offers an inclusive perspective of women and relationships.
45. Newman and Newman, p. 270.
46. Newman and Newman, p. 273.
47. Newman and Newman, p. 273.
48. Viorst, p. 175.
49. Newman and Newman, p. 264.
50. LeShan, p. 2.
51. Sheehy, *Silent Passage*, p. 80.

52. Gould, p. 218.
53. Gould, p. 218.
54. Newman and Newman, p. 318.
55. Gilligan, pp. 171–172.
56. Fonda, pp. 146–147.
57. Erikson, p. 267.
58. Newman and Newman, p. 325.
59. Zweig and Abrams, p. xxv.
60. Gerzon, p. 195.
61. Gerzon, p. 194.
62. Gerzon, p. 195.
63. deBeauvoir, p. 17.
64. deBeauvoir, p. 14.
65. deBeauvoir, p. 421.
66. Newman and Newman, p. 350.
67. Erikson, p. 269.
68. Gerzon, p. 188.
69. Gerzon, p. 186.
70. Gerzon, p. 210.
71. From a letter from Chief Seattle to President Franklin Pierce in 1855.
72. Mountainwater, p. 112.
73. Walker, p. 72.
74. Walker, p. 72.
75. Levine, p. 203.

Chapter 3: Cycles of Relationships

1. Rudhyar, p. 15.
2. Rudhyar, p. 32.
3. Rudhyar, p. 33.

4. Johann Wolfgang von Goethe, source unknown. This has held a prominent place in my refrigerator collage for so long, I have forgotten whence it came!
5. Harding, pp. 75–76.
6. *The American Heritage Dictionary of the English Language.*
7. Johnson, p. 23.
8. Gardner, p. 102.
9. Rudhyar, p. 23.
10. Sams, pp. 246–247. Poem from SACRED PATH CARDS by Jamie Sams. Copyright © 1990 by Jamie Sams & Linda Childers. Reprinted by permission of HarperCollins Publishers, Inc.
11. Sams, p. 242.

Chapter 4: New Moon Cycle

1. Tennov, p. 16.
2. Tennov, p. 20.
3. Tennov, pp. 23–24.
4. Minuchin, pp. 54–55.

Chapter 5: Waxing Moon Cycle

1. M. Scott Peck, p. 81.
2. Adapted from audiotape of Melody Beattie's *Codependent No More.*
3. Gordon, p. 64.

4. Gordon, pp. 237–242.
5. Virginia Woolf's *A Room of One's Own* provides us with a classic view of the importance, especially for women, of reclaiming our own space.
6. Virginia Satir first identified as the basic feelings, mad, sad, glad, scared, in her book *People Making.*
7. Ferder, p. 2.
8. An excellent guide for dealing with money issues is Joe Dominguez and Vicki Robin's *Your Money or Your Life.*
9. Branislaw Malinowski, cited in Viorst, p. 207.
10. Viorst, p. 224.
11. Gibran, excerpt from "On Love," p. 15. From *The Prophet* by Kahlil Gibran. Copyright ©1923 by Kahlil Gibran and renewed 1951 by Administrators C T A of Kahlil Gibran Estate and Mary G. Gibran. Reprinted by permission of Alfred A. Knopf, Inc.

12. Fulghum, pp. 6–7. From *All I Really Need To Know I Learned In Kindergarten* by Robert L. Fulghum. Copyright © 1986, 1988 by Robert L. Fulghum. Reprinted by permission of Villard Books, a division of Random House, Inc.

Chapter 6:
Full Moon Cycle

1. LeShan, p. 150.
2. Indianapolis *Star*, Feruary 21, 1993, pp. H1–3.
3. LeShan, p. 186.
4. Gibran, excerpt from "On Love," p. 15.
5. Words spoken by the Peacemaker, founder of the Iroquois Confederacy, circa 1000 AD, cited in Wall and Arden, p. 7.
6. From an address by Kay Gardner at the National Women's Music Festival, June 1989.
7. VanArsdall, pp. 12–13.
8. Gould, p. 291.

Chapter 7:
Waning Moon Cycle

1. Olsen, p. 115.
2. Sheehy, *Passages,* p. 506.
3. Sue Saniel Elkind, cited in Martz, p. 113.
4. Estes, p. 385.

5. Rabbi Rami M. Shapiro, cited in Roberts and Amidon, p. 325.
6. Estes, p. 448.
7. Gibran, p. 71.
8. Wendell Berry, cited in Roberts and Amidon, p. 321.
9. Tilker, p. 447.
10. Levine, p. 292.
11. *A Reckoning* by May Sarton is a deeply touching portrayal of such a woman.
12. Levine, p. 292.
13. Viorst, p. 295.
14. Estes, p. 385.
15. David Ignatow, "One Leaf" from *New & Collected Poems 1970-1985,* © 1986 by David Ignatow, Wesleyan University Press by permission of University Press of New England.
16. Wendell Berry, cited in Roberts and Amidon, p. 321.
17. Adapted from Levine, p. 243.

Chapter 8:
Dark of the Moon

1. Chant by Shekhinah Mountainwater in Starhawk, *Dreaming the Dark*, p. 225.
2. John Soos, cited in Roberts and Amidon, p. 288.

Bibliography

ADAMHA News (Alcohol, Drug Abuse, and Mental Health Administration), March/April 1988.

Bateson, Mary Catherine. *Composing a Life*. New York: Penguin Books, 1990.

Beattie, Melody. *Beyond Codependency*. New York; Harper/Hazelton, 1989; Hazelton Audiotapes, 1993.

Beck, Renee and Sydney Barbara Metrick. *The Art of Ritual*. Berkeley, CA: Celestial Arts, 1990.

Berman, Morris. *The Reenchantment of the World*. New York: Bantam Books, 1984.

Blumstein, Phillip, PhD., and Pepper Schwartz, PhD. *American Couples*. New York: Wm. Morrow & Co., 1983.

Bolen, Jean Shinoda, MD. *Goddesses in Everywoman*. San Francisco: Harper and Row, Publishers, 1984.

Brooks, Nan. *Ceremonies For Our Lives*. Bloomington, IN: Spirit Magic Books, 1991.

Butler, Sandra. *Conspiracy of Silence*. San Francisco: Volcano Press, 1978.

Campbell, Joseph. *The Power of Myth*. New York: Doubleday, 1988.

deBeauvoir, Simone. *The Coming of Age*. New York: Simon and Schuster, 1984.

Dominguez, Joe and Vicki Robins. *Your Money or Your Life*. New York: Penguin, 1992.

Downing, Christine. *The Goddess*. New York: Crossroad, 1984.

Erikson, Erik H. *Childhood and Society*. New York: W.W. Norton, 1950.

Estes, Clarissa Pinkola, PhD. *Women Who Run With the Wolves*. New York: Ballantine, 1992.

Ferder, Fran. *Words Made Flesh*. Notre Dame, IN: Ave Maria Press, 1986.

Fonda, Jane. *Women Coming of Age*. New York: Simon and Schuster, 1984.

Friedan, Betty. *The Feminine Mystique*. New York: Dell, 1963.

Fromm, Erich. *The Art of Loving.* New York: Harper and Brothers, 1956.

Fulghum, Robert. *All I Really Need to Know I Learned in Kindergarten.* New York: Ivy Books, 1986.

Gardner, Kay. *Sounding the Inner Landscape.* Stonington, ME: Caduceus Publications, 1990.

Gerzon, Mark. *Coming Into Our Own.* New York: Delacorte, 1992.

Gibran, Kahlil. *The Prophet.* New York: Alfred A. Knopf, 1926.

Gilligan, Carol. *In a Different Voice.* Cambridge, MA: Harvard University Press, 1982.

Gordon, Thomas. *Parent Effectiveness Training.* New York: NAL/Dutton, 1975.

Gould, Roger L., MD. *Transformations.* New York: Simon and Schuster, 1978.

Harding, M. Esther. *Woman's Mysteries: Ancient and Modern.* New York: Harper Colophon: 1971.

Jamplosky, Gerald. *Love is Letting Go of Fear.* Berkeley, CA: Cogent, 1989.

Johnson, Sonia. *The Ship That Sailed Into the Living Room.* Estancia, NM: Wildfire Books, 1991.

Lacey, Louise. *Lunaception: A Feminine Odyssey into Fertility and Contraception.* New York: Coward, McCann and Geoghegan, 1974.

LeShan, Eda. *The Wonderful Crisis of Middle Age.* New York: David McKay, 1963.

Levine, Stephen. *Who Dies?* Garden City, NY: Anchor Press/Doubleday, 1982.

Martz, Sandra, Editor. *When I Am an Old Woman, I Shall Wear Purple.* Manhattan Beach, CA: Papier-Mache, 1987.

Miller, Jean Baker, MD. *Toward a New Psychology of Women.* Boston: Beacon Press, 1976.

Minuchin, Salvador. *Families and Family Therapy.* Cambridge, MA: Harvard University Press, 1976.

Monaghan, Patricia. *The Book of Goddesses and Heroines.* New York: E. P. Hutton, 1981.

Mountainwater, Shekhinah. *Ariadne's Thread.* Freedom, CA: The Crossing Press, 1991.

Newman, Barbara M. and Philip R. Newman. *Development Through Life*. Homewood, IL: Dorsey Press, 1975.

Olsen, Tillie. *Tell Me A Riddle*. New York: Dell, 1960.

Passmore, Nancy, Editor, Publisher. *The Lunar Calendar*. Boston: Luna Press, 1979, 1989.

Peck, M. Scott, MD. *The Road Less Traveled*. New York: Simon and Schuster, 1978.

Peck, Teresa A. "Women's Self-definition in Adulthood: From a Different Model?" *Psychology of Women Quarterly,* 10, 1986, 274–284.

Rich, Adrienne. *The Dream of a Common Language*. New York: W.W. Norton, 1978.

Roberts, Elizabeth and Elias Amidon, Editors. *Earth Prayers: From Around the World, 365 Prayers, Poems and Invocations for Honoring the Earth*. San Francisco: HarperCollins, 1991.

Rudhyar, Dane. *The Lunation Cycle*. Boulder, CO: Shambala, 1971.

Rush, Anne Kent. *Moon, Moon*. New York: Random House, 1976.

Sams, Jamie. *Sacred Path Cards*. San Francisco: Harper, 1990.

Sarton, May. *A Reckoning*. New York: W.W. Norton, 1978.

Satir, Virginia. *People Making*. Palo Alto, CA: Science and Behavior Books, 1972.

Schaef, Anne Wilson. *Women's Reality*. Minneapolis: Winston Press, 1981.

Sheehy, Gail. *Passages*. New York: Bantam Books, 1976.

Sheehy, Gail. *The Silent Passage*. New York: Random House, 1992.

Spretnak, Charlene. *Lost Goddesses of Early Greece*. Boston: Beacon Press, 1978.

Starhawk. *Dreaming the Dark*. Boston: Beacon Press, 1982.

Starhawk. *The Spiral Dance*. San Francisco: Harper and Row, 1989.

Stein, Diane. *Casting the Circle*. Freedom, CA: The Crossing Press, 1990.

Stone, Merlin. *Ancient Mirrors of Womanhood*. Boston: Beacon Press, 1979.

Tennov, Dorothy. *Love and Limerence*. New York: Stein and Day, 1980.

Tilker, Harvey A., PhD. *Developmental Psychology Today*. New York: Random House, 1975.

VanArsdall, Nancy. "Ecofeminism: Ancient Values/Contemporary Language," *Branches*, 6:1 (March/April 1993), pp. 12–13.

Viorst, Judith. *Necessary Losses*. New York: Ballantine Books, 1986.

Wagner, Jane. *The Search For Signs of Intelligent Life in the Universe.* New York: Harper and Row, 1986.

Walker, Barbara G. *The Crone*. New York: Harper and Row, 1985.

Wall, Steve, and Harvey Arden. *Wisdomkeepers*. Hillsboro, OR: Beyond Words Publishing, 1990.

Wetzel, James R. "American Families: 75 Years of Change," *Monthly Labor Review,* US Department of Labor, March 1990, pp. 4–13.

Winnicott, D.W. *Home is Where We Start From*. New York: W.W. Norton, 1986.

Woolf, Virginia. *A Room of One's Own*. New York: Harcourt Brace & Company, 1957.

Zweig, Connie and Jeremiah Abrams, editors. *Meeting the Shadow.* Los Angeles: Jeremy P. Tarcher, 1990.

Additional Suggested Reading

Adler, Margot. *Drawing Down the Moon*. Boston: Beacon Press, 1976.

Austen, Hallie Iglehart. *The Heart of the Goddess: Art, Myth and Meditations of World's Sacred Feminine*. Berkeley: Wingbow Press, 1990.

Budapest, Zsuzsanna E. *Holy Book of Women's Mysteries*. Oakland, CA: Susan B. Anthony Coven No. 1, 1979.

Budapest, Zsuzanna E. *The Grandmother of Time*. San Francisco: Harper and Row, 1989.

Chopra, M.D., Deepak. *Ageless Body, Timeless Mind*. New York: Harmony Books, 1993.

Hart, Nett and Lee Lanning. *Awakening: An Almanac of Lesbian Lore and Vision*. Minneapolis: Word Weavers, 1987.

Hart, Nett and Lee Lanning. *Dreaming: An Almanac of Lesbian Lore and Vision*. Minneapolis: Word Weavers, 1983.

Hoffman, Mark S., Editor. *The World Almanac, 1992*. New York: Scripps Howard, 1992.

Kaufman, Gershen. *Shame: The Power of Caring*. Rochester, VT: Schenkman Books, 1985.

Loulan, JoAnn. *Lesbian Sex*. San Francisco: Spinsters Ink, 1984.

Stein, Diane. *All Women Are Healers*. Freedom, CA: The Crossing Press, 1990.

Stein, Diane, editor. *The Goddess Celebrates*. Freedom, CA: The Crossing Press, 1991.

Stone, Merlin. *When God Was A Woman*. New York: Harcourt Brace Jovanovich, 1976.

Walker, Alice. *Possessing the Secret of Joy*. New York: Harcourt Brace Jovanovich, 1992.

Walker, Barbara G. *Women's Rituals*. San Francisco: Harper and Row, 1990.

Index

Other Books from Third Side Press

Fiction

NOT SO MUCH THE FALL by Kerry Hart, $12.95
1-879427-24-9
ON LILL STREET by Lynn Kanter, $10.95 1-879427-07-9
ENTWINED by Beatrice Stone, $10.95 1-879427-21-4
THE SENSUAL THREAD by Beatrice Stone, $10.95
1-879427-18-4
AFTERSHOCKS by Jess Wells, $9.95 1-879427-08-7
HAWKWINGS by Karen Lee Osborne, $9.95 1-879427-00-1

Mystery

TIMBER CITY MASKS: A Royce Madison Mystery, by Kieran
York, $9.95 1-879427-13-3
CRYSTAL MOUNTAIN VEILS: A Royce Madison Mystery, by
Kieran York, $10.95 1-879427-19-2
OUT FOR BLOOD: Tales of Mystery and Suspense by Women
Writers, Victoria Brownworth, editor, $10.95 1-879427-20-6
OUT FOR MORE BLOOD: Tales of Malice and Retaliation by
Women Writers, Victoria A. Brownworth and Judith M.
Redding, editors, $12.95 1-879427-27-3

Drama

SHE'S ALWAYS LIKED THE GIRLS BEST by Claudia Allen,
$11.95 1-879427-11-7

Stories

THE COUNTRY OF HERSELF, Karen Lee Osborne, editor, $9.95
1-879427-14-1
TWO WILLOWS CHAIRS by Jess Wells, $8.95 1-879427-05-2

Erotica

SPEAKING IN WHISPERS: Lesbian African-American Erotica, by
Kathleen E. Morris, $11.95 1-879427-28-1
THE DRESS/THE SHARDA STORIES by Jess Wells, $8.95
1-879427-04-4

Autobiography

ENTER PASSWORD: Recovery, by Elly Bulkin, $7.95
1-879427-10-0

Business

THE WOMAN-CENTERED ECONOMY: Ideals, Reality, and
the Space In Between, Loraine E. Edwalds and Midge
Stocker, editors, $15.95 1-879427-06-0 paper

Health Books from Third Side Press

ALTERNATIVES FOR WOMEN WITH ENDOMETRIOSIS: A Guide by Women for Women
Ruth Carol, editor

Offering hope to the millions of women in the U.S. and Canada who
suffer from endometriosis, this unique book takes the mystery out of
therapies like homeopathy, chiropractic, traditional Chinese medicine,
and others, presenting personal narratives of a dozen women who have
been diagnosed with endometriosis over the past 15 years. Each describes, in personal detail, her efforts—and successes—at finding relief.

*"I highly recommend you read this book. It can open
some new doors for you." —Endometriosis Association
Newsletter*

$12.95 1-879427-12-5

CANCER AS A WOMEN'S ISSUE: Scratching the Surface
Midge Stocker, editor

Women/Cancer/Fear/Power series, vol. 1

This very personal collection of narratives explores how cancer affects women, individually and collectively.

*"If you are a woman, or if anyone you love is a woman,
you should buy this book." —Outlines*

Chicago Women in Publishing, 1992 Women's Issues Book Award

$11.95 1-879427-02-8 paper

CONFRONTING CANCER, CONSTRUCTING CHANGE:
New Perspectives on Women and Cancer
Midge Stocker, editor

Women/Cancer/Fear/Power series, vol. 2

Powerful essays, featuring writing by feminist anti-cancer movement organizers from around the U.S., confront myths about cancer. Introduction by Sandra Butler (coauthor of *Cancer in Two Voices*).

"Questions the usual, concealed reactions . . . and advocates a more open, women-centered, political stance. . . . extends—beyond obtaining medical information, seeking counseling, and recovering—to emphasizing honesty and advocacy as qualities of a normal life." —Booklist

"Written from an unabashedly feminist viewpoint, these essays provide much food for thought, touch the heart, and supply useful information." —Library Journal

"These books [in the Women/Cancer/Fear/Power series] are for everyone, not only those touched by cancer. . . . Include[s] opposing opinions on a variety of topics, counteracting the mainstream media myth of the 'universal' feminist stance." —Sojourner

"Read it and reap." —Chicago Tribune

$11.95 1-879427-09-5 paper

BEYOND BEDLAM: Contemporary Women
Psychiatric Survivors Speak Out
Jeanine Grobe, editor

Upclose and personal writing by women who have survived psychiatric abuse on psych wards and in mental hospitals.

"Could be the book that awakens the world to the ugly reality of loony bins . . . telling not just of shipwrecks on the ragged shoals of psychiatry but of reconstructing meaningful lives in the aftermath." —Mouth

$15.95 1-879427-22-2 paper

SOME*BODY* TO LOVE: A Guide to Loving the Body You Have
Leslēa Newman

SomeBody to Love offers women a chance to look at ourselves as beautiful, powerful, and lovable—challenging what society teaches us.

"*Startling and provocative . . . This book will change many women's lives.*" —Jewish Weekly News

"*A moving experience and a practical tool.*" —Eating Disorders Digest

"*I'd recommend the book even if you can't bear the though of all that writing. . . . Just reading it will make you laugh, loosen up, and who knows, you might even glance at yourself in a plate glass window and see me waving back.*" —The Healing Woman

$10.95 1-879427-03-6 paper

 Third Side Press

P.O. Box 59267, Chicago, IL 60659-0267
312-271-3029 (voice) / 312-271-0459 (fax)
102171.771@compuserve.com

To order any Third Side Press book, or to receive a free catalog, write to us at the address above. When ordering books, please include $2 shipping for the first book and .50 for each additional book.

The book you are holding is the product of work by an independent women's book publishing company.